The Logic of History

We look to historians for reliable information about the past. But modern and postmodern critics have challenged their credibility and objectivity, seeing written history as a product of contemporary culture. Can we find a way to approach history with new confidence?

The Logic of History: Putting postmodernism in perspective reveals the rational basis for historians' descriptions, interpretations and explanations of past events. C. Behan McCullagh defends the practice of history as more reliable than has recently been acknowledged. Historians, he argues, make their accounts of the past as fair as they can and avoid misleading their readers. He explains and discusses postmodern criticisms of history, providing students and teachers of history with a renewed validation of their practice. McCullagh takes the history debate to a new stage with bold replies to the major questions historians face today. Historical reasoning is explained in plain and simple terms, accessible to all with an interest in history.

C. Behan McCullagh is Senior Lecturer in Philosophy at La Trobe University. His many publications include *The Truth of History* (1998).

The Logic of History

Putting postmodernism in perspective

C. Behan McCullagh

Routledge
Taylor & Francis Group

LONDON AND NEW YORK

First published 2004 by Routledge
11 New Fetter Lane, London EC4P 4EE

Simultaneously published in the USA and Canada
by Routledge
29 West 35th Street, New York, NY 10001

Routledge is an imprint of the Taylor & Francis Group

Typeset in Goudy by The Running Head Limited, Cambridge
Printed and bound in Great Britain by TJ International Ltd, Padstow, Cornwall

British Library Cataloguing in Publication Data
A catalogue record for this book is available from the British Library

Library of Congress Cataloging in Publication Data
McCullagh, C. Behan.
The logic of history: putting postmodernism in perspective / C. Behan McCullagh.
p. cm.
1. History—Philosophy. 2. Postmodernism. 3. Historiography.
4. History—Historiography. I. Title.
D16.8.M3858 2003
901—dc 21   2003008975

ISBN 0–415–22398–9 (hbk)
ISBN 0–415–22399–7 (pbk)

I dedicate this book to my wife
Janice Elizabeth McCullagh
with gratitude and love

Contents

Acknowledgements

I would like to thank Professor Tor-Egil Førland, Dr Hugh Jackson and Professor Christopher Lloyd for very useful comments upon an early draft of this book. I also benefited from the comments of anonymous readers for Routledge, for which I am grateful. Finally, I thank God for giving me the strength and wit, day by day, to do what I have done. The book's limitations and imperfections, of course, reflect my own.

Introduction

This book is designed to show how historians' descriptions, interpretations and explanations of past events can be rationally assessed and justified. When historians begin their inquiries, they choose a topic which interests them and ask some questions about it. To answer the questions, they read widely and search for evidence which might help produce answers to them. They interpret the evidence they collect by drawing upon an informed imagination which reflects their general knowledge of human nature and social processes, and their particular expertise in the field. Imagination and insight provide most of the interesting hypotheses in history. In answering their questions, historians' attitudes to their subject often influence their thoughts about it, so that once they have formed hypotheses in answer to their questions, it is important that the hypotheses be tested. It is at this point that the present book becomes relevant, explaining how historians' descriptions, interpretations and explanations can be rationally assessed and justified.

Historians often learn how to assess their hypotheses by studying debates in history in the course of their education. They acquire a capacity to evaluate their hypotheses critically, without always being aware of the standards of rationality they are applying. Awareness of those standards, however, will make it easier for historians to ensure that their work is rationally defensible.

There are many good books which explain how students of history should undertake their inquiries, but they contain very little guidance as to the logic of historical reasoning. They are almost entirely about searching for answers to one's questions, and writing up the results. Yet the point of all the good practical advice is to gather information from which sound inferences about the past can be formed. Those inferences and arguments are at the heart of historical practice.

This book is designed to introduce the reader to historical arguments, not to analyse them in all their detail. In many cases, a fuller exposition can be found in my earlier works (McCullagh, 1984 and McCullagh, 1998), though many of the points made in this book are quite new. In several places I address views which I have not considered before, and almost all the examples analysed here are fresh, making use of recent scholarship. This book differs from my previous ones in being addressed primarily to students of history. It does not assume any knowledge of philosophy, and uses as few philosophical terms as possible.

One cannot write in defence of the rationality of history today without addressing some well-known objections to its credibility. Sceptics see historians as influenced by their culture, producing works which reflect the values, beliefs and rhetorical practices expressed in its discourses. They also note that the books historians write often reflect their individual interests, promoting groups like those to which they belong. The sceptics conclude that historical descriptions, interpretations and explanations are expressions of historians' cultural milieu and social interests rather than accurate accounts of the past. Such views have been referred to as relativistic, postmodern, and as part of 'the new historicism'. I explain and address them in the first chapter of the book, which is consequently much more philosophical than the rest. Nevertheless it is relatively brief, as its intention is not to cover every nuance of their arguments, but to provide an idea of how the credibility of history can be defended against them. (Many of their arguments are considered at greater length in McCullagh, 1998, ch. 1.)

In Chapter 1 I present historical knowledge as part of our knowledge of the world, all of which is built ultimately upon perceptual experiences which we interpret and explain as caused by things in the world. As the book unfolds, one can see that the chain of inference has several links: from their perceptions historians infer the presence of evidence of a certain kind; from that they draw inferences about the actions and circumstances which produced it; and on the basis of these descriptions of the past they draw further inferences about such things as the ideas, attitudes, practices and psychological states of people, about the events they reported, and about the structures of their society.

Historians often begin their investigations by reading texts written in the past. They assume that the texts were written to convey information in a conventional manner, so they read them to grasp their conventional meaning. So long as historians know the language in which a text was written, interpreting its conventional meaning is seldom difficult. Chapter 2 begins by briefly describing this process of interpreting a text, and then settles down to consider a range of objections that have been made in recent years to the possibility of fixing the conventional meaning of a text. They involve worries about the stability of language, the possibility of knowing the context in which a text was written, the social function of texts, the subjectivity of their interpretation and a problem of hermeneutical circles. The last section is on the meaning of actions, events and practices in history.

Historians use texts to draw inferences about the circumstances of their composition and the events to which they refer. They have to draw upon general knowledge to form hypotheses about these things. This general knowledge is sometimes just commonsense knowledge about the world, and sometimes it is specifically about the culture and society in which the evidence was created. The forms of these inferences from evidence are described in Chapter 3, by means of some vivid examples. On the basis of the particular facts they discover about the past, historians then make generalizations about the society they describe, and draw conclusions about its social structures. These forms of inference are also illustrated and described in Chapter 3.

An important part of historical research involves the explanation of human actions. Various theories have been offered about the sorts of thing that can cause human actions, and all point to types of causes of interest. Chapter 4 notes the contribution of Classical and Enlightenment theories of human nature, which emphasize its rationality; modern theories of Marx, Freud and Nietzsche, which see human behaviour as motivated by interests, instincts and the pursuit of power; and finally recent cultural theories which attribute human behaviour to the discourses, practices and expectations of society. All these theories provide insights into causes of human behaviour, and responsible historians will search for causes of each kind when explaining decisions and actions.

Historians often accumulate a lot of information about their chosen subject, all fairly detailed, and they must then decide what to do with it. One solution is to write a narrative account of the subject, and Chapter 5 describes three kinds of historical narrative: commonsense narratives, which use just commonsense notions to tell the story of some historical subject; colligatory narratives, which describe a kind of pattern of events the historian has noticed; and summary interpretations, which illustrate a general summary account of a subject. Historians have to resist the temptation to accept a fashionable assumption about a pattern inherent in the events they are studying, and illustrate that, without checking to see whether it truly represents the subject. I call this practice 'top-down' history, and it is more common than you might imagine.

Chapter 6 is a short chapter discussing the credibility and fairness of historical interpretations. All interpretations are expected to be credible, but only those which purport to describe a particular historical subject are expected to be fair. Colligatory narratives, which pick out interesting patterns in the past, when they are not summarizing an historical subject are not intended to give a fair description of anything. Several objections to the possibility of narratives providing credible or fair accounts of their subjects are considered, and are shown to be unjustified. But in some cases new evidence might destroy a general interpretation of an historical subject, so in those cases the degree of credibility placed upon the interpretation should not be high.

The difference between a chronicle and a narrative is that narratives describe causal relations between many of the events they narrate, whereas chronicles merely list them. In recent years little attention has been paid to causal statements in history. Writers have been more interested in continuities in social and linguistic practices without attending much to the causes of historical change. In practice, however, historical narratives abound in causal claims. Even reasons for actions are uninteresting unless it is thought they influenced the agent to perform the actions they explain. It is vital, therefore, that responsible historians know what causes and explanatory conditions are like, and how particular instances of them can be detected. Chapter 7 provides all that information, with telling illustrations.

Once a number of the causes of an event have been identified, how are historians expected to select and arrange them to explain the events that interest them? Some have thought there is no principle of selection. Others have set out *a priori* models of historical explanation which they expect historians to follow. My approach to the understanding of historical explanations is descriptive and analytic. I examine cases of historical explanation to see what structure they actually have. In Chapter 8 I describe two common forms of explanation in history, which I call genetic and contrastive. Genetic explanations trace the origins of events from the first event which substantially increased the probability of their occurrence in the circumstances. Contrastive explanations point to conditions which made the kind of event that did occur more probable than another. Historians sometimes elaborate upon these basic forms of explanation, accounting for unexpected or very interesting features of them, producing what I call profound explanations. The last section of the chapter briefly discusses explanations which refer to social structures: those in which social structures are said to influence individual behaviour, and those which offer explanations of changes in the social structures themselves.

In discovering the standards of justification adopted by responsible historians, I have been instructed by numerous examples of historians defending their conclusions. The book is full of such examples, partly to illustrate the theories of historical knowledge and understanding presented, and partly to demonstrate their applicability.

I hope that this introduction to the logic of history will quicken historians' interest in the rational justification of their accounts of the past. It should help guide historians in the rational assessment of their own work and that of others. And it will help students of history to understand the point of many of the debates about the past that they study.

Chapter 1

The possibility of historical knowledge

Before we can decide how to create arguments which will justify historical knowledge, we need a clear idea of what it is we are trying to justify. The traditional answer is that historians want to justify the claim that their descriptions of the past are true. Fine, but what is meant by 'true'?

This has become a very difficult question to answer. Indeed some have decided we simply cannot know whether our descriptions of the world are true, and we should give up pretending that we can. Postmodern critics consider methods of historical inquiry and argument to be traditional practices which cannot yield truths about the past and so might as well be abandoned. They urge us to admit that traditional beliefs about the truth of history cannot be justified. For example, Keith Jenkins has written of 'history whose end is signalled by postmodern thinking' (Jenkins, 1999, p. 2). He says 'it really is history *per se* that radical postmodernism threatens with extinction . . . [T]he optimum conditions for the creation and sustaining of history now lie behind us, and . . . we should now . . . embrace a non-historicising postmodernism' (ibid., p. 9).

In this chapter I will state, as briefly and clearly as I can, the traditional reasons for thinking we can discover truths about the past, and then the objections to that traditional view which render it no longer acceptable. But rather than becoming sceptical of historical knowledge, I prefer to build upon the insights of postmodern critics to create a more sophisticated theory of historical knowledge and historical truth. With this theory, although no knowledge of the world is infallible, it is often reasonable to believe many descriptions of the past are true. The traditional theory of truth is one of naïve empiricism. I have called the more sophisticated theory 'a correlation theory of truth' (McCullagh, 1998, ch. 1), but it could also be called 'a critical theory of truth'.

Having established that there is an intelligible and appropriate sense in which historical descriptions can be understood to be true, I shall move on in the second section of this chapter to consider some objections which stem from a conviction that historians construct their accounts of the past from elements of their own culture, particularly its language and beliefs, so that they could not possibly tell us anything true about the past, which is 'another country'. Those who do not enjoy philosophy could skip this chapter, as it really just clears an intellectual space for the chapters on justifying historical knowledge and understanding which follow.

Theories of truth

Naïve empiricism

The beliefs which historians have traditionally held about their capacity to discover what happened in the past are just commonsense beliefs which most people accept most of the time without question. They still do so without much harm. Strictly speaking, however, these commonsense beliefs are not warranted, as will be seen. The beliefs are as follows:

1. Our senses mirror the world. Well, more precisely, the world is as we sense it. It contains the objects we sense, with the features we sense them to have: the shapes and colours we see, the sounds we hear, the smells we detect and the textures we feel. (A theory of sensation.)

2. On the basis of our sensations and our knowledge of both language and the world we identify the things we sense, and draw inferences about their nature. (A theory of perception.)

3. A description of what we perceive is true if what we describe really is the thing we describe it to be, with the characteristics we describe it as having. If it does have those characteristics, then we say it 'corresponds' to our description of it. Strictly speaking, its having those characteristics warrants our description of it and our assertion that it exists. (A correspondence theory of truth.)

4. It follows from 1, 2 and 3 that historians can sense and know what evidence of the past is before them, and can describe it truly.

5. There are forms of inference, such as statistical inferences and arguments to the best explanation, which allow historians to draw true conclusions about the past from the evidence available to them. To say that the historical descriptions are true means that the things described really did exist and that they really had the characteristics they are described as having.

This is an empiricist theory because it bases historians' knowledge of the world upon their sensory experiences of the evidence available to them. It is a naïve theory because it takes no account of the criticisms which have been levelled against it.

Criticisms of naïve empiricism

1. We have no uninterpreted access to the world. Even our simplest sensations are structured according to concepts we possess: for example we see people and trees, not just shapes and colours. The concepts we use to structure our perceptions are provided by our culture: we are taught to perceive things in terms of them.

Furthermore, we are prone to exaggerate slightly the characteristics of things that interest us and to ignore things that do not.

Consequently, it is wrong to say that the world is simply as we sense and perceive it.

2. We interpret our experiences linguistically, and our knowledge of the world is constituted by our descriptions of it. So our knowledge of the world is not something we discover, but something we create.

3. Our knowledge of the world is something we construct, on the basis of our concepts and according to our language. We have no way of knowing what the world is 'really' like, independent of our culturally determined perceptions and descriptions of it.

4. Consequently, the correspondence theory of truth is useless, since we can never know whether there are things in the world with precisely the characteristics we perceive them to have and describe them as having.

Critics of the naïve correspondence theory often argue that there is no good reason for believing any descriptions of the world to be true. Common reasons for their scepticism are as follows:

5. The only sense in which we can show a description of the world to be true is a coherence sense, in that we can show it coheres well with other beliefs commonly held about the world.

6. There are common forms of argument for drawing inferences about the past from descriptions of evidence, but there is absolutely no way of proving that the conclusions reached by means of them are true, as we have no independent access to the world to check their truth. The forms of inference are taught by the culture and accepted as standards of rationality within it.

7. Consequently, there is no good reason to suppose that historical knowledge reached by means of such inferences is true or correct. The most one can say about historical knowledge is that it conforms to current standards of rationality.

There are further reasons for being sceptical about historical knowledge:

8. The meaning of words and sentences cannot be fixed and, consequently, their truth cannot be ascertained. Words and sentences acquire their meaning by their relations with other words and sentences. Words and sentences are defined by their implications, synonyms and contrasts, and also by their associations. There is no known limit to these. So the meaning of words is found in other words; and that meaning is, as they say, constantly deferred and consequently quite imprecise. Therefore one cannot be quite sure what historical descriptions are affirming.

9. It is impossible to capture the complexity of any historical event adequately. This became most obvious when historians tried to represent the Holocaust. The life and death of every victim of the Holocaust was a story of tragic misfortune worth telling. And what of each of those who killed them and those who facilitated their deaths? Their deeds should be exposed as well. Even if the history of every individual involved could be told, no words could accurately capture their emotions and attitudes. As Max Silverman writes: 'Auschwitz becomes the present absence, that which lies behind all human discourse, whose traces (for that is all we have) we are obliged to interrogate' (Silverman, 1999, p. 25).

Historians should stop attempting the impossible and simply point to places where events took place, name them and do no more.

10. Whenever historians explain the causes of past events, or find patterns of significance among them, the account they present reflects their theoretical preconceptions and interests. Their interests direct their attention to some matters rather than others; and their preconceptions determine what causes and effects of events they notice and describe. Consequently historical interpretations and explanations do not truly represent the past, but are constructions which reflect the historian's culture.

These criticisms leave us with the impression that historians do not discover facts about the past; rather they create them. Written history is the product of historians' perceptions, beliefs, interests and assumptions together with a big dose of imagination; and we have no way of knowing what relationship it has to events in the past. Consequently we have no reason to declare any historical description true in a correspondence sense. The most we can claim is that our beliefs about the past cohere well with other beliefs we hold about the nature of the world. It is now easier to understand why Jenkins was inclined to deny the possibility of knowing the truth of history. '[W]e might as well forget history', he writes, 'and live in the ample imaginaries provided by postmodern type theorists' (ibid., p. 12).

In dismissing historical knowledge so lightly, Jenkins and other sceptics fail to appreciate the value of history as the source of our understanding of culture and society. How could we judge the value of our laws and institutions if we did not know why they were created and how they had functioned in the past? Imagination is not reliable enough to guide us. Historical knowledge is a precious source of wisdom and essential to the efficient formulation of social, economic, political and military policy. Indeed everyone in the community who votes for parliamentary parties will draw upon historical knowledge to judge the value of the parties' programmes. Historical knowledge is much too important to be lightly lost. The question is, can it be rendered intelligible again, and is there any way its credibility can be restored?

We cannot simply ignore the critics and assert naïve empiricism once again. We need a new, more sophisticated theory of historical knowledge to inspire us. I propose that it be called 'a critical theory of truth'. This name highlights the fact that credible history is history which has survived criticism and is rationally justifiable, not merely the product of an historian's imagination. The theory is also a kind of critique, a critical analysis of historical judgement. (It is not, however, a critique of social processes, such as is associated with critical social theories, for example those of Marx, the Frankfurt School and Habermas (see Held, 1980).)

A critical theory of truth

1. According to our best theories of perception, our perceptions are a product of the things in the world which cause them, as well as of the preconceptions

which frame them and the interests which direct them. That is why we say they are perceptions of whatever we have reason to think caused them.

Our experience of the things we perceive, their shape and colour for instance, is partly given and partly constructed. It is certainly not purely a product of our imagination. We know it might not perfectly mirror reality, but we also know that attributing it to reality in normal circumstances produces reliable beliefs about the world. Consequently we form the belief that the world is more or less as we perceive it. We hold this belief for practical reasons: we need a picture of the world in order to survive and flourish in it, and this is a good enough picture for our everyday purposes.

We cannot compare the world to our perceptions of it: all we have to go on are our perceptions. But we normally accord our perceptions, made in reliable conditions, more credibility than other beliefs about the world because they are generally more reliable. To say they are reliable means that other experiences implied by assuming them to be true are borne out in practice. It is because we accord our perceptions more reliability than other beliefs that we use them to check and correct our other beliefs about the world.

Sometimes perceptions occur, even in normally reliable conditions, which are mistaken. For example, it is easy to mistake plastic or cloth flowers for real ones, even under a bright light. Further tests, such as touching the flowers to determine their texture, reveal the mistake. So it is not the case that all perceptions made under normally reliable conditions are true. However, generally it is much more probable that they prove more reliable than other kinds of beliefs.

2. There are two important problems with the traditional correspondence theory of truth. The first is that it is unintelligible. The theory is that to say a description of something in the world is true means the thing is correctly picked out by the subject of the sentence and the predicate really applies to it. What are unintelligible are the concepts of 'correctly picked out' and 'really applies'. Suppose I said: 'There is a computer in my room'. For this to be true according to the correspondence theory, the thing I am referring to must really be a computer and it must really be in my room. What do correspondence theorists mean by saying there really is a computer in my room? Perhaps they mean there exists something which regularly appears to me to be (i.e. causes me to perceive) a computer in my room. But appearances can be deceptive. What appears to be a computer could be just the shell of a computer; or it could be a hologram, or a mirror image of a computer. Perhaps they mean that there is something that appears to God to be a computer in my room, assuming that God is never mistaken and that he knows the rules of our language.

The second problem with the traditional correspondence theory follows from the first: the theory is useless, for it follows from that theory that we can never know that any description of the world is true, since none of us is divine, nor have we certain knowledge of the mind of God.

3. To overcome these problems, I propose we adopt a theory rather like one produced by Charles Peirce. He said that a description of the world is true if it is

part of an ideal theory which explains all possible observations of the world, and I would add that for an ideal theory of the world to be true there must exist in reality something which could cause all those perceptions, were people in a position to make them. This is not what people normally mean when they call a description true, but it states the conditions under which it is reasonable to believe a description true. This theory does not tie truth to an unintelligible, unknowable correspondence. And it explains our method of deciding the truth of descriptions of the world remarkably well. You recall how we test our perceptions by checking out their implications: if something which looks like a natural flower does not also feel like a natural flower, then we judge that our perception of it was mistaken. This is the process of testing an explanation of one perception by checking it against another. Historians interpret the evidence available to them very largely by constructing plausible explanations of it, thereby building up an account of what happened in the past. Scientists also develop laws and theories to account for their observations of the world, thereby enlarging our ideas about what exists.

If the truth about the world resides in an ideal explanation of all possible observations of it, then the truth would seem to be unknowable, since we have no such ideal explanation at hand. Still, we might reasonably claim to know parts of it when we know some descriptions of the world which explain such a large amount and variety of perceived evidence that we have good reason to believe they would be part of an ideal theory if we had it. Certainly our knowledge is fallible and the most we can justify is the credibility of those descriptions of the world which provide excellent explanations of a large range of observations. We are never in a position to prove their truth beyond all possibility of error. Nevertheless, the truth is a goal which all serious inquiry about the world is trying to attain.

As things stand, part of the best explanation of our experiences is that they are caused by things outside us, things in the world which we say we perceive. We have no idea what those things in the world are like independent of our beliefs about them. We cannot make sense of the notion of a correspondence between our beliefs about them and their intrinsic nature without appeal to the view of a relatively unknowable God. All we can intelligibly assert, it seems, is that there are things in the world which help to produce the perceptions we experience.

For an ideal theory to predict human perceptions, it would have to include a hypothesis about the nature of the external world, together with a hypothesis about the state of the perceiver – the perceiver's sense organs, language, preconceptions, interests and values and so on – as all these contribute to any perceptual experience. Of course the state of the perceiver is a fact about the world just as much as the state of trees and houses. The concept of perception will have vague limits, because it is not always clear what is perceived and what is inferred from a perception. 'I can see you are frowning' reports a perception of a physical state; may one also say 'I can see you are angry'? I think so, though you might want to say 'I infer you are angry'. When we say that our knowledge of the world is designed to account for perceptions, however, it is the perceptions of physical states which are given priority. It might be that the person who is frowning is not angry but just worried; but it is certain that he or she is frowning. The perceptions of physical states are given priority because they provide us with the most reliable hypotheses about the state of the world.

If an ideal theory is designed to account for all possible perceptions of the world, you might ask are they part of the ideal theory, and so true, or not? I am inclined to say that perceptions are data which are neither true nor false, whose significance depends on how they are explained. Some will be explained as veridical, some as mistaken, some as hallucinations, some as dreams. Descriptions of perceptions are treated as *prima facie* correct (according to the rules of language), that is, as correct unless or until there is good reason for thinking them mistaken. Occasionally the best explanation of a lot of reports gives reason to doubt that another reported perception really occurred as described, in which case it is not accepted as correct. Explanations of perceptions give an account of how a perception came about, and they do so by using descriptions of those perceptions. For instance, they explain an historian's perception of a letter by saying 'the historian can see the letter because the letter is on the table before her'. The existence of the letter explains the historian's perception of it, but the explanation itself is provided in words which describe the perception and the letter.

When we call an historical description of the world true, we mean that there were things in the world that could have produced the possible perceptions which the description implies, had there been someone present to perceive them. We are justified in believing this according to our best explanatory theory. That theory also provides a description of a causal process which produced those perceptions. Our best theory is a scientific one, though historians use everyday beliefs about the world when constructing explanations of their perceptions of evidence. Scientific theories explain scientific observations, and commonsense theories explain everyday perceptions. An ideal theory is one which will relate the various theories of reality to one another. Historians draw upon specialized scientific theories occasionally to explain otherwise inexplicable events, but normally their explanations are of a commonsense variety.

Our knowledge of reality is an edifice built upon the perceptions people experience, and they constantly serve as the basis for increasing and modifying that building. It is possible that more than one ideal theory could explain perceptions equally well. In that case, for a description of the world to be true, it must be a member of one of the ideal explanatory theories, and its truth would be relative to that theory.

If an ideal explanatory theory is at present unknowable, why should we believe any descriptions of the world true, as at the end of science they might well be false? The reason is that from experience we have found most of our everyday explanations of perceptions are quite reliable guides to experience, helping us anticipate the experiences we can expect to have in the world. If the best explanation of my experience of a tree is that it exists, then I can expect to see it again next time I look in its direction. So reliable is our knowledge of the world that we plan and act successfully on the basis of it. We believe it for practical reasons, even though we know it is fallible. Believing that a description of the world is reliable normally entails assuming that there are things in the world just as described. People assume that there are things in the world with the perceptible and imperceptible properties ascribed to them, even though they cannot prove this to be the case.

Notice, by the way, that I am not saying the best explanation of perceptions is true because it is useful, which Peirce was inclined to say. I am saying that we believe our best explanations to be true, because it is useful to do so. An ideal explanation is true if, as I said before, the perceptions it implies are of the kind which the world supplies.

Clearly the task of fully elaborating a theory of truth along these lines is a big one, and the above remarks simply sketch some of its features. It is promising enough, however, to show that the abandonment of the naïve correspondence theory need not entail general scepticism about the possibility of knowing the truth about the world.

4. Can we know the truth about the past? Traditionally philosophers have defined knowledge as justified true belief, and although this simple analysis has been found inadequate in some ways, philosophers still insist that knowledge entails truth. If the truth about the world lies in an ideal theory, and we never have access to that theory, then we clearly can never know the truth about the past.

What we can have, however, are reasons for believing that some descriptions of the world are probably in an ideal explanatory theory, that is reasons for believing the descriptions to be true. This is the case when a description of the world is supported by such a variety of perceptions that the chances of falsifying it are minute, and when the description does not depend upon some high level theory which is likely to change in time. Perceptions of historical evidence are normally couched in everyday terms, and when there is a lot of evidence of different kinds explained by the same description of the past, then it is very unlikely that the description will be falsified in time.

If there is good reason for supposing a description of the past to be true, then we can call it 'credible'. In everyday speech we normally use the word 'knowledge' to refer to beliefs that are very credible, acknowledging that such 'knowledge' is fallible. I think this is a good practice, as one cannot prove that one knows anything about the world in the strict philosophical sense of the word 'know'. However, rather than distress traditional philosophers, I will confine myself to saying that historians can provide credible descriptions of the past, even though they cannot strictly know what happened. There are degrees of credibility, corresponding to degrees of justification for one's belief in an historical description. Descriptions supported by a great variety of evidence are generally more credible than those for which the evidence is slight.

Critics sometimes point to historical descriptions which are contested, for which the evidence is inconclusive, as proof that we can never justify descriptions of what happened in the past. What they ignore are the millions of historical facts that are attested by masses of evidence and are never disputed. For instance, historians are often uncertain about the motives of great leaders, but know without question most of the important things they have done. The evidence of their deeds often lies in official reports, newspaper accounts and private letters, not to mention radio and television bulletins. These reports can, of course, be biased, but when they come from different sources with different perspectives, and there is no strong reason for the sources to falsify their descriptions, then there is good reason to believe them true. Their truth best explains the variety of witnesses to them.

In creating explanations of evidence and of the historical events implied by that evidence, historians form generalizations which can then be used in drawing further inferences about the past. In those cases the credibility of each inference rests, not in the amount and variety of evidence it explains, but in the knowledge of the frequency with which the kind of evidence that is available was associated with, or brought about by, an event of the kind described. For instance, historians can often identify the source of a script by noting its resemblance to other examples whose source they have been able to identify. For inferences of this kind to be reliable, the general correlation between a feature of the evidence, such as the style of handwriting, and a kind of cause of that feature, for instance the author of the script, must be lawlike and not accidental. We commonly assume a correlation to be lawlike in order to account for the frequency with which it has been observed to occur.

Descriptions of regular features of the world employ general concepts. Such concepts are often related hierarchically, in ascending degrees of generality. Some historical descriptions are justified simply by reference to the rules of language. For instance, if a document has a certain format, it might reasonably be classified as a letter, and a collection of letters between two people might be said to constitute the correspondence between them. If an area of land has certain markings, posts and net, it might correctly be classified as a tennis court, and an activity upon it which followed the rules of tennis be said to constitute a game of tennis. If a group of people regularly obey another person, they might be called a social organization. If people regularly respond to a certain kind of situation in a similar way, this could be called a practice. The relations involved are those of classification or constitution, and they are justified by rules of language which are sometimes elements of a theory: a document can be classified as a letter; a group of people can be said to constitute a social organization. One finds structural hierarchies in nature too: atoms form molecules which form elements and compounds; proteins form cells which form organisms, though biological patterns are much less regular and stable than chemical ones. Inferences involving classification or constitution of things in the world clearly depend upon rules of language which name them and to theories which refer to them.

Sometimes historians are interested in a social structure in the past as it was understood by the people contemporary with it and affected by it. To discover this, they have to find contemporary descriptions of it. At other times, historians wish to describe the social structure of a past society in terms of a modern theory which would not necessarily have been known to the people involved in it. To do this, they need only be familiar with the modern theory, though they need to take care that its concepts really apply to the period in question.

Historians can justify the credibility of their descriptions of the past in any of the three ways just described: by an argument to the best explanation of available evidence, by an inference from a generalization, or by appealing to rules of language. There remain five common sources of scepticism about the credibility of history which will now be briefly addressed. Some will be discussed at greater length later in the book.

Some common reasons for scepticism

1. Some, such as F.R. Ankersmit (1983), think that because historians describe the same event differently, their descriptions cannot be credible. On 19 May 2000, George Speight led a group of armed gunmen into Fiji's democratically elected parliament and held its members hostage for 50 days. Some have described this event as an attack upon democracy in Fiji and others have portrayed it as an assertion of traditional rights by the indigenous Fijian people. Clearly both descriptions are warranted and credible.

It is easy to see that many different descriptions of the same thing can be credible. Each description has a range of conditions whose existence would conventionally warrant it. Thus the imprisonment of the members of parliament could have taken place in any number of places, under a whole range of severe conditions, and still be called 'imprisonment'. As long as what happened fell within the range of conditions that warrant the description, it is justified. Both the descriptions of the event given above are justified and credible: it was an attack upon the practice of democracy in Fiji and it was an assertion of traditional indigenous Fijian authority. It was also a criminal act of imprisonment. Which description people give will certainly depend upon their interests, but all can be credible.

2. Some think that historians' interests in a subject will inevitably distort their accounts of it, so that no historical descriptions are credible. There is no doubt that people's emotions can not only direct but also actually distort their perceptions of things in the world. Lovers are famous for finding beauty in people which others cannot see and, I suppose, haters attribute evil to others unjustly. At all events, historians' attitudes to historical people and events can influence their selection and interpretation of evidence about them. And it normally influences them quite unconsciously.

Even when historians know how their descriptions of the past should be justified, they can be moved to marshal the evidence for their preferred account unjustly, including what supports their preferred view and omitting what tells against it. Bias in historical argument can only be checked by other historians familiar with the material, but coming at it from another point of view. This is why consensus among historians is important. Not because this guarantees credibility, but because it helps to eliminate individual bias in historical thinking. Widespread cultural bias is more difficult to detect and remove. (For a much fuller discussion of bias in history, see McCullagh, 2000.)

The likelihood that historians' hypotheses about the past are biased, as well as their arguments in support of them, shows how hard it is to achieve truly rational beliefs. Still, while historians are free to criticize the findings of their colleagues, there is a good chance that they will often be achieved. In totalitarian states, however, history is normally unchallenged propaganda.

3. Some think that because historians employ concepts and beliefs drawn from their own culture in describing the past, their descriptions of the past cannot be worthy of belief. But this overlooks the fact that historians apply their concepts critically. At one stage Marxist historians described the English Civil War as part of a bourgeois revolution in which emerging agricultural capitalists tried to free themselves of feudal bonds. This interpretation was generally discarded as false once it was recognized that its implications were not supported by the evidence: opponents in the Civil War were not divided along class lines, for there were feudal aristocrats fighting on both sides.

The concepts used by historians are normally those of their own culture and language. Sometimes they also use concepts belonging to the times they are describing to show how contemporaries viewed the events occurring around them. Once again, the fact that there are many languages, and different sets of concepts, does not mean that no description of the past can be true. If the conditions which warrant a given sentence in a given language are satisfied by what it is reasonable to believe true of the historical subject, then it is correctly applied in describing it.

4. Some have argued that because historians are unable to capture past events in all their unique detail, they inevitably misrepresent them.

It is true that historical descriptions are usually couched in words of some generality. Sometimes the subject of an historical description is a class of things and sometimes it is an individual. Even when it is an individual, however, the predicate ascribed to that subject is usually of a general kind. For instance, if an historian said that Hitler hated the Jews, that is a singular statement about one individual – Hitler – but the predicate 'hated the Jews' is general and does not give us much detail about the content and ferocity of the hatred.

Clearly such general predicates can be true when the conditions which warrant those predicates are satisfied. But in that they are general, they are a bit vague. Is that a good reason for refusing to believe them? If the purpose of history was just to admire the unique in all its particularity, then they would be inadequate. Indeed, then historians would have to be silent, or merely gesture towards the inexpressible. But the reason we describe the world, and do not just admire it, is in order to understand it and learn how to act effectively within it.

The point of writing and studying history is not just to contemplate the unique, but to understand processes of historical change.

Jean-François Lyotard thought of historical generalizations as descriptions of very general processes of historical change, such as those produced by Hegel and Marx, which have been used as the basis of political programmes aimed at making people conform to patterns of behaviour which will, on these theories, yield progress. But the generalizations which people value from an education in history are not these grand narrative accounts of historical progress. They are more everyday generalizations about the causes of historical change which they find illustrated in the past and, at times, refined by their study of unusual events in the past. General knowledge of this kind is an immensely important product of an education in history.

5. Finally, there is the argument that the meaning of words and sentences depends upon that of other words and sentences to which they are related in the minds of those who read them, and that these associations are more or less limit-less, so that it becomes impossible to define the meaning of sentences at all precisely. Indeed each sentence means something different to each person who reads it, so it has no fixed meaning to be deemed credible or incredible.

Be that as it may, for each sentence there is a range of sets of conditions necessary and sufficient for it to be justified according to the rules of language. These constitute the conventional meaning of the sentence, the meaning which is judged to be more or less credible or incredible. Other associations that sentences have for individual readers will, of course, vary, but they are irrelevant when judging their credibility.

Conclusion

Historical descriptions are constructed by historians on the basis of the evidence available to them, interpreted according to their general and historical beliefs. In calling them credible, historians are not saying they have magical access to the past which enables them to see what happened, so that they can vouch for their accuracy. Rather, they are asserting that the historical descriptions are part of an excellent explanation of the evidence available to them, indeed part of the best explanation that can be imagined, an explanation which is unlikely to be super-seded in future. (What constitutes a good explanation will be described in Chapter 3.)

The historians who write history books have usually been trained in the rational evaluation of evidence and are experts in their field. So they are well qualified and equipped to come up with the very best explanations of the evidence which relates to that field. In later chapters of this book you will see examples of the reasoning they employ in justifying their descriptions, inter-pretations and explanations of past events. These patterns of reasoning are absolutely vital in enabling them to decide which descriptions, interpretations

and explanations are worthy of belief, and which are not. Every practising historian has to consider the implications of their data as rationally as they can.

This does not mean that their conclusions are always correct. It may be that
their judgements are not as rational as they should be. Or that the evidence
available to them is later found to have been misleading, when more evidence
comes to hand. Or that the general knowledge they used in interpreting the
evidence is found to have been unreliable. Or that their beliefs about the historical context of the events they are investigating are later found to have been
mistaken.

Given these possible causes of error, is it then reasonable to believe what is
written in history books? There are two reasons for saying that it is. First, responsible historians will present only descriptions of the past which they have good
reason for thinking correct. That means there is normally abundant evidence for
them, evidence whose implications can scarcely be disputed. In that case it is
reasonable to believe them to be true, even though it remains logically possible
that they are false, that one day an even better account will be found.

Given this logical possibility, however, you might wonder whether we should
not remain sceptical about historical knowledge. This raises an interesting point
about scepticism in general. All our knowledge of the world could be mistaken,
but we find it useful to believe those descriptions of it which explain our perceptual experiences well. Such beliefs guide our behaviour, and normally do so quite
successfully. So we have practical reasons, a pragmatic justification, for belief.
This applies to historical knowledge just as it does to beliefs about the present
world. For example, our knowledge of how the Nazis treated the Jews is of value
as it reminds us of the ever-present danger of racism and genocide. Historical
knowledge, in very many ways, enables us to understand the present. We accept
it as true, when it is well justified, for practical purposes.

Chapter 2

The meanings of texts, actions and events

When historians begin to investigate the past, they search for evidence of what happened, and that evidence will almost inevitably take the form of a text. How should they interpret that text? Texts can reveal a variety of things about the past, as we shall see, and how historians interpret texts depends upon the kind of information they are after. The first section of this chapter will sketch the kinds of meanings texts can have, and how they are discovered.

The second section considers a number of objections that have been raised against the possibility of arriving at a credible understanding of the meanings of texts. This is quite a philosophical section, so readers with no interest in these arguments could miss it. However, in a book devoted to defending the rationality of history, the objections cannot be ignored, which is why they are discussed here.

This chapter is largely about the meanings of texts. But while on the subject of meaning, it is convenient to discuss the meanings of actions and events as well, so a short section on these has been added to the end of the chapter.

The meanings of texts

When historians examine a text from the past, they usually begin by looking for its conventional meaning, and if they know the language well they can usually grasp it without much trouble. This section starts by noting some problems in discovering and conveying the conventional meaning of the text. Sometimes historians are interested in the way people interpreted the text in the past, and form hypotheses about the way particular people read it, usually to explain their responses to it. Thirdly, historians of ideas also find the content of some texts fascinating, and offer general summaries of what they mean to compare and contrast them with other texts. These ways of reading texts will also be described.

One can know the conventional meaning of a text without knowing anything about the circumstances of its creation. All one needs to know is the language in which it is written and the context to which it refers. In fact most of the books and papers we read and understand are works of whose authors we are content to remain quite ignorant. It is sometimes tempting for historians to read accounts of past events as though they were quite correct, without bothering to investigate the conditions under which they were constructed. But shrewd historians recognize that texts are constructed by individuals, and are derived from their beliefs, purposes, interests and attitudes. If the author was well informed, wanted to convey the truth and to give a balanced account of the subject, and used the language well, then perhaps the conventional meaning of their text could be trusted to give an accurate impression of something that happened in the past. But without considerable knowledge of their authors, historians should not take texts at their face value.

When people write texts, they normally expect them to be understood in a conventional way. So when historians interpret texts, they often ask: why did the author want to convey the information contained in this text? The information in question is the conventional meaning of the text. (We will examine a particular instance of this question at the beginning of the next chapter, on historical inferences.) So although the conventional meaning of a text is not the same as its historical significance, it is nevertheless very important in determining the historical significance of a text.

To understand the conventional meaning of a text, historians obviously need to know the language in which it is written, and the context of the sentences, so that they can tell what people and events they refer to. The context is often given in the text itself, but sometimes it is not. A diary, for instance, might refer to people by initials, and an historian would need to know from other sources the names of the author's friends and colleagues in order to decide who they are.

If the text is from a culture about which an historian knows almost nothing, then it is very hard to interpret. In effect, historians have then to learn the whole language of that culture before they can interpret its individual texts confidently. Impressive examples of this are the success historians have had in interpreting ancient Minoan writing in Crete, and the hieroglyphs of the Mayan people in Middle America (which I have explained in McCullagh, 1984, pp. 111–16; cf. McCullagh, 1998, pp. 164–6).

Once the conventional meaning of a text has been established, historians face the task of communicating it to their readers. This is the task of translation, and its pitfalls have been discussed by historians for ages. David Thelan recently noticed that some historians try to communicate the different world view of those they are describing, whereas others simply look for the closest modern equivalent to their ideas (Thelan, 1999, p. 1294). Those wanting readers to understand the period from which the document came adopt the first approach, whereas those more interested in the message the document has for the present adopt the second. A responsible historian, I suggest, will try to explain the world view of the authors of the document, leaving its modern significance for readers to determine.

There are many more or less technical problems in translation. Sometimes the obvious translation of a term in a text has misleading connotations in the receptor language. W.P. Adams has remarked that the word 'farmer' in America suggests farming wide prairies, whereas the equivalent in French ('fermier') and German ('Bauer') suggests 'more or less gardened landscapes'. To circumvent this problem, Germans have adopted the English word ('der Farmer') to refer to farmers in America, Australia and Africa (Adams, 1999, p. 1286). When there is no direct equivalent in the receptor language, historians are forced to substitute a paraphrase which explains what the original meant. For example, the English concept of 'common law' is translated into German by a phrase meaning 'the unwritten English customary and case law' (das ungeschriebene englische Gewohnheits-und-Fallrecht) (ibid.).

Occasionally the meaning of a term in the original text is uncertain, and historians are sometimes tempted to impose a meaning upon it in translation. Thelan notes the many ways in which people have translated the American Declaration of Independence. It begins: 'When in the course of human events, it becomes necessary for one people to dissolve the political bands which have connected them with another.' It is not clear what Jefferson meant by 'one people'. It could mean 'people with a deeply shared cultural past' (German 'Volk'), or just 'inhabitants of a place' ('Einwohner'). It could mean 'nation' (Polish 'narod'), suggesting a nation ruled by the upper classes, or just 'the people' ('lud'), suggesting the lower classes. Finally, a Japanese translator thought it meant 'a kin group of people', the Americans (ibid., pp. 1296–7). The need to translate the term made people aware of its vagueness. Rather than impose a meaning upon the term through translation, a responsible historian should point out its vagueness, leaving readers to make of it what they can. Perhaps Jefferson himself had no clear idea of its meaning.

Normally the conventional meaning of a text is the one which the author intended to convey, but very occasionally an author writes ironically, satirically, humorously or mistakenly, and intends to say something else. Jonathan Swift, for example, intended his book *Gulliver's Travels* to be a political satire; and Cervantes intended *Don Quixote* to be a parody of knightly chivalry (see McCullagh, 1998, pp. 154–5). To be sure of such interpretations, historians must often discover quite a lot about the circumstances of the text's composition from other sources. At all events, the conventional meaning of a text is not necessarily its intended meaning.

It is almost impossible to guess how people in the past read the texts before them. Even when they are fluent in the language of the text, and familiar with its context, it is common for people to find things in texts which were not there, or to distort what was said in some way. It is only when readers describe a text that an historian can be certain of their reading of it. If a person's reading is inaccurate, then historians sometimes investigate the causes of the misreading, using it as a way into the mind and personality of the reader.

An historian's own reading of a text is not always accurate, because historians usually read texts hoping to find evidence for or against a certain hypothesis about the past, and are prone to overlook what does not suit them. Historians of ideas are more likely to be accurate, as they want to discover precisely what the author thought about the matter which interests them. They will sometimes provide the briefest possible summary of a text, which is a statement of the thesis that the text had been created to defend. A nice example of this kind of summary is provided in Quentin Skinner's lectures entitled *Liberty before Liberalism*, in which he contrasts two schools of thought about the nature of civil liberty, one which he called 'neo-roman' and the other which he called 'liberal' or 'classical'. The first he finds exemplified at the time of the English Revolution in the writing of Parker, Nedham, Milton and Harrington, and in the 1730s by Lord Bolingbroke, whereas the classical liberal view was expressed by William Paley. Skinner sums up the contrast between their views in these words:

> What, then, divides the neo-roman from the liberal understanding of freedom? What the neo-roman writers repudiate *avant la lettre* is the key assumption of classical liberalism to the effect that force or the coercive threat of it constitute the only forms of constraint that interfere with individual liberty. The neo-roman writers insist, by contrast, that to live in a condition of dependence is in itself a source and a form of constraint. As soon as you recognize that you are living in such a condition, this will serve in itself to constrain you from exercising a number of your civil rights.
>
> (Skinner, 1998, p. 84)

The processes of thought which enable people to understand texts are much too complicated to describe. There have been several objections, however, to the possibility of reaching a credible interpretation of a text, and these will be described and responded to in the next section.

Problems about knowing the meanings of texts

There are seven problems about knowing the meanings of texts which deserve discussion:

(i) The meaning of languages is not as uniform or stable as is commonly supposed, so there is no such thing as a 'conventional' reading of a text.

(ii) Since the 'linguistic turn' in cultural studies, the context of a text is sometimes thought to be other texts, not conditions in the world at all. There is a sense in which the social contexts of texts are linguistically constructed. So is it reasonable to believe they have actually existed as the points of reference for people's descriptions of them?

(iii) Some postmodern writers view texts as products of the discourses in which they were produced, and not expressions of their authors' intentions at all. Indeed they see the production of texts as ways in which authors fashion their social persona. If there are no authors' intentions outside of texts about them, then there cannot be intended meanings of texts.

(iv) Texts only have meaning when someone reads them. Their meaning is what the reader takes them to mean. In that case, there is no 'conventional' meaning of a text, only the various meanings it has for various readers. Furthermore, as was said in the last chapter, texts produce associations, contrasts and resonances in the minds of their readers which have no limit. Therefore, any attempt to state what a text meant to some reader is bound to be inadequate.

(v) Some think that every summary interpretation of a text is inevitably subjective, so that every such interpretation is as good or bad as the others. They overlook the conventional expectation that such interpretations be accurate and comprehensive, as well as informative.

(vi) There are ways in which the reading of a text can be biased. Can bias ever really be avoided?

(vii) Finally, there are problems of hermeneutical circles. Is not the interpretation of a text judged by its coherence rather than its credibility?

These are the main difficulties critics have raised against the possibility of arriving at a rational understanding of the various meanings of a text which would be acceptable to all. Each can be answered, as I shall now show.

(i) The uniformity of meaning

To discover the literal meaning of a text, historians have to acquire mastery of the language in which it was written. This involves discovering the world view which the language expresses. As soon as historians begin to investigate the languages of a society, however, they find that there are several different discourses being used, and that these are by no means stable. In an interesting discussion of the topic, David Harlan reports that J.G.A. Pocock found that 'every language system is a melange of "sublanguages, idioms, rhetorics and modes of speech, each of which varies in its degree of autonomy and stability"' (Harlan, 1989, p. 591). He also quotes Michel Foucault, who found that medical discourse in France changed enormously between 1780 and 1830. Foucault wrote: 'In the space of forty or fifty years everything has changed: what one talked about, the way one talked about it; not just remedies, of course, not just the maladies and their classifications, but the outlook itself' (ibid., quoted on p. 590). Such changes in discourse come about through innovation by users of the discourse, so historians have to be prepared for unconventional usage in the texts they interpret.

Not only do discourses change over time, historians sometimes find that different individuals and social groups in a community use the same word in different senses. Peter Lake, for example, has identified three different ways in which groups thought of 'Puritans' in early seventeenth-century England. All agreed about the nature of Puritan beliefs and practices, but they disagreed about the Puritan character. There was the view of Puritans themselves, who considered their pious practices as proof of their election for salvation; there was the view of some who mocked them, who saw them as 'self-righteous and self-selecting groups whose high opinion of themselves made them the object of a good deal of ill feeling and satirical humor' (Lake, 1993, p. 15). And third, there was the view of the Laudians, the high Anglicans, of a stereotype of Puritan deviance and subversion; word centered, sermon obsessed, and sermon gadding, at best indifferent and at worst hostile to the rites and ceremonies of the church and the demands of the beauty of holiness, sacrilegious in its attitude to the physical site and possessions of the church and the rights and tithes of the clergy, obsessed with their own status as elect saints, semi-separatist in their addiction to their own conventicles and meetings, bizarrely superstitious on the matter of the sabbath.

(ibid., p. 21)

Lake sums it up when he says: 'Viewed both from inside and outside, then, there was considerable agreement about what Puritan godliness looked like, accompanied, of course, by complete disagreement about what it meant' (ibid., p. 22). Within each of these groups, there were variations of view and emphasis. Lake notes, for example, that 'the Laudian vision of Puritanism was comprised of many strands developed by various anti-Puritan and conformist authors, both popular and élite, since the 1570s' (ibid.).

If the meaning of words in a language in a community can vary so much, how can historians be confident that they have correctly interpreted texts written by members of that community? What helps historians to understand texts is that most of the words and concepts employed in past texts are common within the community where the texts were created. Many of the words are common to the whole community. Some are common to subgroups within it, to medicine and the law, for example, and so require special knowledge of their vocabulary. Extensive reading within those subgroups eventually produces the familiarity needed to understand them. When the meaning of a word is uncertain, or its normal meaning does not make sense, the context of the particular text in which the words occur will often limit the range of its possible meanings. Historians then try the various possible meanings to see which best fits the context, both the immediate textual context, and the historical context in which the text was produced. The conventional (and intended) meaning of 'Puritan' in a seventeenth-century document would depend upon the nature of the group in which it originated and for which it was written: Puritan, mockers or high Anglican.

(ii) Are the contexts of texts just other texts?

Sometimes the literal meaning of a sentence leaves the precise meaning of specific words uncertain. For instance, if a document said 'I wrote to him last Thursday', it might not be clear who the words 'I' and 'him' refer to, nor which Thursday was 'last Thursday'. To clarify the meaning of these words, an historian must consider their context. The context will include other parts of the text, as well as what the historian knows about its author and the circumstances in which the document was written. If the document is a letter, a date at the beginning would fix the date of 'last Thursday', and the signature at the end would reveal who 'I' was. The identity of 'him' might also be given in the letter, or else-where in the correspondence of which the letter was a part.

The meaning of a text in which uncertainties are resolved by reference to the context of the text is what I call the 'basic meaning' of the text (see McCullagh, 1998, ch. 5), which is the text's conventional meaning. To test whether or not an interpretation of the conventional meaning of a text is satisfactory, historians consider its implications and check whether they are consistent with what is known of the author's beliefs and attitudes and the author's situation and behaviour.

There are two general objections to the suggestion that historians under-stand documents by considering their historical context. The first can best be explained by considering how historical writing can be deconstructed. For example, if you ask an historian how he knows who the author of a letter is, he points to the signature at the foot of the letter, which is not the author himself writing the letter, but a text with his name on it. If you press him to explain why he thinks this was written by that person, he will, let's say, point to the author's letter book, in which he recorded the letters he wrote, in short to another text. It seems that historians' knowledge of historical contexts is always provided by texts about that context. So really, historians interpret texts by reference to other texts they have at hand. It seems there is no reference to actual past events and people at all. A natural response is to point out that the texts to which historians refer are evidence of the historical context. But to say that, the critics go on, is just to supply another text about them. All talk about evidence is just part of a discourse of historical justification, the sort of text historians like to produce. It seems we can never get outside the world of texts. These could be said to constitute the world for historians, for they know of nothing besides them. (See the exposition and discussion of this point by Spiegel, 1990.)

In practice, historians refuse to agree that they cannot interpret texts by refer-ence to their original historical contexts. Spiegel's words are echoed by many:

> In analyzing the meaning of texts, we need to do more than juxtapose them beside the 'circumambient' cultural 'scripts' of the period in the fashion of New Historicists, a procedure that inevitably aestheticizes culture and trans-forms text and context into a species of intertextuality. We should, rather, seek to locate texts within specific social sites that themselves disclose the political, economic, and social pressures that condition a culture's discourse at any given moment. Involved in this positioning of the text is an examina-tion of the play of power, human agency, and social experience as historians traditionally understand them.
>
> (ibid., p. 85)

Notice there is no argument here, just a refusal to deny the reality of the social contexts of texts.

The second recent objection to the possibility of discovering the social context of a text is well expressed by V.E. Bonnell and L. Hunt in the Introduction to *Beyond the Cultural Turn. New Directions in the Study of Society and Culture* (1999). They explain that postmodern theorists have substituted language about society for social realities themselves. They write: 'In the poststructuralist view, language or discourse did not mirror some prior social understanding or positioning and it could never penetrate to the truth of existence: it itself configured the expression of social meaning and functioned as a kind of veil between humans and the world around them . . . Social categories only came into being through their expressions or representations' (p. 9). If this were true, then historians could not interpret texts in their social context, but only by referring to other texts about society. In practice, however, historians retain belief in the reality of society, as we have seen. The editors note: 'Although the authors in this collection have all been profoundly influenced by the cultural turn, they have refused to accept the obliteration of the social that is implied by the most radical forms of culturalism or poststructuralism' (p. 11). They add: 'All of them emphasize empirical, comparative, and theoretically informed and informing studies. They have not given up on social or causal explanation; rather, they seek better explanations' (pp. 24–5).

Clearly practising historians have rejected the suggestion that they confine their interpretation of documents to consideration of other texts. They know how to reconstruct the social setting in which the documents were produced, and quite properly relate their meaning to that. What the sceptics have ignored is that the documents to which historians refer in the process of their research provide evidence of social realities which it is reasonable to believe really existed. Those who have the law, money, guns or status on their side can exercise real power, making others obey their will; those without any of these can easily be victimized. Social relations, such as those of relative power, are clearly not just texts. Certainly an historian's reconstruction of a social setting is expressed in a text, using the language of social sciences, but that is no reason for denying that what is described in the text really existed. As was said above, virtually all our knowledge of the world is linguistic, but we have rational ways of distinguishing descriptions of the world that are credible, and strong practical reasons for believing them.

The social context of a document can be fairly readily defined, given adequate evidence. But what of the intellectual context? Sometimes one needs to be familiar with the intellectual history of authors to acquire a full understanding of what they say. And one also needs to be aware of the intellectual context in which they write, to appreciate the intended point, or force, or their words. As David Hollinger has written, the relevant context for interpreting a text may have to include all 'the theoretical knowledge, literary and religious traditions, and other cultural resources that historians know to have been accessible to most well-informed members of a given society at a given historical moment' (in 'Historians and the Discourse of Intellectuals', quoted in Harlan, 1989, p. 594). This, of course, is an exaggeration. To decide uncertain references or meanings in a text, historians seldom need do more than read the works the author was likely to have had in mind when writing the text in question. Admittedly this assumes that the author's culture was in the same historical tradition as the historian's own, and that the historian has already a good background knowledge of the historical subject being investigated. Without this degree of familiarity with the author's culture, the task of interpreting texts would indeed be great.

(iii) Are there authors with intentions?

Traditionally it has been very important to know writers' intentions in order to understand their texts. As well as judging the conventional meaning of a text as evidence of what the author wished to convey, historians have always been interested in the author's intention in publishing the text. This often provides an important indication of possible bias in the text. Was it written to win favour with someone, or to justify some action, or to destroy a reputation? A text is likely to be biased according to the purpose for which it was written.

Some people, such as Michel Foucault (see below, pp. 95–8), have gone so far as to deny the reality of an author as a subject. They are impressed with the degree to which what people write and say is a product of the culture and society of which they are a part. People so often think, speak and act as convention dictates, that it seems they contribute nothing of their own at all. Foucault was impressed with the ways in which prevailing discourses shaped people's thought and behaviour. We used to think that people had a non-material, or transcendent, spirit, and that they were autonomous, able to deliberate and exercise their will in new, creative ways. Now this theory of human nature is rejected by some as unnecessary. Although we continue to speak about ourselves and others, as Bonnell and Hunt put it: 'the self as a meaningful conceptual category has largely been effaced; the self has been reduced to an entirely constructed, and therefore empty and wholly plastic, nodal point in the discursive or cultural system. Since poststructuralists and postmodernists have celebrated "the death of the subject", they have left little in the self to resist social or cultural determinations' (1999, p. 22).

Of course people talk about their thoughts, beliefs, desires and so on, but according to postmodern writers, this talk refers to nothing real at all. It is part of what they call 'self-fashioning', largely connected with the social roles they adopt. This idea was developed and illustrated particularly by S.J. Greenblatt (1980). He showed how different historical individuals drew upon traditions of their own culture to form their 'characters'. John Martin, in a useful discussion of this idea, summarizes a couple of Greenblatt's examples from sixteenth-century England thus: '[Sir Thomas] More's self-fashioning, for example, is portrayed as taking place in the interplay of his submission to the authority of the church and his opposition to heresy and the monarchy, while [William] Tyndale's self is depicted as developing out of the tensions between his opposition to the church,

on the one hand, and his submission to Scripture as authority, on the other'
(Martin, 1997, p. 1315). According to Greenblatt, '[t]here is no layer deeper,
more authentic, than theatrical self-representation' (quoted by Martin on
p. 1317 and p. 1319). Stephen Shapin has observed that people's identity is not
fixed, but is modified from time to time with changing circumstances. He writes:
'a personal identity has to be continually made, and is continually revised and
remade, throughout an individual career in contingent social and cultural settings' (quoted by Martin on p. 1320).

Martin's response to the theory of self-fashioning is quite subtle. He agrees
that people develop their ideas about their own nature from discourses prevalent
at the time, but he shows how people have individual, private characteristics, as
well as conventional, public ones. 'There are multiple layers in the make-up of a
particular person: a natural temperament, a cluster of (often conflicting) emotions, a primary language, a particular family and education, as well as broader
political, social, and cultural forces – all of these go into shaping us, making us
who we are. Accordingly, we are never purely the roles we play . . .' (ibid.,
p. 1337). He notes how Montaigne contrasted the private self, developed in
childhood, from the mask one adopts in certain social settings. He develops this
contrast by describing how, during the Renaissance and the Reformation, the
virtues of prudence and sincerity were promoted, each having to do with what
the private self should allow to be displayed in public. There were pressures to
adopt different public masks ('The fashioning of selves . . . is overdetermined . . .'
ibid., p. 1339), and there were incompatible pressures to behave with prudence
and sincerity as well.

> The language of prudence and sincerity points to a sense of interiority, albeit
> constructed, that cannot be viewed purely reflectively in relation to the cul-
> tural poetics of a particular place and period but was in fact relatively
> immune to the sort of ideological forces and totalizing pressures of the
> church or the monarchy that Greenblatt and other New Historicists have
> seen as determining if not as wholly hegemonic in the formation of Renais-
> sance identities . . .
>
> The very vocabulary of prudence and sincerity, moreover, enabled dissent
> and opposition, a salient feature of Renaissance political life that the New
> Historicism, with its emphasis on the self as 'unfree' has either ignored or
> failed to explain.
>
> (ibid., pp. 1339–40)

And this theory of human nature with its private and public aspects, which pre-
dates the Renaissance, has been with us ever since. It is superior to the shallow
reduction of human nature to patterns of discourse related to social roles, because
it explains the possibility of prudence and sincerity, the contrast between private
and public opinions, which the postmodern theory, denying the reality of the
contrast, cannot.

So, with the concept of the author restored, it makes sense to inquire about what authors intended to say, allowing that authors might not have said that at all, or not expressed themselves clearly. Sometimes the intended meaning of a text is in addition to its literal meaning. Jonathan Swift's book *Gulliver's Travels* was intended to be a satire upon King George I of Britain, and the politicians of his day. Knowing this, the reader can conclude that Swift meant his text to have two sets of meanings: its literal meaning, and another satirical meaning. If we believed it was intended to be nothing more than a whimsical story, then we would assume it had only one meaning, namely its literal meaning.

Following Foucault, historians are very sensitive these days to the political significance of the texts people have written, that is, the way they were intended to confirm or alter relations of power in the community. Spiegel rightly thinks the intended political significance of texts is very important, and insists it can only be discovered by taking the social and political context of a text into account when interpreting it. She discusses a document called the *Pseudo-Turpin Chronicle*, describing Charlemagne's expedition to Spain, which was translated from Latin verse into French prose and published in France in the early thirteenth century. This work celebrated the glory of the French aristocracy, and was published by French-Flemish aristocrats at a time when they were resisting the power of the Capetian king of France. Spiegel says that 'it inscribes . . . a partisan and ideologically motivated assertion of the aristocracy's place and prestige in medieval society' (Spiegel, 1990, p. 82). It was the work 'of a failing aristocracy in search of ethical and political reassurance' (ibid., p. 83). This purpose gives us a clue as to how those who published the translation intended it to be read. Spiegel notes that this meaning was 'completely different from what it had possessed in the hands of its original clerical authors' (ibid.).

How does one discover an author's intention? It was once thought that this was done through an act of empathetic imagination. This involved historians imagining the circumstances in which authors found themselves when writing, taking into account their beliefs, values and attitudes, and then imagining how they would have responded in precisely those conditions. We commonly use this technique to interpret what is going on in the minds of those around us, and it seemed natural to apply it to history. (See, for example, W. Dilthey's theory of understanding in Gardiner, 1959, pp. 211–25; and Collingwood, 1946, Pt V., sect. 4.) There are a couple of problems with this procedure, however. The first involves the assumptions being made about an author's beliefs, values and attitudes. How are these arrived at in the first place? Without specialized knowledge of their state of mind, one could only imagine that their views of the world were like ours, but that is bound to be wrong. So one cannot really discover the mental state of others by empathetic imagination, though often this technique is useful for suggesting possibilities. The second problem is that this method is quite uncritical. Once the historian imagines what someone intended to say, so long as this hypothesis seems to cohere quite well with what is known about the subject and their situation, it is accepted. But there could be other hypotheses even better supported by all the relevant evidence. Coherence is not enough.

The appropriate method for discovering authors' intentions is, once again, that of finding the best explanation of all the relevant evidence. An informed imagination can produce plausible hypotheses, but these must be checked against alternatives to discover which is most worthy of belief. People's intentions are often very difficult to discern, and responsible historians will admit to uncertainty when lack of evidence requires it. (For example, see several quite different interpretations of the intended point of Plato's *Lysis* and *Phaedo* in McCullagh, 1998, pp. 152–4.)

(iv) Do texts have objective meanings?

I have been discussing literal, basic and intended meanings of texts as though meanings had an existence of their own. But should we say that the meaning of a text is the meaning it has for someone who reads it? In that case it is a mental state of the reader, it is what the reader takes a text to mean. And it would presumably follow that a text has as many meanings as it has readers.

In fact, however, we often contrast the literal, basic and intended meanings of a text with what individuals take it to mean. We do so when a person reports the meaning of the text incorrectly. This practice alone shows that we contrast these kinds of meaning, and do not reduce all meanings of a text to their meaning for someone. You might think that when we correct another person, we are simply asserting the meaning which a text has for us over against the meaning it has for the person we are criticizing. But we allow that we too can be in error. The literal, basic and intended meanings are indeed objective, established in the ways indicated above. Public documents, such as laws and instructions, have an objective meaning which is generally recognized, and appealed to in courts of law. People are expected to interpret them, not in a personal, idiosyncratic way, but according to the procedures mentioned before. These procedures normally suffice to fix the meaning of the texts, so that all educated people would be expected to understand them correctly. Once the language, context and intention of a text are known, its meaning can usually be fixed.

But how can a conventional meaning of a text be fixed if the implications, associations and contrasts of its words and statements are without limit? The answer is, I think, that only some of those implications are deemed relevant for practical or argumentative purposes. In literary contexts, the various extraneous associations of a text are deemed to add to its richness, and are sometimes important in determining its significance. This is particularly the case with poetry. There is much less inclination to suppose a work of literature has a 'conventional' meaning than in the case of other texts. Instead it is normal to speak of there being various readings of literary works.

(v) Are summary interpretations inevitably subjective?

One way in which historians report the significance of a text is by giving a general summary of its themes or theses. Historians of ideas, for example, study texts in politics, philosophy or religion, and often try to summarize their main points. They do this primarily to enable them to compare and contrast the theories of one writer with the views of others.

The ever-present danger for historians of ideas is that they will attribute ideas to people in the past which they assume they had, without checking carefully to see whether they in fact held them. To avoid such mistakes, responsible historians strive to provide summaries which are accurate, comprehensive and informative. Accurate summaries are supported by the details of the text, and are not inconsistent with any of them. For a summary to be comprehensive, it must relate to all major points in the text. And an informative summary is not so general that it could apply to lots of different texts, but picks out the distinctive characteristics of the text in question.

Let me illustrate the first two conditions from discussions of general interpretations of the political writing of John Locke. It is particularly important for historians to observe these two conditions, for summaries which fail to respect them give a misleading impression of the text.

C.B. Macpherson, in his book *The Political Theory of Possessive Individualism*, said that in Locke's view, only people with property could be regarded as citizens of a state. Alan Ryan has pointed out that this part of Macpherson's summary is quite inconsistent with passages in which Locke clearly states that all rational adults should be regarded as citizens (Ryan, 1965, p. 223). Macpherson's mistake was possibly the result of his Marxist assumption, that Locke wrote to justify claims by the bourgeoisie to a greater say in government. Be that as it may, Ryan showed that on this point his summary was inaccurate. He was inaccurate on another point as well. Macpherson said that when Locke wrote of 'property' he meant material goods, whereas Ryan showed that for Locke, people's property included everything to which they had a right, and which others had no right to take without their consent. This included their life, liberty and health, as well as any material goods they owned. Ryan remarked that 'the force of Macpherson's account challenges one to produce some alternative picture that fits the text better than this' (ibid., pp. 227–8).

The importance of a summary interpretation being comprehensive is brought out by another discussion of Locke. John Plamenatz assumed that Locke was a great liberal philosopher who thought that people should obey a government if it governs with their consent. But John Dunn has pointed out that this is only part of Locke's theory. Locke also thought people should obey the government out of duty to God. God wills people's preservation, he said, and this is only possible in a good society. People should obey the government in order to maintain a society in which their preservation can be more or less ensured. By ignoring the religious aspect of Locke's thought, Plamenatz had produced an inaccurate account of his theory of political obligation (Dunn, 1980, pp. 29–33).

These examples show how historians check the misinterpretations of their colleagues, by appealing to standards of interpretation which are widely acknowledged. Professional historians expect general summaries of texts to be both accurate and comprehensive.

(vi) Historians' bias

When an historian's preconception of the past is motivated by an attitude of approval or disapproval of whatever the past is assumed to be, then the resulting history may be not merely mistaken but also biased. Sometimes it results in unjustified inferences being drawn from evidence; sometimes in descriptions of historical subjects that are unfair, in that they are misleadingly partial, given what is known about the subject; and sometimes a strong preference leads an historian to find evidence of one kind of cause, ignoring evidence of other causes of an historical event. Here are two examples of biased history resulting from understandable admiration of Thomas Jefferson, one of the eighteenth-century fathers of the American revolution against Britain, and author of the American Bill of Rights.

Stephen Conrad (1993) has described some of the different ways people have read an early essay which Jefferson wrote, entitled *Summary View of the Rights of British America*, first published in 1774. It discusses the justice of British rule in America, and justifies independence from British rule as it was then exercised. Conrad begins by noting how historians have generally seen this essay as an early defence of individual natural rights. They have seen it like this because Jefferson is famous for subsequently drafting the declaration of independence adopted by Congress on 4 July 1776, which opens with these famous words: 'We hold these truths to be self-evident, That all men are created equal, that they are endowed by the Creator with certain unalienable Rights, that among these are Life, Liberty and the pursuit of Happiness. That to secure these rights, Governments are instituted among Men . . .' and so on. He is also famous for drafting the amendments to the American constitution known as the Bill of Rights in 1789. Jefferson is so famous for promoting individual rights, that historians read his early essay as a defence of these. As Conrad put it, Jefferson has become a symbol for human rights, so that 'distinguished scholars can feel . . . a "sense of obligation to the symbol" entailing an "obligation" even to compromise "the historical truth" about the man behind the symbol' (Conrad, 1993, p. 256).

Conrad then argues that to read Jefferson's essay as a defence of individual rights is to misinterpret it. He says that the essay in question scarcely argues in favour of individual rights at all. Much of it is devoted to historical examples of the failure of rights to ensure justice, and Conrad notes that 'in more than one place in his account, he suggests that the mere act of claiming a right simply makes matters worse' (p. 263). So Jefferson turns from considering rights to consider the justice of British rule. (pp. 265–6) Conrad concludes: 'I would argue that the basic thrust of his argument does not depend on rights talk at all' (p. 273).

What Conrad has shown is that historians' interpretation of the essay has generally been quite biased by their preconceptions as to what they believed it must have contained. They read back into it a commitment to individual rights which in fact it did not strongly support.

Conrad also explains how the British saw the essay. They interpreted it 'as little more than "the determination of Virginia tobacco planters [of whom Jefferson was one] to repudiate their large debts to British merchants".' (p. 270). He goes on: 'Some of our most knowledgeable historians continue to read the *Summary View* as a manifesto of purely economic self-interest, if not necessarily as a ploy to repudiate debts' (ibid.). So here is another way of viewing the document, reflecting British concerns with the money owed them, and thinking that independence of British rule would effect a cancellation of Virginian debts to British merchants, which were enormous.

The moral is, historians' preconceptions and interests strongly influence the way they read documents. The point is not new, but it has led some philosophers of history to become very sceptical about historical knowledge.

A natural response to such scepticism is to point out how historians regularly correct such misperceptions, just as Conrad did. By examining the essay afresh, and in detail, he was able to point out that little of it defended individual natural rights, but that it examined other grounds of complaint against British rule. And a careful consideration of both its contents and its publication history led him to conclude that it was probably intended 'to consolidate American Whig sentiment' both within and beyond Virginia, to foster a sense of national identity in the face of British injustice (p. 271). The relief of Virginian debt was, if anything, a minor concern.

Another example of the influence of historical bias resulting from admiration for Jefferson is evident in the debate over the relationship between Jefferson and his slave, Sally Hemings. After his wife had died, it was rumoured that from 1784 Jefferson had a 38-year liaison with his slave woman named Sally Hemings, and that he fathered several of her children. This was denied by Jefferson and by many white historians who admired him. Annette Gordon-Reed, professor of law and no mean historian, has discussed the debate which followed in a book entitled *Thomas Jefferson and Sally Hemings* (1997). She says: 'most Jefferson scholars decided from the outset that this story was not true (p. 224). Gordon-Reed marshals the witnesses and all the relevant evidence, and considers the implications of it, both individually and collectively, very carefully. Some have thought that Jefferson was too much of a gentleman to do such a thing, that being an intellectual he lacked sexual passion (!), that his love for his family would have prevented him, and finally that his racism, his view that negroes were inferior people, would have made it impossible for him to take one as a mistress. In fact he trained several of her children, Beverley, Madison, and Easton, to become carpenters and musicians, and Harriet to become a wife, and gave them their freedom.

The case for Hemings being Jefferson's mistress is very strong. Both Madison and Easton Hemings long claimed to be Jefferson's children; the children's names were from the Jefferson family; Jefferson and Sally were living together at his house, Monticello, when each of these children would have been conceived; Sally and her children were the only slaves of Jefferson to be freed, the rest being auctioned after his death; and the children looked remarkably like him, as many people remarked. The hypothesis that Jefferson fathered those four children by Sally would help to account for all these facts, and clearly Gordon-Reed is persuaded of its truth, though she is cautious about admitting that outright. She is right to admit that the evidence does not provide incontrovertible proof, though its cumulative effect is persuasive (see ibid., p. xv).

It used to be thought that the best way to avoid bias in history is to urge historians to remain impartial and detached when considering the evidence in answer to their questions. But detachment cannot be guaranteed. I suggest that a better antidote is a strong, conscious commitment to rationality in the writing of history. This would involve the deliberate search for evidence inconsistent with a preferred hypothesis before being willing to assert its truth. It was a careful consideration of the relevant evidence which corrected the biases just noted concerning Thomas Jefferson. (For a full discussion of the problems of overcoming bias, see McCullagh, 2000.)

In practice, errors arising from the personal bias of historians are commonly corrected by their colleagues, especially by those who do not share their preferences. But culture-wide bias is much more difficult to correct. National histories used to praise the leaders of the nation, admire the achievements of its people, and blame others for any calamities that may have occurred. The bias would become especially prominent in histories of the nation at war, where the virtues of the nation would be extolled and the wickedness of its enemies exaggerated. It often requires other nations to correct such bias, resulting in a more balanced account. (See Berghahn and Schissler, 1987, p. 15.) Other kinds of culture-wide bias have been detected over the last few decades among Western historians. Until the Second World War, histories were written mostly by well-educated white males, and they commonly overlooked the historical significance of the actions of working-class people, coloured people, and women. Once members of these groups began to complain about their exclusion, the bias became widely recognized, and now would no longer be tolerated. National bias remains the most prevalent, and there are probably now quite strong biases for and against global capitalism. Some view it as the path to world freedom and prosperity, and others see it as the exploitation of the world to the advantage of a few. One just hopes that religious bias will not grow stronger between the Christian West and the Muslim East.

When reading history books, it is certainly wise to take into account the culture of the author, as that will alert you to possible sources of bias in the work.

Responsible historians will be as rational as they can, thereby avoiding easily recognized mistakes arising from their biases. There might remain some residual bias, however, which a critical reader must allow for.

(vii) Is coherence enough?

Coherence is never enough to establish the credibility of an interpretation of a text. One way in which an interpretation of a text can cohere with other credible information about it, is by not contradicting that information, or rendering any of it improbable. This kind of coherence is clearly not enough to establish the credibility of an interpretation. An interpretation needs positive support from credible information, as well as this kind of consistency, to be credible.

For example, it has frequently been remarked that, at a time when contemporaries were appealing to an ancient English constitution and contract between parliament and the crown to justify the revolution of 1688, which saw the Catholic king James II replaced by the Protestants William and Mary, John Locke, in his *Two Treatises of Civil Government*, made no reference to them. Quentin Skinner said that in ignoring the ancient contract, Locke 'was rejecting and repudiating one of the most widespread and prestigious forms of political argument at the time' (Skinner, 1974, p. 286). This implication is certainly consistent with Locke's silence on the matter, but there are other possibilities worth considering. Martyn Thompson, for example, says that Locke did not think the ancient constitutional contract was relevant to the general 'theoretical enquiry into the rational origins, extent and end of civil power' which Locke undertook in the *Two Treatises*, but that he did think it relevant in deciding particular issues in the politics of his time (M.P. Thompson, 1987, pp. 292–3). The coherence of Skinner's hypothesis with the data is not enough to establish its credibility. One needs more positive evidence of Locke's attitude to the doctrines of the ancient constitutional contract to be confident of any hypothesis concerning it.

Positive support for an interpretation of a text, however, is not always enough. If there is evidence that strongly supports a belief inconsistent with it, then the interpretation remains uncertain. Historians can display much ingenuity in explaining away inconsistent evidence to render their interpretation consistent with it, but if the explanation is *ad hoc*, that is without independent evidential support, then it is not credible.

An example of this source of uncertainy is provided by Alison Hanham's hypothesis about the date of the execution of the Lord Chamberlain, William, Lord Hastings, by Richard, later Richard III. After the death of King Edward IV of England, his younger brother Richard sought the throne. The chief minister of the dead king had been William, Lord Hastings, and Richard ordered his execution, perhaps fearing his support for Edward's son as successor to the throne. There is some uncertainty over the date of Hastings's execution. Some thought it occurred on Friday 13 June 1483, and others think it happened a week later, on the 20th. Alison Hanham argued for the later date and referred to a letter written on Saturday 21 June which described the execution as having taken place 'on Friday last'. She admits the phrase is ambiguous but declares that 'the context really resolves all ambiguity' (Hanham, 1972, p. 238). Not only do linguistic conventions imply that the phrase 'on Friday last' suggests 20 June, but that date fits neatly into the accounts of events at that time given by witnesses and others.

Mancini and all the Tudor accounts, with the exception of the Crowland chronicle, make it quite clear that Hastings's death occurred very shortly before Richard's claims to the throne were openly stated (on 22 June), and after the seizure of the Duke of York, which took place on 16 June. This order of affairs is not only well attested, but presents by far the most likely and logical sequence (ibid., p. 240).

In fact there is evidence in support of both hypotheses. Many official documents give the date of Hastings's execution as 13 June. To make her preferred hypothesis cohere with these, Hanham has to assume that they were deliberately falsified. She writes: 'it is difficult to suggest any explanation of the three facts that the error [in official documents] appeared very early, was admitted to official records, and eventually gained universal acceptance, without positing some official countenance . . . by the government of Richard III' (ibid., p. 243). B.P. Wolffe, in reply to Hanham, cites evidence for the earlier date and even conjectures that the letter referring to 'Friday last' might have been written a few days before the 21st (Wolffe, 1974, p. 841). Wolffe also notes that falsification of the records would have to have been connived at not just by Richard, but also:

> by both archbishops and by both chief justices, by their successors in office who took their places as feoffees, by several other prominent legal men and by other leading citizens in their capacity as feoffees and executors for the Hastings family. This is not credible on the sole basis of one rather doubtful entry in a sixteenth-century copy of the records of a London company.
>
> (ibid., p. 844)

(Hanham replied, defending her position, in Hanham, 1975.) If no explanation is clearly superior to all others, responsible historians will admit as much and not insist on the interpretation they prefer. Hanham gets close to doing so when she writes: 'I fully agree that the need to postulate official falsification of the records is a major stumbling-block in accepting the date of 20 June for the execution' (ibid., 1975, p. 826).

Sometimes it is thought that historians must proceed in hermeneutical circles, from which it follows that they must rely upon coherence as the only criterion for the acceptability of their conclusions. Here are three ways you could envisage hermeneutical circles occurring:

(i) Suppose the meaning of a phrase in a text is uncertain, then historians will prefer one which fits the meaning of the text as a whole. But to discover the meaning of the text as a whole, they have to know the meaning of the phrases which constitute the text! They must decide the meaning of the whole and its parts together, by judging which interpretation is most coherent.

(ii) Historians discover what happened in the past by interpreting documents. But if historians need to know the context of a document in order to interpret it appropriately, how can the document provide evidence of that context? They must decide the historical origins of a document and the context of its creation together, by judging which story is the most coherent.

(iii) Or perhaps the interpretation of the meaning of a document depends upon an historian's judgement of the author's purpose in producing it. Then once again, how can the document provide evidence of that purpose? Historians must interpret the meaning and purpose of documents together, accepting the most coherent account of them.

These three accounts misrepresent historical practice. What really happens is this:

(i) In most texts, the meaning of the vast majority of phrases is quite unambiguous, so that the meaning of the text as a whole is quite easy to determine. In that case, there is usually no trouble interpreting an ambiguous word or phrase. In English the word 'bank' is ambiguous: it can refer to a steep slope or to a financial institution. If I said that I enjoy sitting on a river bank reading a book when the weather is fine, you would have no trouble deciding which sense is appropriate, as no other word in the sentence is ambiguous and only one of the possible meanings of 'bank' fits the verbal context.

(ii) Sometimes an ambiguity about the historical significance of a document can be resolved only by studying the context in which the document was produced. We saw a case of this above in the debate over the date of Hastings's execution. But, as in that instance, it is almost never the case that the document itself is the only evidence of that context. If it were, historians might have a problem. Usually other documents yield much information about the context so that the uncertainty about the historical significance of a document is not difficult to resolve.

(iii) The same is true when historians search for the author's intention in writing a document. Often there is a lot of independent information about the author and the circumstances in which the document was written that enables historians to get a fair idea of the author's intention.

Often one interpretation of the author's intention is vastly superior to all others, as none other fits the context, both textual and historical, nearly as well. But, when historians have so little evidence that the only thing going for a hypothesis is its coherence, responsible historians are very wary about attributing much credence to that hypothesis.

The meaning of actions, events and practices in history

So far we have been considering the meaning of texts. Now we turn briefly to the meaning of actions, events and practices in history. There are three basic approaches to the meaning of these. The first is to ask what they meant to those involved in them. Cultural historians have been interested in this form of meaning. The second is to ask what important consequences the events had, or whether they were part of an important pattern of change. The third is to note what particular events signify in relation to some general, theoretical account of what was happening.

The meaning of events for those involved in them

Over the last few decades, some historians have been influenced by the anthropologist Clifford Geertz to look for the meaning of actions, events and practices in the culture of the society in which they occurred. The assumption seemed to be that culture determined the way agents envisaged their actions and the way others interpreted them. Another assumption made by Geertz was that historians could infer the values of a culture from the behaviour of people within it. Geertz was quite aware of the distinction between the meaning of an action for the agent, for others who viewed it and for the historian, but in his practice these distinctions were often ignored, as he attributed the meanings which he found in common practices to the individuals who performed them. For instance, in a famous essay about the significance of Balinese cockfights, Geertz attributes attitudes to the Balinese about their fighting cocks which he detects in their behaviour. Vincent Crapanzano has rightly criticized him for this. According to Geertz, says Crapanzano:

> In the cockfight man and beast, good and evil, ego and id, the creative power of aroused masculinity and the destructive power of loosened animality fuse in a blood drama of hatred, cruelty, violence, and death. It is little wonder that when, as is the invariable rule, the owner of the winning cock takes the carcass of the loser – often torn limb from limb by its enraged owner – home to eat, he does so with a mixture of social embarrassment, moral satisfaction, aesthetic disgust, and cannibal joy.
>
> (Crapanzano, 1986, p. 72)

It is highly unlikely that Balinese men involved in cockfighting would interpret their activity in these terms, or even experience all the emotions Geertz attributes to them. Responsible historians are careful to distinguish between the three sources of meaning, the agent, the onlooker and the historian.

Cultural historians who find evidence of a certain idiom or pattern of thought in a culture are prone to imagine it was influential without taking care to discover whether in fact it was and, if it was, how it influenced events and to what extent. An example of such vagueness is Lynn Hunt's book, *The Family Romance of the French Revolution* (1992). In this book she examines depictions and discussions of the family in French literature, art and law in the eighteenth century, and notices how sometimes the revolutionaries used family metaphors in describing political relations in France. She found passages in speeches, books, pamphlets and pictures likening the execution of Louis XVI and Marie Antoinette to the killing of a bad father and mother, and notes that 'fraternity' was one of the slogans of the revolution, along with 'liberty' and 'equality'. The revolutionaries saw themselves as a family of brothers (Hunt, pp. 67–9). Clearly some people involved in the French Revolution interpreted events by means of the analogy of a fight within a family in which the brothers turn upon their parents.

What remains quite uncertain in Hunt's book is the connection she sees between ideas about the family and the political process. Sometimes she uses the family metaphor to present her own interpretation of the events of the Revolution. After the king had been executed, and laws passed to limit the authority of fathers (ibid., pp. 40–2), Hunt remarks: 'The republic had displayed its anti-patriarchal direction: the political father had been killed, and ordinary fathers had been subjected to the constraints of the law or replaced by the authority of the state' (ibid., p. 67). She generally presents ideas about the family as both a conscious and unconscious metaphor which helped to shape political discourse. Did it also motivate political action? She notes Sigmund Freud's account of the origins of the social contract in *Totem and Taboo* (1913), where Freud told a story of brothers murdering their father, who had kept all the females for himself, and then forming a new society in which they bound themselves to live under certain laws. She takes this as further evidence of the connection between thinking about family relations and political power. At one point she refers to 'the psycho-sexual foundation of the political order' (Hunt, p. 10), hinting that once the king had been identified as a bad father, and the revolutionaries as brothers, the execution of the king was more or less inevitable, as Freud had suggested. Finally, she notes that 'fraternity' was a conscious aim of the revolutionaries, at least until 1794 (ibid., pp. 12–13), and she calls it 'a model for a government based on equality and popular sovereignty' (ibid., p. 73). A commentator found this variety of uses of the family metaphor disconcerting. '*Mentalité*, political idiom, heuristic model, political script and/or ideology – the "family romance" functions in this volume as all of these at different times' (C. Jones, 1995, p. 283).

There is no doubt that many revolutionaries sometimes viewed the state in terms of a family, with the king and queen as father and mother, and the revolutionaries as sons who had finally come of age to rule the country themselves. This was not the only metaphor they used: Hunt acknowledges that the death of the king was seen by some as a ritual sacrifice, performed to cleanse the state of a bad regime (Hunt, p. 11). But how the metaphor of the family influenced events, besides providing a useful way of conceptualizing them, is generally unclear.

The same problem arises in the remarkably similar book by Jay Fliegelman, *Prodigals and Pilgrims. The American Revolution against Patriarchal Authority, 1750–1800* (1982). Fliegelman examines the way in which Americans used the metaphor of the family to interpret their relationship with Britain, and later, the 'founding fathers' of the Republic. He carefully describes a 'revolution' during the eighteenth century in thinking about the nature of fathers, from seeing them as having to curb the natural wickedness of their children by stern discipline, to regarding their role as that of cultivating the mind and character of their children by example and instruction to prepare them for independence (Fliegelman, pp. 1–2). This 'revolution against patriarchal authority', he says, found its 'most important expression' in the American Revolution, by which the American states achieved independence from the government of Great Britain (ibid., p. 5). Precisely how changing ideas about fatherhood influenced political events, he does not say, but in fact he produces evidence that, in writing such as Thomas Paine's *Common Sense*, it helped to justify rebellion (ibid., pp. 103–6).

It is obvious that the revolutions in France and America were motivated by more than metaphors of the family. Indeed, even in the ideology of revolution prevalent at the time, which employed theories about the rights of citizens, this metaphor played a very small part. Responsible historians will not inflate the historical significance of common cultural ideas unduly. The significance of people's understanding of the events in which they participated should be made as clear as possible.

Meaning as historical significance

Until now we have assumed that the meaning of an action, practice or event is to be found in the ideas and attitudes they express. But there is another kind of meaning which historians sometimes study, which locates the meaning of an action, practice or event in terms of its relation to other events within the context of an historical narrative. Victor Turner has written: 'Meaning is apprehended by *looking back* over a temporal process . . . The meaning of every part of the process is assessed by its contribution to the total result' (Turner, 1981, p. 153). Thus historians sometimes refer to events as triggers of a war or revolution, or turning points in a process of change. Arthur Danto had made the point previously in these words:

> To ask for the significance of an event, in the *historical* sense of the term, is to ask a question which can be answered only in the context of a *story*. The identical event will have a different significance in accordance with the story in which it is located or, in other words, in accordance with what different sets of *later* events it may be connected . . . To demand the meaning of an event is to be prepared to accept some context within which the event is considered significant. This is 'meaning in history', and it is legitimate to ask for such meanings.
>
> (Danto, 1965, pp. 11–12)

There are several different patterns of historical significance. A common form of historical significance is causal: an event is significant if it caused another event deemed important. Sometimes the historically significant effects of an action are intended. For instance, the publication of some texts, the performance of some plays and the portraits of political leaders can be interpreted as attempts to enhance or diminish the legitimacy and authority of those in power. Their meaning, in other words, lies in their intended effect. Kevin Sharpe refers to this use of a text, play or work of art as 'the politics of representation', in which works of culture are used to persuade those who see them to accept or deny the authority of those depicted (Sharpe, 1999). He explains how these are designed, not only to express ideas held by those who created them, but also to appeal to those who see them so that they will adopt the attitude which the works promote. In this way Sharpe sees many public works as the product of a 'negotiation' between the artist or politician and their audience. Once again it is sometimes unclear whether the political implications of some works are those detected by the historian or intended by their author. Sharpe writes, for example, that 'Dryden's *Absalom and Achitophel* attempted to cleanse patriarchalism of the damaging associations with tyranny and absolutism and to revalidate royal abundance. And he did so to reclaim a prelapsarian state of nature for the king, and – audaciously – to recast his Whig opponents as libertines' (ibid., p. 866). One wonders whether this is precisely how Dryden would have described his intention in writing it.

The consequences of an action, event or practice do not have to be intended to provide their meaning. They may simply be consequences which the historian judges to have been important. Nevins and Commager, for example, have explained how significant was the American massacre of British troops in 'the first great battle of the war' of independence at Bunker Hill. They said it 'had an importance out of all proportion to its immediate results'. They described its significance in these words:

> The battle proved to the Americans that even without proper organization or equipment, they could repulse the best regular troops of Europe, and they gained enormously in confidence. Howe, in immediate command on the British side, was so sickened by the carnage that he never forgot it. When he replaced [General] Gage, who was recalled to England in disgrace, he showed timidity in pressing American troops to battle that helped cost England the war.
>
> (Nevins and Commager, 1966, pp. 82–3)

These were both real historical consequences of the battle, and consequences which the historians judged to be important in the War of Independence which they went on to narrate. The significance of the battle is not merely its significance in the narrative, but nor is it merely its real historical significance. It is the combination of the two.

Sometimes an event is significant, not as the cause of an important effect, but as part of an important whole, a whole pattern of events which historians have detected in the events they study. Notice how Nevins and Commager called the Battle of Bunker Hill 'the first great battle of the war', giving its place in the whole. As Danto said, the one event can have an important place in different patterns. For example, some would see the defeat of Britain in the American War of Independence as the first step in the dissolution of the British Empire, whereas others would describe it as the first step in the creation of a new nation, the United States of America. Patterns of growth and decline are very common in history, as are patterns of revolution and restoration. The practice of seeing historical events as forming patterns like this is called the practice of colligation (see Walsh, 1958, pp. 59–64; and McCullagh, 1978). This is a form of narrative interpretation, discussed in Chapter 5 below.

Historians and their readers often have a particular interest in the significance of historical events, especially when those events are of a kind which might recur in the present or future. Notice the lesson which, according to Nevins and Commager, American learned from the Battle of Bunker Hill, that 'they could repulse the best regular troops of Europe'. Events which affected the economic prosperity, justice and peace in situations relevantly similar to our own are all of interest today.

The significance of particular events on a general, theoretical account

Historians have long been fascinated by the causes of certain kinds of change in societies' social, economic or political structures. Marx, for example, investigated the origins of the transition from feudalism to capitalism, and many scholars have done so after him. Others have sought the causes of democratic revolutions. Chalmers Johnson developed a well known theory of the general elements of revolutionary change which involved 'alienation, recruitment, ideological conversion, protest, and structural conduciveness' (Johnson, 1983, p. 182). Emile Durkheim studied the process by which labour became increasingly divided in society, and also the causes of suicide.

By studying and comparing many particular instances, such historians have been able to identify the major causes of the kinds of events they have investigated. For example, Durkheim found that the rate of suicide among those who belong to the Catholic Church, are married and live in a settled rural community is lower than among Protestants who are single and live in towns where there is much social mobility. His general theory was that 'Suicide varies inversely with the degree of integration of the social groups of which the individual forms a part' (Durkheim, 1952, p. 209). As for the division of labour, Durkheim found that to increase with population and economic competition which produced specialization. With such specialization, people become more dependent upon one another, and so social solidarity is increased (Durkheim, 1964).

Just as the study and comparison of particular cases enables such general theories to be formed, it also produces exceptions to the theories which require their modification. Durkheim, for example, found that social isolation did not always produce suicide, nor did the division of labour always produce an increase in social solidarity. Instead, when some groups feel disaffected, division of labour can promote industrial or political conflict. What social scientists recognize today is that the causes of structural change that they identify do not necessarily cause their effects, but often increase the probability of such effects, other things being equal (see McCullagh, 1984, ch. 10, for many examples of structural history and its vicissitudes).

In the context of structural history, then, individual events can be significant, either as supporting a general theory or as providing an exception to it, which requires a modification of the theory.

Chapter 3

Justifying descriptions of the past

Historians have a social responsibility to produce credible accounts of the past. Communities turn to history to understand the origins of their cultural traditions and to appraise the value of their social practices. They rely upon historians to provide trustworthy information about these and other traditions and practices in the past.

How can historians prove that their descriptions of the past are credible? Roughly speaking, they do so by showing that they can be rationally inferred from evidence available to them, together with other previously established information about the past. This chapter explains and illustrates the forms of argument historians use to justify the credibility of their descriptions of the past.

Historians cannot prove the absolute truth of their descriptions. An absolutely true account of the world is an ideal explanation of all possible sensory experiences, past, present and future, and that is unattainable. But often historians have so much data to support their descriptions of the past that it is reasonable to believe those descriptions would survive all critical inquiry, and eventually be part of the ideal explanatory theory of the world. In short, it is often reasonable to believe that historical descriptions are true.

Although historians cannot prove descriptions of the past true, they can give reasons for believing them to be true. That is, they can demonstrate their rational credibility. There are degrees of rational support for historical descriptions, and there are corresponding degrees of rational credibility. Responsible historians will be careful not to exaggerate the certainty of their conclusions, but will point out how tentative they are when there is not strong evidence to support them.

When historians draw inferences about the past and go on to test them, they bring with them a heap of beliefs about nature, society and history, which they assume to be true. It is by drawing upon this knowledge that they can interpret their perceptions of evidence, and make new discoveries about the past. Occasionally their presuppositions are corrected by historical discoveries; indeed quite often common assumptions about their period of history are altered by what they find. The point is that historians cannot possibly establish the credibility of all the information they draw upon in making new inferences about the past, and in testing them. The rationality and credibility of their conclusions is always relative to that of the assumptions they employed in reaching them. This is a matter of no concern, so long as those assumptions are themselves well supported by other perceptions, scientifically validated you might say. If the assumptions are rationally credible, then so may be the historical inferences which depend upon them.

It is interesting to see how historical discoveries build upon one another. Evidence will point to some past actions, these actions will suggest the mental state of the agents, and that will reflect more facts about the context in which they acted. The relations are explanatory: descriptions of the actions help to explain the evidence; descriptions of the mental state of the agents help to explain their behaviour; and descriptions of their environment help to explain their mental state.

You may have noticed that I said historical descriptions 'help to explain' certain facts about the past. When historians investigate the past, they normally begin wanting to discover facts of a certain kind. They do not want a complete explanation of the evidence available to them. Rather, they want to know what it can tell them about the kind of information that interests them. In fact they scan available evidence to find pieces of evidence which they believe will point to the information they want. Indeed to call a letter, a report, a photograph or some other material object 'evidence' is strictly speaking an incomplete description: it must be evidence of something, and historians select as relevant evidence those things which they think might imply facts of the kind they wish to discover.

To explain the existence of some observable evidence, historians draw upon their general knowledge of the probable, or possible, causes of its creation. Sometimes their general knowledge is so appropriate that the conclusion they reach can be accepted as credible without further consideration. Inferences of this kind can be called 'direct inferences'. On the other hand, sometimes historians have no direct knowledge of the information they want, and have to draw upon very general knowledge of the possible causes of the evidence to form hypotheses about the circumstances of its creation. Sometimes historians feel confident that the correct hypothesis is probably one of the possible ones listed, and they then attempt to show that one is much more credible than the others. This form of inference is called 'an argument to the best explanation'. Most often the inference lies somewhere between these two extremes: general knowledge renders one hypothesis considerably more probable than the other possible hypotheses, but to confirm this impression historians look for other support for their favoured hypothesis as well. I call inferences of this kind 'hybrid inferences'.

Historical inferences depend upon general knowledge, knowledge of the usual causes of the evidence historians study, and knowledge of the usual implications of the hypotheses they form about the past. The sources of this general knowledge are various. Some is common sense knowledge about human nature and everyday events in the world; some is knowledge of the meaning of a language, the historians' mother tongue or other languages they have learned; occasionally historians use general theories developed by natural scientists and social scientists. Historians themselves provide general knowledge of cultural and social regularities, of the meanings of some words, symbols, actions and events, and of regular practices, be they technical, legal, commercial, military or whatever. In every case the general knowledge must be of a regularity which is so regular as to be 'lawlike'. The nature of these lawlike regularities will be discussed in the second section of this chapter. It will also say something about how their credibility can be established.

The inferences described so far are those that arrive at conclusions about single events. Historians are sometimes also interested in generalizing about people and events in the past. The generalizations I am referring to now are not lawlike, not necessary, but accidental. The third section of the chapter will look at two common kinds of accidental generalizations, those which describe the general characteristics of a class of things, and those which describe a common causal process by which a certain kind of event normally came about in a particular society.

Another kind of general description in history is one which provides a general interpretation of an historical subject. For convenience I have reserved a discussion of general interpretations for a later chapter, Chapter 6.

Finally, some historians are very interested in social institutions and structures of various kinds and the relations between them. The existence of such structures has been doubted, but there is good reason to believe they exist. The justification of descriptions of social structures will be discussed in the fourth and final section of this chapter.

Justifying descriptions of single events

Historical research normally begins when historians want to know more about an episode or a period of which they have already read quite a lot. Usually it begins with historians asking particular questions about what they already believe happened in the past. Historians search for information of a certain kind.

With their questions in mind, historians look for evidence from which they expect to be able to infer the information they want. To interpret that evidence they draw upon both their knowledge of particular events that occurred in the period they are investigating, and their knowledge of the processes which generally operated in that period. Some of these processes will be universal truths of human nature; others might be quite specific to the subject being investigated; and some will be true of the period in general.

There are three common ways of inferring descriptions of particular events in the past from available evidence. I call the first 'a direct inference', the second 'an inference to the best explanation', and the third 'a hybrid form of inference'.

Direct inferences

Direct inferences move from information about a piece of evidence to a description of the past by means of a generalization that relates the two.

For example, suppose an historian were studying a heap of letters which all seemed to have been written by the same person. Suppose, further, the historian, or other historians, had established the authorship of a large number of the letters. When the historian came to examine yet another letter, and observed it to have the same handwriting as the others, the same vocabulary and turns of phrase, and the same address and signature as the others, there would be no need to doubt that it was written by the same author as the others. All letters having these characteristic features could reasonably be attributed to the same author.

The basic logical form of direct inferences is quite simple:

(i)   This piece of evidence has characteristics of the kind X, Y, Z.
(ii) Everything with characteristics X, Y, Z was created by a process with characteristics of the kind A, B, C.
(iii) So this piece of evidence was created by a process with characteristics A, B, C.

In the example just given, X, Y, Z refer to the characteristics of the letters, and A, B, C refer to the process by which they were produced, a process which makes reference to a particular author and to his or her method of writing, say by dictation or directly with a pen.

This basic form has to be qualified, however, to reflect the degree of rational credibility of each of the premises and the conclusion. If everyone can identify the characteristics of the letters, then it is highly probable that they have the characteristics in question. If these characteristics are uncommon, probably unique, as handwriting and signatures tend to be, then it is highly probable that the author of all the letters was the same person. The probability of the conclusion is a function of the probability of the premises. So if the probability of each premise being true is, say, 0.9, then the probability of the conclusion is 0.9×0.9, i.e. 0.81. So a better summary of direct inferences is as follows:

(i)   The probability that this piece of evidence has characteristics of the kind X, Y, Z is p.
(ii) The probability that everything with characteristics X, Y, Z was created by a process with characteristics of the kind A, B, C is q.
(iii) So the probability that this piece of evidence was created by a process with characteristics A, B, C is $p \times q$.

Usually historians perceive the characteristics of the evidence quite accurately. What is sometimes disputed is the probability of the second premise, the generalization relating those characteristics to the circumstances of their creation. For example, suppose you read that Abelard, a cleric and an outstanding professor of philosophy in Paris in the early twelfth century, seduced one of his bright young students, Heloise; that they were discovered by the girl's uncle, had a baby and married in secret; that Abelard then sent Heloise to a convent; that the uncle had Abelard violently castrated, and that he too retired to live, apart from Heloise, in religious communities. This story is full of drama, and you might like to discover more details of what happened. The most detailed account of the events is given in a document written by Abelard himself, known as the *Historia calamitatum* (history of a calamity).

You might assume that since Abelard was writing about his own life, his account of what happened would be pretty accurate. Now let us examine the justification for that conclusion. It rests upon a generalization: people who write accounts of events in which they were involved describe them, for the most part, accurately. This generalization, however, is in need of qualification. Some people write up events falsely to make themselves appear better than they really were. The historian Etienne Gilson thinks we can set aside this possibility, however, for Abelard presents himself as a dreadful character. Abelard writes that he seduced Heloise simply to satisfy his lust, at times acting against her will. Gilson comments as follows:

> We have only the testimony of Abelard at our disposal. Let us add, however, that the pitiless penetration of his self-analysis is of such a character as to inspire us with confidence and that no known fact from any other source entitles us to contradict anything he says.
>
> (Gilson, 1960, p. 1)

In response to Abelard's *Historia*, Heloise wrote letters to him, reflecting upon what had happened. These too, Gilson argues, are to be believed. 'Both of them speak . . . not to sing their personal victory but to mark the extent of their defeat. This is why they can be believed' (ibid., p. 36). The generalization that Gilson is relying upon is this: if people write of events in which they were involved, and in doing so cast themselves in a bad light, then their testimony is probably a faithful record of what they experienced.

Once the generalization has been stated which mediates these simple inferences, it can be examined carefully. A recent scholar, Constant J. Mews, has given us reason to doubt Gilson's generalization. Examining the text of the *Historia*, Mews notes that

> Abelard's professed intention is to relate how the consoling power of the Holy Spirit had enabled him to survive many difficulties and turn from a life of arrogance and debauchery to one devoted to the will of God . . .
>
> He shapes events to fit in with his theme of how a successful, but morally profligate teacher turned to a life lived for God . . .
>
> Abelard plays up his vices in order to show how they are eventually

overcome through divine providence. . . . His thesis is that true consolation comes not from a woman, but from the Holy Spirit, the Paraclete or Comforter and the very goodness of God . . .

The thrust of his narrative is to emphasize that the consolation offered by divine providence is far beyond that offered by carnal pleasure . . .

[He] scarcely acknowledges the significance of the many love letters which he had written over fifteen years earlier.

(Mews, 1999, pp. 31–5)

Gilson had not attended to the didactic intent of the document, thinking of it really as a simple confession. Once the document is considered as an argument, as well as a confession, there is reason to suspect that the truth might have been simplified to hammer home its message. Indeed Mews says some of the phrases used in the text have philosophical significance. 'Dogmatic assertions that Abelard "was driven by lust" or that Heloise "was motivated by pure love" fail to recognize that these are rhetorical phrases, used by Abelard and Heloise respectively, each fulfilling a certain function' (ibid., p. 144). So we should not be quite as confident of the veracity of the *Historia* as Gilson was.

Gilson's original argument took this form:

(i)   The evidence, namely the *Historia*, describes events in which the author was involved, and presents him as wicked.
(ii) Whenever a document does these things, then it is very probable that the events it describes really happened.
(iii) Therefore very probably the events it described really happened.

The observations by Mews reduce the probabilities involved by indicating another generalization, roughly that 'Whenever a document does these things, but is designed to have an effect which is heightened by exaggerating the wickedness of the author, then it is probable that, although most of the events happened, the author was not as wicked as portrayed.' Generally, the more qualified a generalization, the more accurate it is likely to be.

Because the conclusions of historical inferences, even direct inferences, are fallible, responsible historians are always looking for information which might imply that they are probably false. The credibility of an historical description is a function of the evidence both for and against it. Hence the remark by Gilson, supporting his claim that the *Historia* is credible, 'that no known fact from any other source entitles us to contradict anything he says'. Had a known fact contradicted Abelard's account, there would be reason to doubt its veracity. (A much fuller discussion of direct inferences can be found in McCullagh, 1984, ch. 3.)

Inferences to the best explanation

The second kind of historical inference which is quite common is an inference to the best explanation. This is used when there is no evidence to provide strong direct support for a particular hypothesis about the kind of information an historian wants to discover, and so the historian has to draw upon very general knowledge to arrive at plausible hypotheses about its origin. As the name of this form of inference suggests, it proceeds by judging which of the plausible hypotheses provides the best explanation of what is known about the creation of the evidence in question. Strictly speaking, the best explanation is only likely to be true if the historian has considered all the plausible hypotheses, and not left the best explanation out of the list.

This form of historical inference was described and recommended by the philosopher and archaeologist, R.G. Collingwood. He illustrated it with a detective story in which a detective has to consider various hypotheses about who committed a murder, and settles upon one which fits quite a lot of the evidence and is inconsistent with no known facts. The range of suspects is limited to those known to have been near the place of the murder at the time (Collingwood, 1946, pp. 266–82). In his autobiography Collingwood refers to several archaeological inquiries as illustrating this form of inference. One of the most interesting of these concerns the purpose of a Roman wall, known as Hadrian's Wall, built across the north of England, between the Tyne and Solway (roughly between Newcastle and Carlisle).

There is no direct evidence of the purpose of this wall, so historians have had to speculate as to what it might have been. Before Collingwood investigated it, it was assumed to have been designed and built to repel the Caledonians from raiding and plundering the Roman towns south of the border. Historians imagined that Roman soldiers would have fought the invaders from the protected pathway which ran along the top of the wall. But Collingwood noted several facts inconsistent with this hypothesis. The most important was that the path along the top of the wall was only three or four feet wide, a little over a metre. Collingwood wrote: 'There would be barely room for a man to pass behind the actual firing line; no room, if the "firing" line consisted of men throwing, with the necessary freedom of gesture, a heavy six-foot pilum [a heavy javelin]. It would be practically impossible to reinforce a threatened point, even in the most favourable conditions; wholly impossible to move wounded men. And a few corpses . . . would block the walk entirely' (Collingwood, 'The Purpose of the Roman Wall', *The Vasculum*, 1921, p. 5; quoted in van der Dussen, 1981, pp. 226–8). His point is that if the Romans had intended to use the wall to repel the Scots, they would have made it much wider. He also noted that it had no provision for artillery, and no bastions, typical of Roman fortifications. The hypothesis that the wall was designed as a fighting platform to defend England from the Scots is thus inconsistent with its width. It implies that the walkway along the top of the wall would have been much wider than it actually was.

So Collingwood developed another explanatory hypothesis. At regular intervals along the wall were forts, which would have accommodated soldiers. Collingwood suggested that the wall had several functions. First, it marked the border with England, beyond which the Caledonians were not allowed to pass. Second, it provided a barrier to 'smugglers, or robbers, or other undesirables' (ibid., p. 7), making it difficult for them to pass into England from the north. And third, most significant of all, it constituted a raised, protected walk for sentries, who could patrol up and down on the look-out for concentrations of Caledonian troops who might be planning an invasion, and who could be fought on the ground by Roman troops garrisoned in those forts.

Notice that this hypothesis is plausible, given general knowledge of Roman strategy, and that it explains why the wall was as narrow and weak as it was. No more was needed if it were to be just a casual barrier to villains, and a walkway for sentries. It also explains why the wall 'took the line of the crags': this improved the outlook of the sentries (p. 9).

To test his hypothesis further, Collingwood considered one of its implications. At its western end the wall stopped near an estuary, the Solway Firth, and it would have been easy for raiders to sail south across the water and land on the coast. So Collingwood thought there would probably have been a sentry patrol along the edge of the estuary, though it would not have had to be elevated for sentries to see boatloads of invaders sailing across the water. If his hypothesis were right there would, however, have been forts at regular intervals along that sentry walk. And this is precisely what he found, confirming his hypothesis (Collingwood, 1970, 129–30). There are archaeological remains of such forts, just as he predicted. When a hypothesis explains more data than it was originally designed to explain, that strengthens its credibility. As the scope of an explanation increases, it usually becomes proportionately more credible.

Notice that in both these examples, the detective story and the discussion of the purpose of the Roman Wall, there is no direct evidence of the information the historian wants. However, the historian knows a range of possibilities which he draws upon to form a range of hypotheses. These are based upon very general knowledge about possible causes of available evidence, hypotheses which would constitute the kind of information required. The murderer was probably someone in the vicinity of the body at the time of the murder; the purpose of the Roman Wall was probably to enable the Romans to protect Britain from northern invaders. In this way, general knowledge limited the range of possible hypotheses, without providing strong support for any one of them.

Once again, notice that Collingwood's hypothesis accounts for only a few features of the Roman Wall, namely those which seem relevant to the information he wanted, which was information about the purpose for which it was built. He does not explain how it was built, or how the Romans decided where the frontier should be. He has certainly not provided a full explanation of the origin of the wall.

The general form of inferences to the best explanation is roughly as follows:

The observable evidence was probably produced by a process which included something having a certain feature.

The range of things having that feature is very probably as follows: H1, H2, . . . Hn.

There is reason to believe that it was not any of these Hs other than H1.

Therefore, the observable facts were very probably produced by H1.

In this case, the observable evidence was Hadrian's Wall, and the process which produced it probably included an intention to protect England from invasions from the north.

The range of possible intentions having this feature are (H1) that soldiers fight off enemies from the top of the wall; and (H2) that soldiers use the wall as an elevated sentry walk to spot enemies before they reached the wall, enabling soldiers to engage them in the field.

There is reason to believe it was not (H1), because the wall was too narrow for that intention to have been realized.

Therefore, the wall was produced with the intention (H2).

A further argument was also used by Collingwood, which deserves to be noted. He looked for and found further evidence consistent with intention (2) but not consistent with intention (1). If (H1) the wall had been intended as a fighting platform, then (E1) it would have continued beside the estuary. But if (H2) it were merely a sentry walk, then (E2) it would not have been needed there, though the forts would have been present to house the defending troops.

The form of the argument here is roughly this:

If the hypothesis H1 were true, then evidence E1 would exist, but this would not be the case if H2 were true.

If the hypothesis H2 were true, then evidence E2 would exist, but this would not be the case if H1 were true.

Evidence E1 does not exist, but evidence E2 does.

So hypothesis H1 is false, and H2 may be true.

The form of inference to the best explanation presented above is really a form of argument by elimination. If it is known to be highly probable that the true hypothesis lies among a clearly defined list of possibilities, and all but one of those is shown to be inconsistent with the facts, then there is good reason to believe that the remaining hypothesis is the true one.

Occasionally historians are unable to exclude all but one of the possible explanations of their evidence as convincingly as Collingwood did, and they have to weigh up the comparative merits of each. To choose between them, historians consider several desirable attributes of the explanatory hypotheses, and see which provides the best explanation.

In what ways should an explanatory hypothesis 'fit' information already believed about the subject? For a hypothesis to fit such given data well, (i) the data must imply something like the hypothesis in question, which means the hypothesis must *be as plausible as possible*; (ii) the hypothesis must imply the probable existence of a great quantity and variety of the available data, that is it must *have great explanatory scope*; (iii) it must imply the existence of the data with a strong a degree of probability, thus *having great explanatory power*; (iv) there must be no data which either imply that such a hypothesis is improbable, or which the hypothesis implies that are improbable, so that it is *not disconfirmed by other reasonable beliefs*; and (v) it must *not include additional ad hoc components*, designed simply to accommodate data which appear to disconfirm it. Each plausible hypothesis is judged according to these five criteria, and if one exceeds the others in these respects by a considerable degree, so that it is unlikely the others would ever surpass it, then it is judged to be credible. (Note: simplicity is a virtue of theoretical and metaphysical explanations, which are not implied by general knowledge but are created by feats of imagination to account for observed regularities in nature.)

Thus in the case of the purpose for which the Roman Wall was built, (i) it was probably built for defensive purposes, and could well have been designed as a sentry walk to enable approaching enemy forces to be observed easily; (ii) this would explain its height and width, and its absence beside the Solway Firth, features which could not be explained if it were intended to be a fighting platform; (iii) indeed it makes these features of the wall highly probable, much more probable than the alternative hypothesis does; (iv) there are no data which makes the sentry walk hypothesis improbable, whereas the narrowness of the walkway on top of the wall is inconsistent with the hypothesis that it was designed as a fighting platform; (v) neither has any *ad hoc* elements. So the hypothesis that the wall was intended to be an elevated sentry walk is much superior to the alternative, that it was meant to provide a fighting platform. (For a more detailed consideration of inferences to the best explanation, see McCullagh, 1984, ch. 2.)

Hybrid inferences

Sometimes the conclusion of a direct inference is uncertain, and to strengthen it, an historian will argue that it provides the best explanation of certain data, generally facts about pieces of evidence. Thus the historian combines two forms of argument, a direct inference and an argument to the best explanation. That is why such arguments are really 'hybrid'.

Mews has examined a collection of love letters between two people, dated to the early twelfth century (1999, p. 6), and argues that they 'must have been written by Abelard and Heloise' (p. 143). Their content, 'their attitudes, vocabulary, and prose style' (p. 143) were so close to those of Abelard and Heloise, that he believes they were probably written by them. The generalization assumed here is that if one batch of letters resembles another very closely in these respects, then they were probably written by the same people.

However, this attribution of authorship has been disputed by Peter Dronke, who argues that they seem to imply the love between the two had never been physically consummated, whereas in fact it had (Mews, 1999, p. 6). Mews thinks the evidence for this implication is 'fragile' (p. 7; and see pp. 117–18). Even if the letters do suggest a chaste relationship between their authors, Mews says, this does not disprove the hypothesis that Abelard and Heloise had written them, for they could have been written before their union was consummated (p. 118). Anyway, to strengthen his hypothesis, Mews considers alternative possibilities, and decides there is none which could account for the characteristics of those letters nearly so well. He writes: 'we simply do not find anything approaching the depth and sophistication of this exchange' (p. 143). In other words, there is no other writer who could have produced them. 'The only student of Abelard in a position to record this exchange was Heloise' (p. 143).

In hybrid inferences, the historian's general knowledge suggests an historical fact on the basis of some evidence, and the credibility of the conclusion is strengthened by showing that it is the best explanation either of the same data, or of further data. Mews not only thought the characteristics of the love letters suggested they had been written by Abelard and Heloise, but he argued that there was no better explanation of those characteristics available.

Here is another example of the same form of hybrid inference. It concerns Professor M.V. Clarke's account of the meaning of the paintings on the Wilton diptych (Clarke, 1937, ch. VIII). The diptych is a small portable altarpiece, consisting of two hinged panels, each painted on both sides, about half a metre high. There is no written statement of who the figures on the diptych represent, or what they are doing. Clarke argued that certain details of the paintings, the figures and symbols it contains, were closely associated with King Richard II. For example, the coat of arms painted on one panel is known to have been adopted by Richard II in 1394–5; the emblem of a white hart, with chain and crown, which appears on the robe of the kneeling king on another panel was commonly worn by Richard II after 1390; and the broom cods, or pods, which decorate the collar of the king resemble the golden collars given to Richard II by Charles VI of France on the occasion of his daughter's betrothal to Richard in 1395–6. Each of these features suggests that the kneeling king is intended to represent Richard II, but none conclusively proves it. It is logically difficult to assess their joint significance, but if the figure were meant to represent him, that would help to account for the conjunction of all those features in the one painting. So the explanatory strength of the hypothesis serves to confirm it.

Incidentally, notice how limited is the explanation provided by this hypothesis. It explains why the symbols on the diptych were chosen by telling us who it is meant to represent. However, it does not tell us who painted it, who paid for it, or what the occasion was for its presentation. It only explains the intended significance of its symbolism. But that was precisely the kind of information the historian wanted in the first place. Perhaps we should call such inferences 'arguments to *part* of the best explanation' of the data in question. (For an extensive analysis of Clarke's discussion of the Wilton diptych, see McCullagh, 1984, pp. 93–8.)

Here is a third example of a hybrid inference. Else Roesdahl was interested in migration from Norway to Scotland during the ninth century. She says that 'later written sources' provided 'a definite, though sketchy, picture of where the Vikings settled' (Roesdahl, 1991, p. 213). Because the sources were written 'later' and were not very detailed, she was uncertain of their reliability. But she was able to confirm what they said by discovering other evidence implied by the hypothesis, thereby increasing its explanatory scope. If the Vikings had settled in Scotland as the documents said, you might find evidence of their presence there, and that is exactly what she did find. She wrote: 'The distribution of Scandinavian place-names and graves, farms and hoards [of silver] corroborates the later written sources' (ibid.). Presumably the grave stones and silver in particular helped her date the period of settlement to the ninth century. The absence of such remains, after a thousand years or so, would hardly disconfirm the hypothesis, because they could have been extinguished by any number of events.

The three forms of inference described in this section have been presented as ways of answering questions about the past on the basis of observable evidence. They are also used to draw inferences from credible descriptions of particular occurrences in the past to other particular occurrences. They are the standard ways of justifying singular descriptions of the past.

Lawlike regularities

Lawlike generalizations are those which warrant what are called counterfactual claims. A generalization of the form 'All (or most) As are Bs' is lawlike if it warrants the counterfactual 'If this were an A it would (probably) be a B'. That is why lawlike generalizations are so useful in historical inferences and explanations. They justify an inference from what is known to what is not known.

Laws of nature and society are originally designed to account for the regularity of very regular patterns of events. It is a law of nature that pure water boils at 100 degrees Centigrade at sea level, because it can be observed repeatedly to do so, without exception, and to explain that regularity we ascribe it to a law of nature. Similarly, it is a practice of Australian citizens to speak English, because they almost always can be observed to do so, and that regularity is the result of this being an almost universally respected convention. It is not just a matter of chance. We cannot observe that one thing is necessarily associated with another; but we assume a lawlike connection to account for the regularity of that association. Doing so, we are then rationally entitled to predict such an association in particular cases of a kind similar to the antecedent of the generalization which have not hitherto been observed, like many of the cases discussed by historians. Laws of nature are much more reliable than laws of individual and social practice, but they function the same way in inferences and explanations.

Lawlike generalizations are constantly used by historians in drawing inferences about the past. As was explained above, direct inferences are based upon lawlike generalizations concerning the historical significance of evidence of a certain kind. Gilson believed Abelard's testimony because it portrayed him as a wicked man, and Gilson believed the generalization that if anyone writes about events in which they were involved and in so doing depicts themselves as bad, then their testimony is probably a faithful record of what they experienced. This is a generalization about human behaviour applying to everybody; it is of universal scope.

Inferences to the best explanation also use general knowledge, both to suggest plausible explanatory hypotheses to account for available evidence, and to infer the implications of those hypotheses in order to test them. The generalizations which suggest a range of possible causes of a certain kind of event are backward-looking generalizations; whereas those which suggest the likely consequences of certain kinds of events are forward-looking.

The example of Collingwood's inference about the purpose for which Hadrian's Wall had been built is interesting. It involves the use of lawlike generalizations, implicitly, but also involves an imaginative reconstruction of the thoughts of the Romans who built it. First Collingwood assumes a backward-looking lawlike generalization: if people build a huge construction, such as the Roman Wall, it must be done for a purpose that they value considerably, and which they believe its construction will help them attain. This is a universal generalization about human nature. Then Collingwood put himself in the Romans' shoes, or sandals, and tried to imagine why they might build such a wall. To guide him in forming hypotheses about its possible function, he had to draw upon general knowledge of the possible functions of such walls in Roman times. They could be used as a fighting platform or as a sentry walk. The generalization in this case is not lawlike: there is no law that these must be the purposes of building such a wall. Rather this general knowledge is of a common but not a necessary connection. These are common uses for such a wall that Collingwood could envisage from his knowledge of Roman military history, and so they are uses which its builders might have intended.

Collingwood's inferences about the testable implications of the two hypotheses were rational. If the Romans had wanted a fighting platform, they would have judged that a wider wall was necessary as the narrow one would have been much too inconvenient. Historians know this because of their general technical military knowledge about the way the Romans fought. And if the Romans had wanted a sentry walk, they would not have needed a wall beside the sea at Solway Firth, but would still have needed towers to house the soldiers. The generalizations involved in these inferences are too common to be noticed. They are (i) that if people are convinced that a certain large construction is inefficient or unnecessary, they will tend not to build it; and (ii) if they believe certain constructions are indeed necessary, such as towers for the soldiers, then they will tend to build them. I say 'tend to' because these dispositions could be overridden by other dispositions at the time. These are forward-looking lawlike generalizations, representing rational kinds of response to fairly common situations. Many lawlike regularities in history can be justified as rational forms of behaviour in the circumstances.

As was said in the introduction to this chapter, the lawlike regularities that historians use come from many different sources. As we have seen, historians often draw upon general knowledge of human nature and everyday events in the world. This is so widely accepted that it generally needs no justification, unless the inferences based upon it prove inconsistent with other well established beliefs about the past. In recent years, however, theories of human nature developed during the European Enlightenment of the seventeenth and eighteenth centuries, and by Marx, Freud and Nietzsche in the nineteenth century have been challenged by philosophers who think people have no essential nature at all. This challenge is considered in detail in the next chapter. Another common source of general knowledge is knowledge of the meaning of languages, especially of the sense and reference of the words they use. Linguists can usually supply reliable knowledge of languages, present and past. Historians only challenge the meaning of terms when the normal meaning does not seem to fit the context. They will then study the use of the word to determine its sense and reference within the culture they are studying. Finally, historians sometimes draw upon special theories developed by natural or social scientists, to help them understand natural events and changes in social structures. While they do not challenge the known laws of nature, they sometimes dispute regularities presented by social scientists, which are much less certain. Regularities which make sense of social changes in one society do not always apply without modification in another.

This raises the question of the scope of the regularities used by historians. It is widely acknowledged that cultural and social regularities hold true only of the cultures and societies which have been seen to manifest them, and not necessarily of any other culture or society. While these are examined by a variety of social sciences, including anthropology, ethnology, sociology, economics and politics, they are also occasionally studied by historians. There is a detailed study of social practices and their importance in explaining human behaviour towards the end of the next chapter.

How regular does a pattern of behaviour have to be for it to be lawlike? This is a very hard question to answer. Scientists normally study a large number of instances under a variety of conditions before they feel confident that a regularity is lawlike. If they can derive the regularity from a respected theory, that adds to their confidence. Historians, however, do not need to follow this procedure. They generally assume that a few cases of a cultural or social regularity are enough to establish that it constitutes a norm within the culture or society being examined. The only problem they then face is that of determining the scope of that culture or society. Some words are used in small sub-cultures, and some practices are peculiar to particular institutions in society. You have to salute superiors in the armed services, but not yet at a university!

It is very difficult to construct general theories of social change which cover a wide range of cases. The best thing that general theories can do, it seems, is suggest a range of possible causes of major changes, allowing that the influence of each kind varies in each particular case of such a change. It is then up to historians to determine precisely what the influence of each kind of cause might have been. Here are a couple of examples in which historians look to economic theory to account for the growth of industries during the Industrial Revolution in Britain in the eighteenth and nineteenth centuries.

Economic theory has suggested that the growth of industries can be attributed to a growth in demand for the goods they produce, among other things. Joel Mokyr, considering the importance of increasing demand for industrial goods, comments that 'In a historical event like the Industrial Revolution, demand factors can only play a role under certain assumptions that have to be examined carefully' (Mokyr, 1999, p. 59). For example, an increase in demand for goods will only result in an increased supply 'if the economy has large underutilized resources that can be brought into production' (p. 60). In fact when Mokyr considered evidence of increased demand during the Industrial Revolution he found little. The only instance of increased demand being a significant stimulus to industrial growth was a strong demand for cotton goods, which stimulated inventors to increase output in that industry (p. 63). Recently even this modest conclusion has been challenged by experts who 'deny that the breakthroughs of the 1760s can be explained by demand pressure' (Crafts and Mills, 1997, p. 955).

A second example can be taken from the work of N.F.R. Crafts (1995). In a rather technical paper, he has argued that theories of neo-classical growth economics fail to account for certain features of the growth and subsequent decline of industrial production in Britain during the Industrial Revolution. He explains the theory, called an 'endogenous growth model', briefly as follows:

> At the heart of endogenous growth models is the proposition that investment in a broad sense, including human as well as physical capital and the production of knowledge through research, drives the growth process and that growth is based on the accumulation of reproducible factors of production that does not experience diminishing returns. Long-run growth in per capita incomes occurs without the need to invoke exogenous technological progress.
>
> (Crafts, 1995, pp. 746–7)

Crafts remarks that such a theory, which sees growth as a product of investment, cannot account for 'the speeding up of economic growth during the Industrial Revolution' between 1776 and 1834, or 'the post-1873 slowdown' (p. 755). Microinventions, which are improvements in techniques of production developed within an industry, account for some of the growth, but not all. This leads Crafts to argue, following Mokyr, that macroinventions played a significant part (p. 757). 'This view', he writes, 'is one that allows for exogenous technological shocks' (ibid.).

Crafts later defended his conclusion by noting that periods of intense research and development within industries in the late nineteenth century, and in the OECD in the late twentieth century, failed to produce any striking increases in productivity (Crafts and Mills, 1997, p. 954). Clearly endogenous innovation was not enough to account for the spectacular growth during the Industrial Revolution. Crafts writes 'there is no reason to think technological change can be explained entirely through endogenous innovation – there is still room for (exogenous) macroinventions that trigger off subsequent (endogenous) micro-inventions' (ibid., p. 955).

The difficulty of proving general social and economic theories has made them unpopular with some historians. Ronald Berger, for instance, reviewing a book by Donald Woodward on labourers and building craftsmen in early modern Britain, writes:

> Early modern urban historians face a dilemma: spend months – even years – analyzing quantitative data from voluminous administrative sources to achieve scientific rigor, or utilize eclectic methods to draw a well-rounded picture but face criticism for lack of rigor . . . Perhaps it is time to abandon our reliance on the time-consuming search for statistical certainty and so-called scientific rigor and return to the creative approach of economic historians like Eileen Power, who provided a rich and varied portrait of laborers in the pre-industrial period.
>
> (Berger, 1996, pp. 1539, 1540)

The trouble is one has no way of telling how typical these portraits are without statistical information about the kinds of people they portray.

Not only are some historians impatient with the methods of statisticians. There is also a concern with their accuracy and utility. For instance, to discover that the rate of industrial production was sometimes a response to demand could be useful in confirming a macro-economic theory, but it was not uniformly true, and even when it was true, this fact reveals nothing about the process by which industrialists noticed the increase in demand and responded to it. It does not do much to enable us to understand the causal processes involved at a micro-level.

In response to these objections, I would urge that macro-history can be of great value to society. Governments forming social and economic policy want to know what the macro-effects of their policies will be. If they stimulate demand for goods, will that produce a growth in manufacturing industries or not? Knowing how individual industrialists made decisions about growing their industries does not give you any idea of how general or extensive responses like theirs are likely to be. We should not abandon macro-history just because it is difficult and general. Indeed we should foster it, in the interests of good government. (David Cannadine (1984) has shown how interpretations of the Industrial Revolution have reflected the interests of the societies which produced them.) The only qualification I would add is that theory must not be limited by the availability of statistics. For instance, government policies on public ownership of assets, taxation, debt control, research and development and education can influence an economy in ways which may not be quantifiable (see for example Davis, 1989, pp. 63–7).

Accidental generalizations

Once historians have inferred a lot of credible information about an historical topic, they sometimes want to sum up certain common features of what they have found. They do this by making generalizations which do not represent a lawlike regularity, but just happen to reflect the information they have acquired. That is why they are called 'accidental generalizations'.

There are two kinds of accidental generalization frequently found in historical writing. Some generalizations describe properties of all or most members of a reference class, and others describe common causal processes. We shall look at each of these kinds of accidental generalization in turn.

Generalizations about properties

To discover the accidental properties of a class of things, one has to examine instances of that class. (Intrinsic, essential properties can sometimes be inferred from a definition of the thing being described.) After examining instances of the reference class, historians often find that their initial impressions have to be qualified. Take the example just given, which asserted that 'British industries grew markedly between 1760 and 1830'. When historians examine British industries in this period, they find that the predicate was true of some of them but by no means all. Historians will often allow one or two exceptions to their generalizations, but when the predicate is false of more than half the instances of the subject, it must certainly be abandoned as grossly misleading.

Joel Mokyr, in a brilliant discussion of the Industrial Revolution, contrasts 'the traditional economy', which 'contained agriculture, construction, domestic industry, and many traditional "trades"' with 'the modern sector' that 'consisted of cotton, iron smelting and refining, engineering, heavy chemicals, mining, some parts of transportation, and some consumer goods such as pottery and paper' (Mokyr, 1999, p. 12). He then offers the following, more discriminating, generalizations about economic change during this period.

> Utilizing the distinction between a modern and a traditional sector allows us to summarize what happened to the British economy during the Industrial Revolution as a three-pronged economic change. First, a small sector of the economy underwent quite rapid and dramatic technological change. Second, as a consequence, this sector grew at a rate much faster than the traditional sector so that its share in the overall economy continued to increase. Third, the technological changes in the modern sector gradually

penetrated the membrane of the traditional sector so that part of the *traditional* sector eventually became modernized.

(ibid., p. 15)

It was easy for Mokyr to justify these generalizations because he knew the principal industries in the modern and traditional sectors and could examine the changes of each in turn.

Sometimes the reference class has so many members that it is impossible to examine them all. Historians are then forced to rely on representative samples of the membership of the reference class to justify their generalization. Statisticians have developed several quite technical methods of sampling, each useful in different conditions. Here I shall do no more than illustrate the importance of ensuring that the sample is truly representative. The example also shows that sometimes members of a reference class do not all have the same attributes.

Joanne Meyerowitz has provided an interesting example of how misleading a generalization can be when based on an inadequate sample. She examined the thesis which Betty Friedan had presented in *The Feminine Mystique*, that after the Second World War, women, who had worked independently during the depression and war years, endorsed a philosophy of subordination and domesticity. Friedan, Meyerowitz said, had 'focused primarily on short story fiction in four women's magazines' for evidence of her thesis (Meyerowitz, 1993, p. 1457). Meyerowitz chose 'nonfiction articles in a larger sample of popular magazines', including some with a relatively small circulation, to represent the diversity of American society (ibid.). 'All of the magazines sampled', she writes, 'advocated both the domestic and the non-domestic, sometimes in the same sentence. In this literature, domestic ideals co-existed in ongoing tension with an ethos of individual achievement that celebrated nondomestic activity, individual striving, public service, and public success' (ibid., p. 1458).

Why had Friedan got it so wrong? It was partly that the sample she used was small, and not truly representative of the attitudes of American women. But there were other reasons as well, according to Meyerowitz. The first was an assumption of uniformity rather than diversity in social attitudes. Friedan assumed that there was one dominant view of the role of women in society, and that she had found it in the magazines she read. Today historians are much more aware of 'contradictions, ambivalence, and competing voices' in society (ibid., p. 1457). The second reason Friedan got it wrong is that she discounted evidence in favour of women's independence as insignificant (pp. 1479–80). Perhaps this was because she was convinced in advance that only one attitude was dominant.

The third problem historians encounter when testing generalizations is that of finding reliable and useful indicators of the attribute in question. A reliable indicator invariably marks the presence of the attribute, and it is useful if it is readily ascertainable.

At one stage Mokyr considered evidence for the generalization that for people living in Britain between 1760 and 1850 the standard of living improved (Mokyr, 1999, pp. 116–26). The main problem encountered by historians trying to verify this generalization was that of identifying a reliable and useful indicator for 'standard of living'. Different indicators yielded different results.

Two indicators of standard of living used by economic historians were aggregate consumption and real wages. Plotting these they found that 'living standards remained more or less unchanged between 1760 and 1820 and then accelerated rapidly between 1820 and 1850' (ibid., p. 116). But the usefulness of these indicators has been questioned. Aggregate consumption was measured as the difference between output and investment, and estimates of these was based on 'highly speculative data' (p. 117), so the evidence for average consumption was not very reliable. Plotting real wages proved difficult too, as the years for which data were collected might not have been representative of the whole; and the data were for adult male wages, ignoring the wages of women and children, whose wages are known to have varied differently. Early investigations also ignored the 'wages' earned by the self-employed, such as independent artisans, farm workers and domestic workers, whose income did not rise as did the income of those being paid a formal wage in factories. Nor did it make allowance for areas of unemployment, especially in agriculture. Finally, the reliability of real wages as an indicator of standards of living has been questioned too: 'a rise in real wages may not be an indication of rising living standards if these rising real wages were a compensation for deteriorating labor conditions. If factory work and life in industrial towns and villages became more onerous, dangerous, or unpleasant, rising real wages would have the interpretation of a compensating differential' (p. 121).

Another set of indicators used to measure the standard of living were those which Mokyr calls 'biological': the mortality rate; life expectancy at birth; infant mortality; and human height, all considered sensitive to improved nutrition and life style. Mortality rates did decline over the period, but these 'are flawed indicators for many reasons, primarily because of their dependence on the age structure of the population' (ibid., p. 122). Life expectancy and infant mortality improved until about 1820, and then remained static or increased slightly. The same is true of human height: 'indeed, the cohorts born in 1850–1854 are shorter than any cohort born in the nineteenth century' (p. 123). These data are inconsistent with the data derived from economic indicators, some of which found a marked improvement in the standard of living after 1820. Mokyr concludes: 'At this stage, therefore, it has to be inferred that the evidence of a rise in living standards before 1850 is simply too weak to be convincing' (p. 124). The most it seems one can say with confidence is that the wages of adult males in factories improved over the period.

So accidental generalizations about the properties of members of a reference class are justified if there is reliable evidence that most or all members of the reference class had the properties attributed to them.

Generalizations about causal or explanatory relations

A cause is an event which sets in train a tendency to produce a certain kind of outcome, its effect. In certain circumstances, causes always do this; the consequence occurs with lawlike regularity. (The nature of causes is more fully explained below, in Chapter 7.) Causal chains, however, are often accidental, not lawlike. If I hit a cricket ball at a window, it will tend to break the glass; and the breaking glass will tend to make a loud noise; and if there is a baby present who is asleep, the noise will tend to wake the baby. The impact of the ball on the glass regularly makes it break and cause a noise, but it does not regularly waken the baby. Historians often find accidental causal sequences occurring commonly in certain contexts, and they describe these with accidental causal generalizations.

An excellent example of this point is provided by R.J. Holton's book *The Transition from Feudalism to Capitalism* (1985). Holton describes three general theories that historians have developed to account for the transition from feudalism to capitalism, but none of them is satisfactory.

> Neither the inexorable drives of rational economic man, nor the expansion of the productive forces bursting through outmoded patterns of social relations, nor the fateful march of rationalisation, seem at all adequate as underlying explanations of the transition to capitalism in Europe. In this way no unifying causal principle has been successfully demonstrated to lie behind the historical emergence of capitalism . . .
>
> [W]hat seems called for is a greater tolerance of causal pluralism, multilinear patterns of social change, analyses of particular unrepeatable historical conjunctures and explanation in terms of contingent rather than historically necessary patterns of social development.
>
> . . . There is no single pattern of capitalist development within the nation-states of early modern Europe . . . this is largely because of exogenous as well as endogenous influences in the successful consolidation of capitalism in different parts of Europe.
>
> (pp. 145–6)

Holton explains how the pattern of development differed in various European countries, notably in France, England and Prussia, varying with local conditions. His descriptions of the common patterns of development within each country therefore constitute accidental causal generalizations. They depend upon economic theory to identify important causes of industrialization, but they emphasize the diverse ways in which governments affected the process. In France, in the eighteenth century the Crown and aristocracy drained money from the economy for personal use, and capitalist interests in trade and manufacture proceeded without state support. Under the strong legal and administrative framework of the Napoleonic state, capitalist enterprises began to flourish (pp. 174–5). In

England, from Elizabethan times the crown had fostered industrial projects, and after the Revolution of 1688, the state supported business with the 'mercantilist system' of legal protection (pp. 178–80). The Industrial Revolution in England enormously stimulated trade, under the protection of the state (p. 203). Prussia enjoyed a strong central government from the early eighteenth century, and it permitted the Junkers to develop strong agrarian businesses. In the nineteenth century industries grew in the West, and the economy was protected by a customs union (pp. 181–5).

From a philosophical point of view it is important to distinguish causes and explanatory conditions. Causes are events which produce tendencies for change. They are dynamic. Explanatory conditions, on the other hand, are states of affairs or events which make one outcome more probable than another, in certain circumstances. In short, they are useful for contrastive explanations. (Again, this will be explained more fully in Chapter 7.) To identify explanatory conditions which account for similar contrasts, historians look for conditions which seem to make the difference in every case. To judge their relevance, they have to see how they contributed to the outcome they possibly explain. For instance, Holton saw the presence of a strong state as a condition which explains why some countries prospered more than others did. The Dutch republic, for example, had a loose federal system of government which was unable to protect capitalist interests adequately (pp. 203–4). In some cases, particularly in England and Prussia, the state actually fostered industries ('capitalism from above'), and those activities causally contributed to the growth of capitalist enterprises in those countries

Descriptions of social structures

When historians have accumulated a number of lawlike generalizations about social interactions, they are sometimes able to identify patterns of social relationships which can be called social structures. Theoretical analysis of social structures is rather tentative at present, but I think the following can be said with some confidence.

It is convenient to distinguish three basic kinds of social structure, which I shall call social organizations, social systems and general social structures. What distinguishes social organizations is that their structures are planned to produce certain goods or services in a given environment. In many cases it would be more accurate to say the organization evolved, rather than was planned, but it is nevertheless examined and adjusted from time to time to improve its intended performance. Factories and shops, universities and hospitals, armies and governments are examples of such organizations. They consist of a number of offices defined by their roles (responsibilities), which are related to one another by sets of rules and conventions, and which perform their duties by means of more or less defined practices. Large organizations are composed of a number of smaller organizations, each with its own function and responsibilities within the whole. As well as having an internal structure, organizations have systematic relations with external authorities, organizations and environments, which usually develop as a means of achieving their goals.

Social systems are social structures which are not planned, but nevertheless involve a number of agencies interacting in a regular manner. The agencies may be aggregates of individuals, but often they are social organizations. Part of an economic system, for example, relates manufacturers and primary producers to retail outlets, and the latter to customers. Each of these relations is planned, usually governed by contracts, but the whole system in free market economies is unplanned. Similarly, a political system might involve the formation of political parties, supported by a variety of sponsors, which put forward candidates for election. This part of the political system is unplanned, though the procedure for electing and running a government is planned. An education system involves a number of organizations, schools, colleges and universities, which offer qualifications of different kinds. They are related in that children who qualify at school are admitted to college or university, and universities and colleges often train school teachers. But the education system is not planned as a whole.

Finally, there are general social structures which differentiate groups of people according to their wealth, their power (economic, ideological or coercive), their status (social, economic, educational, etc.), their occupation, their culture, their education or whatever. Historians are often interested in changes in such structures.

As soon as historians start to investigate social structures of these kinds, they find that further distinctions have to be made. The first is between ideal social systems and actual ones. For instance, there might be written statements setting out the roles and rules of an organization, an ideal account of its structure. But these might not have been followed very strictly, so that the roles and rules actually observed are slightly different. Historians have to decide whether to study an ideal or an actual social structure.

There is another contrast between the ideal and actual which is also worth mentioning. Theorists sometimes develop models of an ideal economic or bureaucratic system, in which people make perfectly rational decisions, which can approximate to certain real social systems, but seldom describe them accurately. Historians are seldom interested in such modelling, but it pays to be aware of it nevertheless. The models can suggest regularities within a system which historians can then investigate.

Then again, often historians are interested in the way a person's beliefs about their place in a social structure influence their behaviour. It is possible that a person's belief about an ideal or actual social structure is not entirely accurate. So historians have to be aware of the difference between peoples' beliefs about the structures of their society, and the reality, as far as historians can discern it.

Historians frequently discover regularities in social structures of which members of the society were entirely unaware. This is one reason for refusing to reduce social structures to ideas people have had about them. But does historians' discourse about society refer to anything real? This is a difficult issue, but it is worth saying a little about it.

We often observe complex objects, whose existence depends upon the relatively small objects of which they are composed. A tree exists if its trunk, branches and leaves do; a house exists if its frame and walls and roof do; and so on. Scientists have discovered that this relation of dependence, or supervenience as philosophers call it, is very extensive. The leaves of a tree, for example, depend upon the existence of the cells which compose them; and the cells depend upon the existence of molecules, and molecules upon atoms, and so on. We cannot always see natural systems, but can infer their existence. We cannot see the particles which make up an atom, for example; nor the natural processes which produce weather in different parts of the world; nor the solar system of planets revolving around the sun. But we accept that a complex system is an existing whole if the system is generally stable, and not just an accidental configuration of elements. Once such complex entities have been identified, we are then able to study relations between them.

Social structures are kinds of complex entities with more or less stable, lawlike structures, which is why people generally have no difficulty in accepting their reality. The fact that we cannot see them in the same way as we can perceive middle sized physical objects like trees and houses is no reason for denying their existence. We cannot see physical forces or fields, such as gravitational force or a magnetic field, but we assume they exist, to account for their effects. Similarly, we cannot see the solar system, but since Galileo we accept that it exists, to account for the orbits of the planets. To account for the regular relations between people who hold office in an organization, we talk of the rules, roles and practices of the organization which govern their behaviour. To explain why a loss of markets causes unemployment in an industry, historians draw upon elementary economic theory, which is both rational and generally accurate as a description of how capitalist economic systems work: a loss of markets causes a loss of income which in most cases means the industry cannot afford to pay as much in wages, so it has to dismiss staff to remain viable.

Whereas the relations between the elements of social organizations and systems are lawlike, the relations between the elements of general social structures are not, but are dependent upon chance events. In some countries those in political power are the most wealthy, but in others this is not the case. In some countries the better educated people are among the wealthier, but in others there is no correlation between the two groups. Nevertheless, because in most societies the general structure of society as measured by several such variables remains fairly stable for some time, that structure is identified as an object of historical inquiry.

If changes to social structures have causal powers, then that is an excellent reason for accepting them as real. In some societies, an increase in unemployment causes an increase in crime. Certainly this causal generalization is dependent ('supervenient') upon the behaviour of individuals who, being out of work, decide for a variety of reasons to commit crimes. But that does not make it less true. Compare the generalization that rainwater will rust an iron roof. This is a true causal generalization, even though it depends upon the behaviour of individual molecules of water interacting with molecules of iron.

Just as the regular behaviour of plants and animals depends upon the regular behaviour of the cells which constitute them, so too the regular behaviour of social groups depends upon the regular behaviour of the individuals who constitute them. But historians can discover regularities about groups without referring to the individuals of which they are composed. Here is a conclusion, for example, which Charles Tilly drew after studying many peasant rebellions in seventeenth-century France.

> Where peasant communities have a measure of solidarity and some means of collective defence, where new or increased claims clearly violate publicly known agreements or principles, where some visible person or group that is close at hand stands to gain by the new demands on the peasants, and where effective coalition partners are available to the peasants, collective resistance become likely. When that resistance is sustained and involves organized attacks on the enemy, we have peasant rebellion.
>
> (Tilly, 1981, p. 139)

The vocabulary used to describe social structures contains terms which have special meanings, and to employ them accurately in describing a social structure, historians must know their meaning. A rule, for example, is not just a common pattern of behaviour. That is no more than a common practice. A rule is a statement of how people ought to behave in certain circumstances, which has been authorised by someone with legitimate authority. And what is a legitimate authority? Max Weber proposed the following answer to this question:

> There are three pure types of legitimate authority. The validity of their claims to legitimacy may be based on:
>
> 1. Rational grounds – resting on a belief in the 'legality' of patterns of normative rules and the right of those elevated to authority under such rules to issue commands (legal authority).
>
> 2. Traditional grounds – resting on an established belief in the sanctity of immemorial traditions and the legitimacy of the status of those exercising authority under them (traditional authority); or finally,
>
> 3. Charismatic grounds – resting on devotion to the specific and exceptional sanctity, heroism or exemplary character of an individual person, and of the normative patterns or order revealed or ordained by him (charismatic authority).
>
> (Weber, 1947, p. 328)

This is how Weber spelled out the conditions under which people have normally held an authority to be 'legitimate'. Historians can use his theory to determine whether or not an authority issuing a rule is legitimate. Most of the book from which this extract is taken is devoted to the definition of special terms used to describe social structures, and to a general description of some common social structures as well. Once historians have mastered the vocabulary, they can then formulate descriptions of a social structure and social change using the words of social theory.

Social historians carefully consider what words in social theory best describe the societies they study. T.P. Wiseman, for example, said that nineteenth-century historians looking at the Roman Republic 'saw a two-party system of nobles and *populares*; in the twentieth, they have seen "factions" based on aristocratic families and their allies.' He goes on: 'Of course there were sometimes alliances, but they were temporary and *ad hoc*; of course there were sometimes great issues which divided the political élite, but never into "parties" in any sense even approximately analogous to what modern English means by the term' (Wiseman, 1988, pp. 18–19).

Sometimes the criteria for using a term are uncertain and debated. Economic historians who advocate the use of statistics, to bring maximum mathematical precision into their discipline, are prone to define terms in ways which enable instances of them to be measured. But not all terms in social theory can be defined in a way which allows instances of them to be measured. Consider again the concept of 'the standard of living'. Roderick Floud has described this as 'the level of success or failure which people achieve in fulfilling their desire to consume' (Floud, 1988, p. 33). Economic historians who assume that they can measure the standard of living by measuring 'the value of national income per head', he said, are mistaken. First, there are other components to a good life, such as good health and leisure, which it ignores. And second, in most societies the enjoyment of life has been very unequal, a few wealthy having a good time and the majority working hard, 'so that average national income tells us little about the nature of life in a society' (ibid.).

Historians are frequently commissioned to write the history of social organizations. When it comes to describing social systems, which are much more extensive, they have to be particularly careful about the accuracy of their generalizations.

To maximize accuracy, it is important to designate the precise area of the society being described. Considering economic growth during the Industrial Revolution, Peter Mathias remarked that

> it is important to escape from the tyranny of nationally determined statistics, which can obscure reality. To understand the process of growth the focus of analysis must often concern localities and regions – whether regions within the frontiers of a national state or regions lying across political frontiers.

(Mathias, 1989, p. 22)

Growth of the cotton industry, for example, was not a national phenomenon in Britain, but was confined to some districts of Lancashire and Cheshire.

The temptation to make sweeping generalizations about social and economic history is constantly being resisted in the interests of accuracy. Because production in the cotton and iron industries was vastly increased as a result of technological inventions, some historians, notably W.W. Rostow, attributed the growth of the whole British economy during the second half of the eighteenth century to those industries. But Mathias argues that the contribution of those industries was in fact quite small. There was growth in other industries as well, including handicraft industries such as spinning, and also in agriculture and service industries.

> The leverage exerted by the expansion of the cotton and iron industries, even at the margin, upon the national aggregates – whether by labour employed (and wages paid), by investment and profits, by inputs and outputs of all kinds – is not sufficient to explain the national experience as a whole. The economy was not being dragged forward just on the coat-tails of a single industry, however dynamic.
>
> (ibid., p. 20)

To check the accuracy of a social or economic generalization, historians carefully consider both its credibility and its fairness. It is credible if the conditions which would make it true did in fact exist. For example, it is credible that there was an expansion in the cotton and iron industries because investment and output in those industries increased dramatically. But it is not fair to say that this was responsible for the growth of the national economy, because that implies no other sources of growth were nearly as significant, which is false. To say that cotton and iron were responsible for national economic growth is to give a misleading impression of its causes. (Explanations of social change are discussed in Chapter 8.)

When historians consider the general social structures of a society, it is important to realize that there is no single correct way of describing those structures. As was indicated above, historians can structure society according to a wide variety of variables: economic, political, ethnic, educational, religious and so on. In some simply structured societies, these various structures converged to a large extent. In some such societies the wealthy members of the society were the most powerful and the best educated; the poorest were of a particular racial or ethnic group and least well educated. It might then be possible to describe the society under almost all interesting variables by identifying the different groups concerned. But in a modern society there is much less convergence. The wealthy are not always the best educated, and the latter are not always the most powerful. (For an extensive discussion of problems in classifying social groups, see McCullagh, 1998, pp. 102–8.)

Conclusion

This chapter has provided a glimpse into the ways in which singular and general descriptions of the past can be logically justified. Each topic deserves much more thorough discussion (offered for example in McCullagh, 1984), but the intention of this book is to arouse interest in the logic of history, not to expound it in full detail.

One important point to emerge from this chapter has been the importance of lawlike generalizations in drawing inferences from evidence of the past. Often the evidence is an artefact, and to discover more about the past, historians want to know the circumstances of its creation. The first step they take is to discover why the person who made it did so. If they can discover this, they can often find out details about the world of the agent, what the agent thought had happened and what he or she hoped to achieve by creating the artefact. Why did Abelard write his history? By answering this question, historians can draw interesting conclusions about his life. Why did the Romans build Hadrian's Wall? Answering this question leads to an understanding of some of the problems faced by the Romans on their northern frontier, and how they hoped to cope with them.

Inferences about the reasons for actions are based upon some general assumptions about the kinds of things which cause people to act. These assumptions are so critical to historical inquiry that I have decided to explain and discuss them at some length – in the next chapter.

Chapter 4

Causes of human actions

Historians draw upon their general beliefs about the causes of human actions in two quite different contexts. The first is when interpreting evidence. Once historians have decided who created a piece of observable evidence, they are interested in the circumstances of its creation so as to learn more about the past, particularly those features of the past which interest them. The second context is when historians want to explain an action of some historical significance, and then the causes they look for depend upon the kind of explanation they desire. It may be they want to know all the important causes of the action; or just the most important; or the conditions which account for one action being performed rather than another.

General theories about the possible causes of human actions are developed and tested by philosophers, psychologists and brain scientists (neurophysiologists). My intention in this chapter is to point out some of the theories commonly used by historians, to help the reader appreciate current historical practice and the vital role general knowledge of causes plays in historical inquiry. Historians are amazingly casual about their knowledge of theories of human action, scarcely looking further than the commonsense theories prevalent in their community. I also draw attention to well-known objections to some of these theories, and consider the strength of the arguments that have been presented. For instance, I find objections to some forms of psychoanalytic explanation compelling, but postmodern attacks upon the essential nature of a person quite unconvincing.

Theories about the causes of human actions postulate some strange entities, strange in that they cannot be observed. Among these are people's beliefs, values and intentions; their interests, instincts and concerns; the rules of their culture and the expectations of their society. All of these are theoretical concepts which are widely accepted for their extraordinarily impressive explanatory value. In the past theorists have sometimes focussed on just one or two of these causes, usually for certain practical reasons. But they have generally done enough to establish the importance of each, and historians should therefore be willing to consider them all.

For convenience I have divided this chapter into two parts. The first is about mental causes of human actions, and the second about cultural and social causes.

The mental causes are of roughly two kinds: those of which people are conscious and those of which they are unconscious. The classical, commonsense theory of human behaviour attends to causes of which people are conscious, particularly to those which people commonly offer to explain their actions. It explains rational actions by referring to the desires, beliefs and values which influence people in deciding how to act. And to explain irrational behaviour it often refers to passions, emotions and habits. Unconscious causes of human action were explored particularly in the nineteenth century by Marx, Freud and Nietzsche, and by subsequent investigators building upon their work. Marx showed how much behaviour is driven by people's material interests; Freud wrote about the pervasive influence of basic human instincts for self-preservation and reproduction; and Nietzsche focussed on the pursuit of power. The first part of the chapter ends by considering postmodern criticism of the notion that people are moved by these mental states, and finds the criticism unconvincing.

The second part of the chapter is about cultural and social causes of human actions. It notes the way in which discourses, practices and roles can influence human behaviour, and then asks why this is so. The section concludes with a brief consideration of the objection that cultural and social influences do not really exist.

Mental causes of human actions

Mental causes of which people are conscious

Although I referred to the classical, commonsense theory of human behaviour, strictly speaking there is not one theory but a collection of insights which have been published by writers during the history of Western culture. Most of these, at least until the nineteenth century, referred to mental experiences associated with actions, which seemed influential in producing those actions. Let me mention a few of those, to give you an idea of their nature.

Socrates, teaching in Athens in the fifth century BCE, was very impressed with the ability of humans to think, to deliberate about what they should do. This clearly distinguishes humans from other animals. He taught (see Plato's dialogue Meno) that people always act according to their judgement as to what they should do. Their judgement is not always wise, but he believed no-one would act contrary to their judgement. His pupil Plato admitted that people are sometimes moved by other desires, for example by natural bodily appetites for food, shelter, sex and so on, and also by a stubborn wilfulness which was not always in accordance with wisdom. Each of these was important for a good life, he believed, just as a city needs merchants and warriors if it is to prosper. The challenge people face is to ensure that their appetites and will are subordinated to their wisdom. (See The Republic by Plato, Book IV.) Aristotle, who succeeded Plato, advocated strict training of people's natural desires to ensure they were moderate enough to enable people to act rationally. (See his discussion of virtue in the Nichomachean Ethics.)

Critical inquiry into human nature resumed during the Roman Empire, then again during the Renaissance and the Enlightenment in Europe, between the fifteenth and eighteenth centuries, in the writing of men like Macchiavelli, Montaigne, Hobbes, Locke and Hume, largely in connection with their interest in ethics and politics. In recent years the analysis of commonsense experiences of human action has become very refined. The work of American philosophers, Donald Davidson, Harry G. Frankfurt, John Martin Fischer, Alfred R. Mele, Robert Audi and Bennett W. Helm trace the major philosophical discussions.

Historians are seldom familiar with philosophical and psychological analyses of the causes of human actions, but prefer to operate with commonsense notions. They assume (i) that people normally act as a result of deliberation, in accordance with some of their desires, beliefs, values and principles. When they behave irrationally, they attribute their behaviour to (ii) an overwhelming passion, or (iii) a strong emotion. Sometimes (iv) people simply act from habit, according to convention. The habit may be that of uncritically obeying those in authority over them. Each of these is a mental cause of action of which the agent can be aware. Let me say a little more about each, and illustrate instances of them in historical writing.

(i) Historians often begin by supposing that an action they wish to explain was performed for reasons. That is, they suppose that the action was the result of a process of deliberation which involved the agent thinking about their desires, values, beliefs and principles, and which resulted in the formation of an intention to act. Such intentions incline the agent to act in a certain way. Some writers make room for free choice here, and allow that whether people act according to their intentions is up to them. Others think actions are determined by whatever intention is most influential at the time. If there is an element of free choice in human action, then it is easier to hold people responsible for what they have done. If actions are entirely determined, people can claim they could not help acting as they did, and so should not be held responsible for their actions.

The process of deliberation is not necessarily a very rational one (though some philosophers of history, such as W.H. Dray, have assumed it is. See Dray, 1957, ch. 5.). The goals a person decides to pursue might not be ones they value very highly; and the means they choose to pursue them might not be the best they could have devised. However, without that deliberation historians believe the intention and action which followed would not have occurred. So the deliberation was necessary for the action. If the desires, values and beliefs were strongly held, it would even have made it quite probable.

The points made in the last two paragraphs present the general structure of a causal theory of action. Historical explanations provide the content of the values, desires and beliefs which contributed to agents' deliberation. This content is the cognitive dimension of the explanation. These are values, beliefs and desires that the agent knows about. Here is a neat illustration of the way values and beliefs led to the formation of an intention to act. It is J.M. McPherson's explanation of the reasons why the South seceded from the Union in 1861, an act which triggered the American Civil War.

> With complete sincerity the South fought to preserve its version of the republic of the founding fathers – a government of limited powers that protected the rights of property and whose constituency comprised an independent gentry and yeomanry of the white race undisturbed by large cities, heartless factories, restless free workers, and class conflict. The accession to power of the Republican party (in the U.S. Congress), with its ideology of competitive, egalitarian, free-labor capitalism, was a signal to the South that the northern majority had turned irrevocably toward this frightening, revolutionary future . . . secession was a pre-emptive counter-revolution to prevent the Black Republican revolution from engulfing the South.
>
> (McPherson, 1988, pp. 860–1)

The first sentence describes those aspects of southern society that southerners valued. The next sentence states their beliefs about the ideology of the northern Republicans, which had clearly captured the imagination of the majority of those who elected representatives in Congress. And the last sentence describes the conclusion that they drew as to the most appropriate course of action: to defend the society they valued from the threat of Republican central government, they must secede from the Union. That decision was a fairly rational one, given the values and beliefs stated, and once formulated, became the content of their will. These are the particular values, beliefs and intentions which the leaders of the South knew about, and which moved them to act.

Historians are interested in the distinction between the reasons which actually moved people to act, and the reasons which they sometimes offer for their actions, in justification of them, which did not really motivate them. To make sense of this distinction one must allow that certain values and beliefs can produce a strong tendency to act in a certain way, but that ultimately agents are free to act otherwise. McPherson provides an interesting discussion of the part slavery played in motivating both the North and the South at the outbreak of the Civil War. Historians are sometimes suspicious that Lincoln was opposed to slavery in the South, and that Davis wanted to defend it. However, neither admitted as much. Lincoln said that the North was fighting to preserve the Union, not to abolish slavery; and Davis said the South was fighting to protect its society from a Northern invasion and the devastation which would follow in its wake. McPherson remarks that 'an explicit avowal that the defence of slavery was a primary Confederate war aim might have proven more divisive than unifying in the South' (p. 312). Certainly Lincoln would have alienated a number of his supporters in the North had he declared an attack on slavery as an aim of the war in 1861, though he was to proclaim the emancipation of slaves after the battle at Antietam, on 22 September 1862 (p. 557).

(ii) When people behave irrationally, for no reasons that the historian can imagine, then historians look for an everyday psychological, rather than a rational, explanation. Psychological explanations explain actions as instances of a general kind, not as unique events. During the dreadful battle at Antietam (which the South called Sharpsburg), on 17 September 1862, Union soldiers were described as 'loading and firing with demoniacal fury and shouting and laughing hysterically.' The result was nearly 6000 dead and 17,000 wounded. To explain this behaviour, McPherson considered several psychological possibilities. First, he noted the 'grim determination' of the soldiers to defeat the enemy.

> Yankee soldiers were not impelled by fearless bravery or driven by iron discipline. Few men ever experience the former and Civil War soldiers scarcely knew the latter. Rather, they were motivated in the mass by the potential shame of another defeat and in small groups by the potential shame of cowardice in the eyes of comrades.

Then he considered the effect of a terrifying battle ground, of 'the hiss of bullets and the hurtle of grape-shot', which produced an extraordinary psychological strain in the soldiers. 'This psychological state produced a sort of fighting madness in many men, a superadrenalized fury that turned them into mindless killing machines heedless of the normal instinct of self-preservation' (ibid., p. 540). Clearly such psychological explanations draw upon the historian's general knowledge about the typical causes of the kind of behaviour they are considering.

(iii) Emotional explanations are not always without cognitive content. When an emotion has an object, as is normally the case, an emotional response to that object has a rational dimension. One of the Southern commanders at the battle at Antietam was Robert A. Toombs. Why was he fighting? McPherson offers this explanation: 'Disappointed by his failure to become president of the Confederacy, bored by his job as secretary of state, Toombs had taken a brigadier's commission to seek the fame and glory to which he felt destined' (p. 543). He disliked working for the Southern administration, which frustrated and bored him, and he wanted fame and glory which he associated with a commission in the army. So he left the one and joined the other. People generally avoid what they dislike, and are attracted to things which appeal to them: that is the simple causal theory. But to explain particular emotional behaviour one has to add the cognitive dimension: one has to state the objects of repulsion and attraction, as they were known to the agent. Toombs eventually became disappointed with life in the army, when he did not get an expected promotion, 'and subsequently resigned to go public with his anti-administration exhortations.' (ibid.) – another set of emotional responses!

(iv) When people behave in a conventional way, following the normal practices of their society, it often seems that their behaviour is no more than a conditioned response to a situation. At the battle of Fredericksburg, on

13 December 1862, wave after wave of Union soldiers attacked Confederate troops who were shooting from behind the protection of a stone wall, 'loading and shooting so fast that their firing achieved the effect of machine guns.' (p. 572). The Confederate troops were responding as they had been trained, more or less automatically shooting those who attacked them.

Even in cases of a conditioned response such as this, however, there is a cognitive element. The soldiers had to identify the enemy and point their guns in his direction in order to fire. Conventional behaviour always involves an interpretation of the situation that triggers the response, and perception of its configuration so as to act effectively within it.

Historians use their general knowledge of the possible causes of human actions to draw inferences about the causes of particular actions. A famous instance of this in recent historiography is Daniel J. Goldhagen's explanation of what moved so many Germans to persecute and kill defenceless Jews during the Nazi regime. To conclude this section, readers might find it an interesting example to study. It illustrates a lot of the difficulties involved in justifying a description of people's reasons for acting.

There is almost no direct evidence of the motives of the perpetrators at the time, but years after the Second World War, police and others interrogated many of those involved. Could these accounts be used to reveal their motives? No, said Goldhagen, because the 'motivations for lying, for not announcing that they were among history's greatest criminals, were powerful indeed' (Goldhagen, 1996, p. 467). In fact, he found, they did lie repeatedly, 'by word and omission', to minimize their culpability.

To discover the motives of the perpetrators, therefore, Goldhagen turned to an inference to the best explanation. He asked what were the possible motives for such behaviour, which were universally present. Previous historians had suggested a number of motives, and Goldhagen lists the more important of these: coercion, blind obedience, group pressure, self-interest and ignorance (ibid., pp. 11–12). However, Goldhagen was convinced that the common and most important motive was an almost universal, unquestioned anti-Semitic conviction, a hatred of Jews as polluters of the Aryan race and enemies of German society. People generally act for reasons, he said, reasons which justify their behaviour. And in his opinion this conviction is the only reason adequate to account for their appalling behaviour (ibid., pp. 13–15). In fact all the possible motives are suggested by general theories of human behaviour. To make his thesis plausible, Goldhagen described the development of anti-Semitic views in Germany over the preceding centuries. These did not advocate the extermination of the Jews, but Goldhagen thought this policy was implied by the attitudes they expressed (ibid., pp. 449–50). More to the point was Hitler's anti-Semitic propaganda which portrayed the Jews as enemies of the new Aryan Reich, which influenced Germans under the Nazi regime (Goldhagen, 1996, pp. 133 ff.). As Richard Ely explains, anti-Semitic attitudes were expressed not only in Nazi ideology, but also in practices at every level of the Nazi state:

it's all very well to express skepticism about 'Nazi ideology' in the narrower, formalistic sense of that term, and to doubt the penetration into everyday life of Nazism's programmatic propaganda. But as soon as we focus on the issue of complicity at all levels of German society after 1933, we immediately need an *extended* understanding of ideology, as being embedded in cultural practices, institutional sites, and social relations – in what people do and the structured contexts where they do it, rather than just the ideas they consciously think.

(Ely, 2000, p. 23; and cf. Goldhagen, 1996, pp. 390–401)

But historians such as Hans Mommsen have shown that Nazi government departments and officials did not always follow Hitler's wishes. So is there any reason to suppose the perpetrators of the Holocaust acted in accordance with Nazi anti-Semitic ideology?

To prove his hypothesis, Goldhagen could have examined the actions of people obviously committed to the programme of the Nazi Party, members of the SS for example. It is quite likely that they would have been strongly motivated by the Party's ideology. But Goldhagen believed all the ordinary Germans involved in the Holocaust were also motivated by anti-Semitic convictions. So to find compelling evidence in support of his theory, he chose to study the behaviour of groups of executioners who were not committed Party members. He chose three groups: Police Battalion 101, which executed hundreds of Jewish women and children in Poland in July 1942; those running work camps in Poland; and a group of 47 male and female guards accompanying a 'death march' of over a thousand Jewish and non-Jewish women from the Helmbrechts camp in eastern Germany. In the first case, Germans from a wide range of backgrounds, many middle aged, slaughtered women and children even though they were given every opportunity not to do so. In the second, camps designed to harness Jewish labour to produce goods supporting Germany's war effort, in fact starved, exhausted and killed its inmates in a most sadistic manner. In the third, the guards starved and beat the Jewish women as they walked till they fell.

Why would people kill Jews brutally, if they were given the opportunity not to do so? Why would they kill them instead of using them for the war effort? Why would they discriminate against them on the long march? In each case, the only plausible explanation according to Goldhagen lies in their beliefs about the Jews, their anti-Semitic convictions. He systematically sets aside alternative explanations (ibid., ch. 15). The Germans were not compelled to obey orders, but did so voluntarily, often taking the initiative. Virtually none was punished for refusing to kill the Jews. Germans are not by nature obedient to the state: many disobeyed both their government and their commanders. Peer pressure played a part, but if the majority had opposed the Holocaust that would have stopped it! Few were concerned about career advancement, as many were quite old, and did not seek a career in the army or government. All would have known the significance of what they did: it was too vivid to ignore. The only explanation which covers all cases is the ideological one: without their anti-Semitic convictions, the ordinary Germans would not have acted as they did.

So far we have a classic argument by elimination. Having listed all the possible causes of Jewish persecution, Goldhagen has eliminated all but one: his preferred rational explanation, that the people who executed Jews acted willingly, from anti-Semitic convictions. Are there any weaknesses in this explanatory hypothesis? There are reasons to think that anti-Semitism is not sufficient to account the policy of extermination, and that habits of obedience to the state might have played an important part.

First, there are many countries in which anti-Semitic convictions have abounded, but they did not lead to a policy of extermination. So it seems they are not enough to account for the Holocaust. Goldhagen agrees that they are not sufficient: in Germany they produced the Holocaust only when the state implemented them in a systematic way (Goldhagen, 1998, pp. 141–2). Second, in that case it seems that a desire to obey the state was an important ingredient in motivating the killing of Jews: without it the Jews may have been isolated and even persecuted, but not killed. Goldhagen responds to this suggestion by citing cases of executioners voluntarily persecuting and killing Jews. The worry remains that these cases might in fact have been exceptional. Respect for the will of the Party and a desire to appear patriotic might have motivated many acts of compliance. Third, if traditional anti-Semitism was not bent upon the extermination of the Jews, the question arises as to why systematic extermination was adopted by the Nazi government. Mommsen's suggestion is that this was a response to the practical difficulties of expelling the Jews from Germany or confining them in reservations once the invasion of Russia began, which brought many more Jews under German authority (Mommsen, 1998, pp. 184–5). So the motivation of the government was partly practical, not ideological, and the people simply followed their leaders.

Goldhagen is inclined to say that if many Germans did not believe in the need to exterminate the Jews, why did they not object to the policy of extermination? 'The absence of evidence is evidence itself' of their agreement with the policy (Goldhagen, 1998a, p. 153). The obvious reply is that people were afraid to speak out against official policy, for fear of being treated as Jew-lovers. Goldhagen simply insists that people could criticize the regime, and that support for the elimination of Jews was enthusiastic (ibid., pp. 153–4). Once again, we are left wondering just how many were so enthusiastic about it.

Fundamentally, Goldhagen's problem is that common to so many historical generalizations, namely the problem of generalizing from a number of cases when one cannot be sure just how representative they are of the whole population. We have no idea how representative his chosen cases are of the whole population involved in the Holocaust. How had the police, for example, been trained? How influential was the fanatical anti-Semite who governed the camp at Helmbrechts? Even within those cases, many soldiers enjoyed hurting and killing the Jews, but what percentage did so, and how many of them did so for ideological reasons, rather than from pure sadism, a delight in making others suffer? We may never know. Like many academics, Goldhagen assumes people almost always act for reasons, rather than from sadistic impulses. Similarly, he is inclined to suppose Hitler's executioners were motivated by ideology rather than by fear. His belief that they nearly all acted for reasons enables him to extrapolate from his limited samples to the whole population.

Sometimes Goldhagen admits that, in all probability, some of those who perpetrated crimes against the Jews were not entirely convinced by the Nazi anti-Semitic ideology, and had to be coerced into complying with it. But he insists that 'the vast majority of perpetrators' embraced the ideology without difficulty. It was both a necessary and sufficient motive for their behaviour (Goldhagen, 1996, pp. 416–18). This is the rationalist assumption with which his investigation began. In the absence of adequate evidence, we must consider his claim unproven.

Mental causes of which people are not conscious

People were aware of unconscious causes of human behaviour before the nineteenth century. St Paul had confessed to a power, the power of 'sin', which made him act in ways he did not approve (*Romans* 7: 14–24). Hume had explained that people's natural desire for happiness, rather than reason, is at the basis of their judgements about what is good and bad (D. Hume's A *Treatise of Human Nature*, Book III, Part I). But the works of Marx, Freud, and to a less extent Nietzsche have had much greater influence on historical writing and understanding. What is particularly striking about their theories is the way they subordinate rational explanation to the fundamental motives they claim to be at work in human nature.

Class, group and personal interests

The assumption that human behaviour is chiefly caused by human reason was challenged in the nineteenth and twentieth centuries by Marx and Freud. One of the most frequently quoted sentences from Marx's writing is this: 'It is not the consciousness of men that determines their existence, but, on the contrary, their social existence determines their consciousness.' (From *The Critique of Political Economy*, quoted in Loptson, 1995, p. 129.) Marx's theory of human nature has two important dimensions: a theory of motivation and a theory of consciousness. Marx believed that history can best be understood as the product of a basic human desire for the goods needed for a comfortable, continuing existence. The structure of a society, he held, was the one which would maximize production, given the available means of production. Once technological developments made factory production efficient, society changed from a feudal one, based upon the wealth derived from agriculture, to an industrial one, with much of its wealth coming from industries. Those who owned the new industries, the capitalists, acquired great wealth and power, supplanting that of the feudal nobility to a large extent. To allow them more say in government, they supported constitutional changes which took influence away from the aristocracy and gave more to democratic political parties, which, with their wealth, they could dominate. Marx saw that those in power normally exploited those who were not, and he described this as a relation between social classes. Capitalists spent as little on the wages and conditions of those who worked for them, the proletariat, as they could. (For an excellent brief introduction to Marxist theory see Rosenberg, 1995, pp. 109–15.)

How were the capitalists able to establish their power and continue to exploit their workers? They depended to a large extent upon ideologies which justified and maintained their position. They could appeal to political theory to justify democratic change, such as Locke's theory of natural rights and Rousseau's theory of the general will. And they could promote Christian teaching about the need to be humble, to obey those in authority, and to look for rewards in heaven, to keep the working class subservient. Such ideologies were often sincerely believed, but Marx called this conviction a 'false consciousness'. According to Marx, the reasons that people give for their behaviour do not really motivate them to act. The reasons merely legitimate their actions, which are motivated by often unconscious class interests. Marx's friend and collaborator Engels wrote: 'ideology is a process accomplished by the thinker consciously, indeed, but with a false consciousness. The real motives impelling him remain unknown to him, otherwise it would not be an ideological process at all.' (Quoted from Engels correspondence by Martin Seliger, 1977, p. 30.)

Marx allowed, however, that sometimes the ideology of a dominant class is so strongly promoted that it is accepted by the subordinate class, which ensures their continued subordination. As Martin Seliger has noted, this fact is inconsistent with the claim that a class's ideology reflects its objective interests. Marx believed that the beliefs of the working class had to be freed from capitalist ideology, and to reflect their true class interests, if they were to achieve the freedom and fulfilment they naturally desired. Seliger remarked that in that case it seems as though ideas determine class action after all (ibid., pp. 71–3).

The importance of a dominant ideology helping to maintain the power of a dominant class was fully understood by Antonio Gramsci, who developed a theory of ideological 'hegemony' to describe it. Carl Boggs has summarized Gramsci's idea of hegemony in these words:

> By hegemony Gramsci meant the permeation throughout civil society – including a whole range of structures and activities like trade unions, schools, the churches, and the family – of an entire system of values, attitudes, beliefs, morality etc. that is in one way or another supportive of the established order and the class interests that dominate it.
>
> (Boggs, 1976, p. 39)

Gramsci realized that if the capitalist system was to be overthrown, then its ideological hegemony would have to be exposed for what it is, a tool of class interests, and an alternative ideology of more universal appeal, particularly to the working class, would have to be promoted instead. As Gramsci noted: 'every revolution has been preceded by an intense labour of social criticism, of cultural penetration and diffusion' (quoted in Boggs, 1976, p. 59). Thus Gramsci accorded to ideology a much more significant role in producing historical change than Marx and Engels had allowed.

The conviction that classes pursue their interests only when made conscious of them underlies the work of Marxist historians such as E.P. Thompson. But he went so far as to downplay the significance of a class's objective social conditions in determining its beliefs. He did this by defining a class as a group conscious of its common interests. He wrote:

> I am convinced that we cannot understand class unless we see it as a social and cultural formation, arising from processes which can only be studied as they work themselves out over a considerable historical period. In the years between 1780 and 1832 most English working people came to feel an identity of interests as between themselves, and as against their rulers and employers.
>
> (Thompson, 1968, p. 12)

Thompson, while admitting that people's values are determined very largely by their socio-economic situation, seems to accept the classical view that people's actions are motivated by their values and beliefs. In the period of English history Thompson studied, social groups commonly spoke and wrote about social classes and their interests, so it is easy to relate classes to groups who were aware of their common interests. It is not an accident that Marx used the language of class in developing his theory of history. Modern historians make use of it too. G. Kitson Clark, for example, called the Chartist movement of the 1830s 'the most notable example in the first half of the nineteenth century of the pattern of the class struggle' (Clark, 1962, p. 133). The Chartists, petitioning for universal male franchise, wanted to restore the dignity as much as the prosperity of the working classes.

> What the Chartists desired was no doubt to return to a society of small masters and skilled craftsmen, or at least a stay to the development of the large factories and high capitalism, a desire which was as impracticable as their proposal to plant out the surplus population in colonies of smallholdings on the land.
>
> (ibid., p. 135)

The Chartists, however, were poorly led and organized, and no match for the power of the government.

Whereas Marx wrote of the interests of the working class as a whole, subsequent historians have noted that different groups within the working class have acted in different ways, depending upon their particular circumstances. Asa Briggs introduced the collection of essays entitled *Chartist Studies* by remarking that 'Conditions of life in various parts of the country differed considerably, not only between city, market town and countryside, but between one city and another, between one rural region and a second' (Briggs, 1959, p. 1). Not only were there regional variations, within each region different groups within the working class fared differently. Briggs distinguished 'a section of superior craftsmen, including printers, cobblers, tailors, cabinetmakers, booksellers and small shopkeepers; factory operatives, concentrated in the textiles districts . . .; and domestic outworkers, including not only handloom weavers but such producers as framework knitters and nailmakers' (p. 4). He went on to explain:

> It was not only rates of remuneration which diverged [between these groups], but the extent of social security, regularity of earnings, the climate of industrial relations, status in the local community, and prospects of future advancement, both for the individual and for members of the family.
>
> (ibid.)

Thompson was, of course, aware of such distinctions, but he said that

> the outstanding fact of the period between 1790 and 1830 is the formation of 'the working class'. This is revealed, first, in the growth of class-consciousness: the consciousness of an identity of interests as between all these diverse groups of working people and as against the interests of other classes. And, second, in the growth of corresponding forms of political and industrial organization. By 1832 there were strongly based and self-conscious working-class institutions – trade unions, friendly societies, educational and religious movements, political organizations, periodicals – working-class intellectual traditions, working-class community-patterns, and a working-class structure of feeling.
>
> (Thompson, 1968, pp. 212–13)

Briggs argues that 'the attempt to create a sense of class unity . . . was never completely successful' (Briggs, 1959, p. 4). However he attributes the failure of the Chartist movement to the failure of the working class to seek the support of the middle class, particularly in London (ibid., pp. 297–9).

Not only has Marx's concept of class been challenged by historians who distinguish many variations within it; the influence of class interests has also been questioned. It is certainly not the case that people always act, consciously or not, in pursuit of their class interests. In some cases social action has been in pursuit of religious or national ideals rather than class ones (Neale, 1985, p. 164). In saying this, Neale and others assume that the ideology of a group can be contrary to its class interests. This is clearly the case when the ideology of members of one class has been accepted from members of another class. But it is also the case when the interests of a group cut across class lines. There have been other exploited groups besides classes, including women, blacks and colonized people, which have organized social action in support of their interests, not class ones. (See Kaye and McClelland, 1990, pp. 4–5; and Neale, 1985, ch. 7, especially pp. 150–2.)

There is quite a severe difficulty in proving that class interests motivate behaviour which furthers them. Consider, for example, a Marxist explanation of the subordination of women. Discrimination against women in the workplace prior to 1970 can be readily observed in capitalist societies. Women were seldom employed in prestigious positions or in jobs requiring the strength and stamina of men, nor were they given a wage equal to that of men. These facts imply discrimination against women in the workplace. Some writers have explained this discrimination by means of a Marxist theory, arguing that it was in the interests of capitalists to pay working women low wages, and to keep middle-class women at home servicing men, and to emphasize the importance of women in producing and rearing children who would in turn contribute to the capitalist economy. The editors of *Sex and Class in Women's History* put it thus:

> As many feminists have pointed out, the sexual division of labor is basic to an understanding of the way in which capitalism has maintained itself, for it has allowed capitalism to divide the work force, to secure lower wages, to maintain a reserve army of inexpensive labor, and to ensure cheap maintenance and reproduction of the labor force.
>
> (Newton *et al.*, 1983, pp. 2–3)

The argument here is that, because the subordination and domestication of women served the interests of capitalists, as these are explained in Marxist theory, those interests account for the general approval given to such discrimination against women. Suppose industrialists were unaware of all the advantages of keeping women down, so that the inferiority of the status of women in capitalist societies was quite unintentional, even though it was convenient. Could the interests of capitalists be said to explain their status then? Jon Elster has called this 'the general functionalist fallacy'. He writes: 'It is true, for instance, that internal cleavages in the working class serve the interest of the capitalist class, but from this we should not conclude that they occur because they have this effect' (1983, p. 60). (See McCullagh, 1998, pp. 198–9.) One suspects that there might have been other causes of the subordination of women. G.A. Cohen, in his analysis of Marxist theory, admits: 'I do not have a good answer to the question how productive forces select economic structures which promote their development' (1988, p. 17).

In fact, Michèle Barrett has argued that while capitalists undoubtedly benefited from cheap labour, they did not need to subordinate women to men. Rather, this practice had its origins elsewhere, in traditions which existed prior to capitalism. She writes:

> A sexual division of labour, and accompanying ideologies of the appropriate meaning of labour for men and women, have been embedded in the capitalist division of labour from its beginnings. It is impossible to over-emphasize here the importance of an historical analysis. I make no claim for the inevitability of this particular ideology as a functional requisite for capitalist production – it is one of several possible options . . . Indeed it can plausibly be argued that the wage-labour relation and the contradiction between labour and capital – the defining characteristics of the capitalist mode of production – are 'sex-blind' and operate quite independently of gender.
>
> (Barrett, 1988, pp. 98–9)

Barrett argues that attitudes towards women had their origin in an ideology which pre-dated capitalism, and were simply included in the social arrangements that capitalism produced. For example, the assumption 'that the relegation of women to domesticity and childcare was natural and desirable' was simply accepted (p. 138). This immediately limited the kind of employment thought suitable for women. 'Women are over-represented in service work and the "caring" occupations, and in manual work such as cleaning which resembles domestic work in the home' (p. 181). 'Furthermore, the construction of a family form in which the male head of household is supposedly responsible for the financial support of a dependent wife and children has militated against demands for equal pay and an equal "right to work" for women' (p. 157). If these attitudes to women were traditional, they might have been adopted from unquestioning habit, rather than have been imposed by capitalists in the pursuit of their interests. It is only when no other explanation is available, that a practice can be attributed to class or group interests with confidence. I would also suggest that if a practice such as the subordination of women suits the interests of a dominant group, that provides members of the group with an incentive to perpetuate it. The subordination of women suited the capitalists because they were men who enjoyed their freedom from domestic duties, not because they were capitalists!

Whereas Marxists ascribe major historical events to people's interest in material prosperity, more recent writers have developed the theory of interests into other directions as well.

Marvin Harris, for example, insists that people's behaviour is best understood as motivated by four unconscious interests, or what he calls their 'biopsychological predispositions'. They can be summarized as (1) a need to eat nutritious food; (2) a tendency to conserve energy by acting as efficiently as possible; (3) a desire for sexual intercourse; and (4) a need for love and affection (Harris, 1979, p. 63). Given these tendencies, and a society's mode of production, it is possible to explain many aspects of its 'sociocultural system' (ibid.,

p. 64). Harris adopts the methodological rule of looking for material explanations of cultural patterns before ideological ones. This is because he believes people can usually recognize what will meet their needs, and act accordingly (pp. 299–300).

Harris gives many fascinating explanations of apparently irrational cultural practices which show how they serve people's basic interests. He explains the Hindu veneration of cows, for example, by pointing to their capacity to bear oxen, and to their use in ploughing fields, pulling carts and providing manure, all vital to the survival of the small farms which support the population of India. Jewish and Muslim abomination of pigs is explained by noting how unsuitable they are for nomadic people in harsh environments, which lack the food pigs need and are often too hot for them to survive. Traditions of potlatch, in which North American chiefs display their status by giving away huge amounts of produce to all who attend, are explained as an efficient means of distributing food and goods to all, especially to those who had suffered from poor seasons (Harris, 1978). Harris allows that people sometimes act in accordance with their values and beliefs and not their interests, but even then he says that their system of values and beliefs is one which is generally directed to furthering their interests (Harris, 1979, pp. 302–3).

Another popular exponent of objective interests is Abraham Maslow. Frank G. Goble has explained his theory thus:

> The average individual is motivated by deficiencies – he is seeking to fulfil his basic needs for safety, belongingness, love, respect, and self esteem. The healthy man is 'primarily motivated by his need to develop and actualize his fullest potentialities and capacities'.
>
> (Goble, 1971, p. 32)

So in addition to the basic needs mentioned, Maslow lists a number of 'growth needs', which superior people quite naturally try to meet. These include wholeness (integration), perfection (moral, aesthetic), completion, justice, aliveness, richness (complexity), simplicity . . . playfulness, truth and self-sufficiency (ibid., pp. 47–8).

I do no know of any historian who has deliberately adopted Maslow's analysis of human nature, but some have suggested that people are not only motivated to meet their basic needs, but look for anything which will increase their happiness and sense of self-fulfilment. The best known historian to appeal to such unconscious interests is Sir Lewis Namier. He argued that many British politicians in the time of George III went into parliament for personal advancement, even though they claimed to be serving the country. He provided numerous examples of the ways in which members of parliament used their position to personal advantage, commenting that such selfish interests were 'almost universal and usually unavowed' (Namier, 1963, p. 7).

According to all these theories, people often act in accordance with interests of which they are unaware. These may account for desires and values of which people are indeed conscious, and which guide their actions. (See McCullagh, 1991 for a full discussion of how objective interests explain actions.)

Freudian and other psychoanalytic theories

Historians normally explain irrational behaviour by referring to emotions which swept people from a rational path, as was explained above when describing classical commonsense theories of human action. Hitler hated the Jews, which helps to explain why he treated them so unjustly. He gave reasons for his hatred, but they were quite unconvincing. So some historians look for a deeper, psychological explanation of his hatred. The kind of psychological explanations given for strong emotions depend upon psychoanalytic theories of human nature.

In this section I shall briefly describe some popular psychoanalytic theories, and give examples of their use in history. Then I shall draw attention to some reasons for commonly finding psychoanalytic explanations unsatisfactory: paucity of evidence of childhood traumas, a problem of reductionism, the possibility of alternative explanations, and the difficulty of proving the truth of psychoanalytic theories. Finally I shall illustrate the difficulty of establishing the truth of such explanations by considering a particular case.

Sigmund Freud began developing his theories of the unconscious when searching for explanations of hysterical and obsessional behaviour, and later when trying to explain the origin of thoroughly irrational dreams and slips of the tongue. Hysterical behaviour he first explained by looking for previous traumatic experiences, memory of which had been suppressed, but which produced violent responses when triggered by certain subsequent events. Dreams he explained as 'disguised fulfilments of repressed wishes' (Freud, 1986, p. 115). He believed quite often the wishes were of a sexual kind, and their fulfilment was represented in symbols which would not offend the dreamer, but had some likeness to the sexual organs involved.

In developing his explanations of irrational behaviour, Freud was led to form quite complex accounts of human nature. Early on he postulated the existence of instincts, notably the animal instincts for survival and reproduction, as the source of people's strong desires. He was also aware of the influence of society upon human thinking, censoring a number of thoughts and desires as unacceptable. He envisaged people has having an 'ego' which was subject to instinctive desires (from the 'id') as well as the constraints of society (internalized in the 'super ego'), and which had also to consider the situation in the external world in which the person had to act. Freud was constantly developing and modifying his theories, which were very elaborate, so this summary is no more than a glimpse of their true nature. For example, he came to develop the concept of 'eros' as an instinct which draws all sorts of things together in nature; and he postulated a death instinct as well, which he called 'thanatos', as an opposite tendency to produce disintegration.

The theory of human nature which Freud developed could clearly help to account for rational behaviour as well as irrational behaviour. Any ordinary attempts to find food and shelter, or to find a mate, can be attributed to the basic instincts for survival and reproduction. Any sensible decisions to act within the bounds of conventional morality can be explained as the function of the super-ego in curbing excessive desire. In these ways his theory of human nature can be seen to have 'deepened' the classical rational explanations of human action. (We shall consider this concept again when we describe 'profound explanations' of human behaviour in Chapter 8.)

Still, Freud's focus was upon irrational acts. To explain a number of these he developed a theory of childhood development, and its influence upon patterns of adult behaviour. He described what he took to be the normal development of sexual relations, particularly between children and their parents, and often ascribed adult abnormalities to deviations from this normal childhood process.

Since Freud demonstrated the importance of unconscious memories and of unconscious instincts in explaining human behaviour, subsequent theorists have searched for other unconscious processes at work in human nature as well. Alfred Adler thought that people instinctively seek to compensate for a natural feeling of inferiority in the world and society by striving for recognition and superiority over others. Jacques Szaluta has outlined several important developments in psychoanalytic theory since Freud and Adler. Anna Freud, Sigmund's daughter, focussed upon the ways in which a person's ego copes with threats to its integrity and with psychological pain by acts of repression, regression, isolation, projection and so on (Szaluta, 1999, pp. 128–9). Melanie Klein, on the other hand, developed an interest in the attitudes of infants towards their mother, suggesting that frustration could cause them to become schizoid (with a split personality), paranoid (subject to illusions), and depressed. These states, she said, could influence their behaviour as adults (ibid., pp. 130–2). Ronald Fairbairn and Donald Winnicott were also interested in how support and affirmation from mother produces a psychologically healthy adult, and how lack of such love can cause problems (ibid., pp. 132–4). (For a fuller summary of their views, see Hughes, 1989.) Another influential theory is that Heinz Kohut, who developed a narcissistic theory of human nature, that people want to feel good about themselves and that rejection in early childhood can cause trouble later on. 'In Kohut's view, the narcissistic person is one who has experienced rejection in early childhood and is marked by a generalized feeling of anxiety, cannot develop mature relationships, has insatiable needs to be admired, and whose alienation from others worsen[s] as he grows older' (Szaluta, 1999, pp. 149–50). Critics objected that he 'neglected feelings of aggression and hatred in the narcissistic person' (ibid., p. 150; pp. 148–56 are on Kohut's theory.) Those writing after Freud actually contrast their 'ego psychology', 'object relations psychology' and 'self psychology' with his psychoanalytic theory, that pays more attention to unconscious instincts. (Note: This is to mention just a few of the developments in psychoanalytic theory which took place during the last century. See Runyan, 1988, for a different list.)

Rather than regard these various theories as incompatible, historians would do well to assume that each draws attention to important general features of human nature which might be relevant to the people whose actions they wish to explain. Each draws attention to unconscious tendencies in human nature, which can sometimes account for human behaviour.

It is important to distinguish two kinds of psychological explanations. There are those which account for irrational behaviour simply by suggesting unconscious motives for it. Some of these are quite plausible. But there are also explanations which attribute adult behaviour to childhood experiences, and these have generally been judged quite inadequate.

Here is an example of the first kind of explanation, which Heinz Kohut offered for the widespread, fanatical support of the Nazi Party by the German people. The Germans had lost pride in their nation after the defeat of the First World War and the further disintegration of society during the Weimar Republic which followed it. Until Hitler emerged, there were no leaders in politics, academia or the arts 'to provide the German group self with the needed resonance that would have encouraged development toward a new self image.' (Quoted in Szaluta, 1999, p. 155.) It was Hitler's charismatic leadership and vision of a greater Germany which met the people's desperate need for self-assurance and worth. The support given to Hitler was not irrational, for he promised great things for Germany. But the breadth and strength of it needs to be explained, and Kohut's narcissistic theory offers such an explanation.

If you accept Kohut's theory of human nature, it is easy to accept this explanation. But here are a couple of explanations referring to childhood experiences which are much less credible.

The first is an explanation of Hitler's hatred of the Jews. Hitler offered reasons for his attacks on the Jews in his writing and speeches. He said that the Jewish community was gnawing at the entrails of the German state, removing its wealth and, consequently, its strength, serving their own interests rather than those of the state. He believed that Germany would have won the First World War, if the Jews had not weakened the country. And so on. The more one reads, the more irrational the reasons appear. So historians ask, why did he believe this nonsense, and why did he act upon it so aggressively?

A full discussion of the various psychological explanations which have been offered in answer to this question is impossible here. (Szaluta, 1999, describes some of them) One respected analysis is that of Robert G.L. Waite, *The Psychopathic God: Adolf Hitler* (1977). This is a large and complex analysis of Hitler's personality, explicitly based upon Freudian theory. Here, for example, is his explanation of Hitler's irrational anti-Semitism. According to Waite, Hitler identified Germany, the Motherland, with his own mother of whom he was fond, and his desire to protect Germany from the ravages of the Jews expresses his unconscious desire to protect his mother, first from a harsh husband, his father, and second from the Jewish doctor who attended her for breast cancer, and injected her with morphia to dull the pain until she died. Waite writes:

he transferred his love for his own mother to Germany and saw himself as the savior of a Motherland menaced by the 'Jewish peril.' Thus he projected his infantile desire – greatly intensified by the primal scene experience [of father having intercourse with mother] – to rescue his mother from being debased by a lecherous father, and to possess her himself.

(ibid., p. 360)

It was at the time of his mother's death that Hitler announced his anti-Semitism, in 1908. Waite remarks: 'The close association between the onset of Hitler's fanatical hatred of Jews and the death of his mother seems clear. It is of course possible that the connection is purely coincidental. But appeals to coincidence are not generally satisfying when there is the possibility of a causal connection' (p. 188).

A second example of a psychological explanation which refers to childhood experiences is Robert C. Tucker's explanation of Stalin's neurotic insistence on the admiration of others. He knew of Stalin's fear of opposition and his ruthless extermination of opponents in the 1930s. After the war, in Moscow he observed the extraordinary state sponsored cult of Stalin; and later still, in 1956 he read a report by Nikita Khrushchev of Stalin's 'arrogant-vindictive' behaviour. Here was a personality which fitted precisely that described by the psychologist Karen Horney. She had described how people who suffer anxiety early in life compensate for it, sometimes by producing an idealized vision of themselves, which they then protect by eliminating all who deny it. Just as Hitler had used the state to attack the Jews, Stalin used the state to promote his image of perfection and to remove any who questioned it. His drunken father had beaten him and his mother regularly when he was young, so there was the source of anxiety which Horney's theory required (Horney, 1988).

W.M. Runyan has drawn attention to three difficulties commonly encountered when providing such psychological explanations in history (Runyan, 1988, pp. 219–44). The first is the frequent lack of evidence about a person's childhood experiences, needed to corroborate the explanation suggested by the theory. Saul Friedlander has commented on the paucity of evidence about Hitler's youth, and even less evidence of how Hitler responded to the few events we do know about. The little we know can be interpreted in various ways. 'Whatever hypothesis one chooses, one can find a way to integrate it into a total context that will appear coherent, for the possible variations are extremely numerous' (Friedlander, 1978, p. 48). The variety of explanations of Hitler's anti-Semitism is evidence of this.

It is sometimes tempting for historians to postulate childhood experiences, in accordance with an explanatory theory, to account of irrational behaviour. Here is a neat example from an interesting analysis of the personality of Lyndon Johnson by H.L. Muslin and T.H. Jobe. They make convincing use of Kohut's theory to account for his dominant personality. 'Narcissistic deficit – low self-worth, ordinarily accompanied by a sense of emptiness and loneliness – plagued

Johnson throughout his life' (Muslin and Jobe, 1991, p. 84). Apparently Johnson found it difficult to relax, and the authors offer this explanation:

> Johnson's life of hyperactivity and inability to achieve peace from human relationships made clear that his infancy and childhood with his selfobject parents did not provide the necessary calming, and because of this deprivation, manufactured his fixation – the repetitious seeking behavior for external sources of calming.
>
> (ibid., p. 86)

Notice the circularity of the argument here: his behaviour must have been caused by a deprived childhood, which caused his behaviour. One cannot help wonder whether other explanations were not possible.

The second problem for psychohistorians that Runyan mentions is what is called the problem of reductionism. This is the tendency to attribute more to childhood experiences than is warranted. Runyan quotes Lawrence Stone saying:

> I just do not think that such things as the extermination of six million Jews can be explained by the alleged fact that Hitler's mother was killed by treatment given her by a Jewish doctor in an attempt to cure her cancer of the breast; or that Luther's defiance of the Roman Church can be explained by the brutal way he was treated by his father or by his chronic constipation.
>
> (Stone, 1981. p. 220)

(This is quoted by Runyan, 1988, on p. 225. The reference is to Erik H. Erikson, *Young Man Luther: A Study in Psychoanalysis and History*, Norton, 1962.)

Hitler's hatred of the Jewish doctor for failing to save his mother is not the same as hatred of all the Jews in Germany, yet psychoanalysts often write as though the first made the second entirely intelligible. Much more is needed to explain his policy adequately.

The third difficulty for psychohistorians is that of eliminating alternative possible explanations. Runyan says that often the available evidence is consistent with several different explanations, so they cannot be regarded as true, but merely as interpretations. A critic of Tucker's explanation of Stalin's personality asked whether his autocratic methods and self-adulation were not part of Russia's traditional political culture, highly developed under the Czars, which Stalin simply continued for his own political reasons (Dallin, 1988, p. 83). People often adopt familiar, traditional roles without question, and not for any special psychological reason.

The three difficulties Runyan has identified are very significant, particularly the last. Even with abundant evidence of childhood experiences, given the range of possible unconscious causes of human behaviour, any explanation which refers to them must be tentative.

There is also a fourth difficulty which is of concern to conscientious historians:

namely the difficulty of judging whether a particular psychological theory is well established. David E. Stannard has argued forcefully that such theories are not rationally justified (Stannard, 1980). He doubts that all people whose parents distress them in childhood end up maladjusted; nor do maladjusted people all have unpleasant experiences in childhood. The correlations just do not exist to support the theory. When exceptions to a theory are produced, then the theory is regularly elaborated to explain them, so that in effect it becomes unfalsifiable. Stannard writes of psychoanalysts'

> wilful effort to resist disconfirmation by claiming that *any* eventuality is covered and can be explained by the presence or absence of the so-called defence mechanisms of reaction-formation, displacement, sublimation, and the like. Although this apparent ability to explain everything has no doubt contributed to the popular appeal of psychoanalysis . . ., it flatly disqualifies psychoanalytic theory from any consideration as a theory of scientific or even logically respectable explanation.
>
> (ibid., pp. 148–9)

Runyan suggests that psychoanalytic theories have been better supported by observations than Stannard allows (Runyan, 1988, p. 220), but even he is uncertain about their credibility.

The difficulty of proving the truth of a psychoanalytic explanation is clearly illustrated by Juliet Mitchell's Freudian explanation of the subordination of women to men, presented in her book *Psychoanalysis and Feminism* (1974). The heart of her theory (in Chapter 12), is this. According to Freud, children respond sexually to their parents. From an early identification with their mothers, he said, girls come unconsciously to desire sex with their father. In order to attract love, a girl offers herself in an attractive form, and tries to please him in every way she can. Mitchell says that this explains why women have always been submissive towards men, and vain. The social consequences of women's unconscious love for their fathers are evident in patriarchal, i.e. father-dominated, culture. Men do not love their father so much as unconsciously wish to kill him to take his place, and they do indeed adopt his role. So the relation between men and women is established in childhood, and simply finds expression in the ideology of patriarchy, which is that women should serve and please men. 'Differences of class, historical epoch, specific social situations alter the expression of femininity; but in relation to the law of the father, women's position across the board is a comparable one' (ibid., p. 406). '[W]omen are everywhere within civilization the second sex, but everywhere differently so' (p. 381).

If Juliet Mitchell is right, Freud's theory certainly implies attitudes of inferiority among women towards men, attitudes which characterize the patriarchal ideology which subordinates women to men. But how can one prove such a theory? So much of the sexual history of children which Freud describes is unconscious and hypothetical that it is hard to find evidence which directly supports it. It is not even certain that patriarchal ideology has a psychological origin at all. It might have originated in a woman's need to stay with her children when they were small, and her husband's need to provide food and shelter for his family. While she was weak, he remained strong, able to lord over her. Here is another completely speculative account of the origin of patriarchy. Certainly, the fact that each theory implies the existence of a patriarchal culture does not mean that it is true. We might never have enough evidence to be certain of the origin of patriarchal ideology. Because the origins of patriarchal ideology are so obscure, most feminist writers have stopped trying to find them.

Nietzsche and the pursuit of power

Friedrich Nietzsche extolled the pursuit of power. '*Not* for pleasure does man strive: but for power', he wrote (quoted in Kaufman, 1956, pp. 226–7). You might think that people seek pleasure rather than power. For Nietzsche, said Kaufman, 'the feeling of pleasure is an epiphenomenon of the possession of power' (ibid., p. 227), and not the main object of desire.

Nietzsche argued that Christian moral doctrines of justice and compassion were promoted by middle classes in their own interests, to protect them from the powerful.

Nietzsche was aware that his doctrine of the natural pursuit of power fits the doctrine of the natural selection of the fittest, in which all species compete for survival. It also fits the practice of liberal capitalism, where businesses freely compete for markets. There is a lot of evidence in history of people pursuing power. His theory was taken up by Michel Foucault, who pointed out how often people promote a vision of society which maintains or increases their power within it. In his book *Discipline and Punish*, for example, he argued that practices of punishment were not designed to satisfy some theory of just desert, but were intended as sometimes public exercises of sovereign power. The public executions common before the revolution in France were quite barbaric in their cruelty. As well as displaying the guilt of the victim, the torture and execution 'made the body of the condemned man the place where the vengeance of the sovereign was applied, the anchoring point for a manifestation of power, an opportunity of affirming the dissymmetry of forces. We shall see . . . that the truth-power relation remains at the heart of all mechanisms of punishment and that it is still to be found in contemporary penal practice – but in a quite different form and with very different effects' (Foucault, 1979, p. 55). I cannot resist quoting this long paragraph, in which Foucault catalogues the kinds of power he thought to be involved in the cruel public executions.

> The fact that the crime and the punishment were related and bound up in the form of atrocity was not the result of some obscurely accepted law of retaliation. It was the effect, in the rites of punishment, of a certain mechanism of power: of a power that not only did not hesitate to exert itself

directly on bodies, but was exalted and strengthened by its visible manifestations; of a power that asserted itself as an armed power whose functions of maintaining order were not entirely unconnected with the functions of war; of a power that presented rules and obligations as personal bonds, a breach of which constituted an offence and called for vengeance; of a power for which disobedience was an act of hostility, the first sign of rebellion, which is not in principle different from civil war; of a power that had to demonstrate not why it enforced its laws, but who were its enemies, and what unleashing of force threatened them; of a power which, in the absence of continual supervision, sought a renewal of its effect in the spectacle of its individual manifestations; of a power that was recharged in the ritual display of its reality as 'super-power'.

(ibid., p. 57)

Although Foucault implies that the motive for social policy is the tendency of those who impose it to maintain or further their power, he is also anxious to point out, rather as Gramsci had before him, that people develop discourses to justify their power in society, discourses which stipulate what is acceptable behaviour and what is not. In 'The Discourse on Language' he wrote: 'I would like to measure the effect of a discourse claiming to be scientific – medical, psychiatric or sociological – on the ensemble of practices and prescriptive discourse of which the penal code consists' (Foucault, 1976, p. 232).

In *Discipline and Punish* (1979) Foucault fulfilled his wish. There he notes that over the last two hundred years or so, the punishment of criminals has been less severe than it used to be. He attributes this change to a change in discourse about the purpose of punishment: it was no longer to provide a public spectacle of horrifying pain upon the body, enough to terrify onlookers; rather it was aimed at converting the soul of the offender, working on his 'passions, instincts, infirmities, maladjustments' and so on (ibid., pp. 16–17). The severity of the punishment now depended upon the criminal's attitude (p. 18). Punishment became private, not public.

Punishment is an exercise of power over the body and mind of the criminal. Foucault saw 'greater leniency in punishment processes' as 'one of the effects of the new tactics of power' (Foucault, 1979, p. 23). The new tactics were to attack, not the body but the mind:

the 'mind' as a surface of inscription for power, with semiology as its tool; the submission of bodies through the control of ideas; the analysis of representations as a principle in a politics of bodies that was much more effective than the ritual anatomy of torture and execution.

(ibid., p. 102)

Foucault's theory that discourse is an instrument of power has been adopted by many historians who study the history of oppressed groups. Edward W. Said, for example, in his book *Culture and Imperialism* (1993) acknowledges economic interests as motives for imperialism, but is more interested in its use of ideology as an instrument of domination. He writes:

> Neither imperialism nor colonialism is a simple act of accumulation and acquisition. Both are supported and perhaps even impelled by impressive ideological formations that include notions that certain territories and people *require* and beseech domination, as well as forms of knowledge affiliated with domination: the vocabulary of classic nineteenth-century imperial culture is plentiful with such words and concepts as 'inferior' or 'subject races', 'subordinate peoples', 'dependency', 'expansion', and 'authority'.
>
> (p. 8)

Similarly, Michele Barrett, investigating the oppression of women, writes of

> the importance of ideology in the construction and reproduction of women's oppression. A particular household organization and an ideology of familialism are central dimensions of women's oppression in capitalism and it is only through an analysis of ideology that we can grasp the oppressive myth of an idealized natural 'family' to which all women must conform. It is only through an analysis of ideology and its role in the construction of gendered subjectivity that we can account for the desires of women as well as men to reproduce the very familial structures by which we are oppressed.
>
> (Barrett, 1988, p. 251)

She adds, however: 'I would resist the suggestion that this ideological level can be dissociated from economic relations. Here I would take some distance from the feminist appropriation of post-Althusserian theories that seek to locate all aspects of women's oppression in terms of a theory of discourse' (p. 253).

Foucault sees human behaviour as conforming to accepted discourses, or ideology, and discourses as the means by which groups of people maintain or increase their power. He denies that actions originate in the values and beliefs of individuals, as has commonly been believed. An historian who has adopted this theory wholeheartedly is Robert Chartier, in his account of the French Revolution. He denies that the Revolution was motivated by ideology, asserting that it involved simply a seizing of power. He says that classic histories ascribing the Revolution to the Enlightenment suppose 'a direct, automatic, and transparent engendering of actions by thoughts. . . . There is neither continuity nor necessity between the one and the other.' Rather, he said, 'we should stress the gap between the (competing) discourses that, in representing the social world, proposed to refound it and the (multiple) practices that, as they came into being, were inventing new ways of dividing things up' (Chartier, 1997, p. 59). Elsewhere he wrote:

the revolutionary event had a momentum and dynamic of its own that were not contained in any of its conditions of possibility. In this sense, the Revolution had no origins, properly speaking. Its absolute belief that it represented a new beginning had a performative value: by announcing a radical break with the past, it instituted one.

(Chartier, 1991, p. 197)

The philosophical and popular literature of the Enlightenment, he said, eroded respect for the old orders of church and state, thus making the revolution against royal government possible. But it did not contain a blueprint for such a revolution.

The gap between democratic theory and practice was most striking, of course, during the reign of terror. The revolutionaries fought for liberty, equality and fraternity, but sought out and killed hundreds whom they judged to be possible enemies of the new state. Chartier comments: 'all regimes of practices are endowed with a regularity, logic, and reason of their own, irreducible to the discourses that justify them.' People's words and deeds, he says, should be understood as 'transformations in relations of domination.' Quoting Foucault he says: 'An event . . . is . . . the reversal of a relationship of forces, the usurpation of power' in response to 'haphazard conflicts'. Like Foucault, Chartier prefers to think of people, not as centres of knowledge and creativity, but as elements in patterns of power. This approach, he says, involves 'considering the individual not in the supposed liberty of his or her own separate "I" but as constructed by the configurations, discursive or social, that determine its historical figures.' Individuals are defined discursively by what people say about them, and socially by the relations they have with others. Indeed according to Chartier 'there are no historical objects that predate the relations that constitute them'. Individuals are thus not instances of a general kind, but are unique, products of a unique configuration at a time and place (ibid., pp. 54–71).

While many of the things the revolutionaries said and did were designed to promote their power, it is implausible to suggest that the political thought of the Enlightenment was of no influence in guiding their actions. It justified the deputies' decision to defy the crown, and guided them in creating and adopting the Declaration of the Rights of Man and of the Citizen. The fact that an ideology does not necessitate the actions it prescribes does not mean it is of no influence in producing them. As Norman Hampson has argued, there were three fundamental, interacting forces at work producing the French Revolution, 'political, economic, and ideological' (Hampson, 1991, p. 46). Montesquieu had praised civic virtue as a condition of liberty in ancient republics, and if they failed, he said one needed a balance of interests to keep the peace. Rousseau had explained how individual freedom should be limited by respect for the common good, as defined by the general will of the people. Hampson reports how widely Rousseau was venerated, and how frequently his ideas were referred to by the deputies at the Constituent Assembly, even if they did not always follow him.

With François Furet he says that to a large extent 'a Rousseauist ideology came to dominate and explain the course of the Revolution' (ibid., p. 51). . . . 'He provided them with their vision of the New Jerusalem and their justification for all the sacrifices they imposed on the French people in order to effect its regeneration' (p. 53). (For the influence of Diderot's writing upon men of property, see Doyle, 1999, p. 34.)

So people are not moved only by the desire for power. Many are moved by ideas which inspire them. Indeed the ideas of Jesus, which he knew would lead to his destruction, have moved people to live a life of compassion at the expense of personal power.

We have a reached a point in this chapter where two theories of human nature stand opposed: the classical commonsense theory that people are moved by their values and beliefs, and the new theory that they simply conform to discourses which have been imposed by people in power. We have already encountered this conflict in Chapter 2, when considering whether authors could have intentions. There is an argument for denying that people have an essential nature which was not considered there, which is worth adding here.

The social and linguistic construction of mental states

The idea that discourse about mental states refers to nothing real was popularized by Ludwig Wittgenstein in his book *Philosophical Investigations* (2nd edn, 1958). He pointed out that when we ascribe mental states to others we are really interpreting their behaviour according to certain linguistic conventions. What we today call different realms of discourse, he referred to as 'language games'. His hermeneutic approach to the explanation of human behaviour was developed by Brian Fay in *Social Theory and Political Practice* (1975). The theory that mental states are nothing but items of discourse is sometimes called 'nominalist' in contrast to a 'realist' one, or 'constructionist' in opposition to an 'essentialist' one.

Michel Foucault has taken the attack on mental realism a lot further. He not only denies the reality of mental states, but denies the reality of a transcendental ego, an immaterial soul, with properties such as various dispositions that influence behaviour. And as we have just seen, he draws attention to the way in which discourse, instead of personal beliefs, has influenced social behaviour.

In the Conclusion of *The Archaeology of Knowledge* (1976), Foucault says that he wants 'to free the history of thought from its subjection to transcendence' (p. 203). To understand what people do, he declares, we need simply note the language they use in describing and justifying their actions. Our language comes to us clustered around different topics: for instance there is the language of punishment, or of mental illness or of sex, about all of which Foucault wrote. Each of these clusters is called a discourse, and when people think about what they will do, they do so in terms of one or more discourses which they have acquired from their culture. Foucault thinks people's decisions and actions are simply a product of the discourses they employ, and should be understood as such. He admits 'how irritating it can be to treat discourses in terms not of the gentle, silent, intimate consciousness that is expressed in them, but of an obscure set of anonymous rules' (p. 210).

The most powerful reason Foucault had in support of his theory was his observation that people's beliefs about what is right and wrong, and about human nature, have changed strikingly over time. This seems to provide evidence of the fact that there are no objective facts about right and wrong, and about human nature, just opinions which are prevalent in a community, promoted, Foucault thought, by people who would gain in power from them.

One the best known examples Foucault has given of the social construction of personal attributes is found in his history of sexuality. In this work he argues that the property of being a homosexual is not an essential natural property of humans, but a socially constructed property attributed to them. The evidence that homosexuality is a constructed property rather than a natural one is to be found in the fact that it has meant different things in different ages. Westerners today distinguish homosexuals by the objects of their sexual preference. We think of a homosexual person as one who prefers to enjoy sexual relations with people of the same sex. But the ancient Romans, it seems, contrasted people according to their sexual roles, whether they were active or passive, penetrating or penetrated. Males who penetrated other men were not thought to be sexually deviant, but the man who let himself be penetrated (the *cinaedus*) was (Karras, 2000, p. 1256). The conclusion that Foucault and others have drawn is that a person's sexuality is not a characteristic of their essential nature, but merely a way of describing them. He wrote:

> Sexuality must not be thought of as a kind of natural given which power tries to hold in check, or as an obscure domain which knowledge tries gradually to uncover. It is the name that can be given to a historical construct: not a furtive reality that is difficult to grasp . . .
>
> (Foucault, 1981, p. 105)

So the constructionist argument is that the terms we use to describe people are cultural constructs which refer, not to some mysterious essential characteristic of a person, but to patterns of behaviour.

James Davidson has illustrated the same point in a discussion of Greek ideas about homosexuality, which differed from the Roman. Davidson says that while Greek homosexual relations were undoubtedly erotic, there was little reference to penetration. Rather the relationship was commonly described as between an older man (an *erastes*: a male who loves) and a younger man he admired (an *eromenos*: a male who is loved) (Davidson, 2001, p. 41). He comments:

> inasmuch as Greek (homo)sexuality was a sexuality of roles and was 'social', it demonstrated, in itself, a non-essential, gestural, social performativity in

the field of (Greek) (homo)sexual identity. In other words, the Greeks under-stood the true spuriousness, the constructed nature, of human sexuality.

(ibid., p. 46)

Foucault was interested in the way people use language, discourses, as instruments of power. People have been called 'homosexual', he said, by those who wish to criticize or reform them.

> There is no question that the appearance in nineteenth-century psychiatry, jurisprudence, and literature of a whole series of discourses on the species and subspecies of homosexuality, inversion, pederasty, and 'psychic her-maphrodism' made possible a strong advance of social controls into this area of 'perversity'; but it also made possible the formation of a 'reverse' dis-course: homosexuality began to speak in its own behalf, to demand that its legitimacy of 'naturality' be acknowledged, often in the same vocabulary, using the same categories by which it was medically disqualified.
>
> (Foucault, 1981, p. 101)

It seems, then, that Romans and Greeks spoke about different patterns of homo-sexual behaviour, rather than about an essential disposition to prefer partners of the same sex. And it also seems that talk about homosexuality in the nineteenth century was often in the context of talk about perversity and immorality, designed to justify forms of punishment or treatment. But neither of these facts proves that homosexuality is not a natural personal trait. Foucault was not at all interested in explaining why some people prefer sexual partners of the same sex and others do not. In many cases we explain homosexual behaviour by attribut-ing a real, essential character trait to the people exhibiting it, saying they have by nature a homosexual orientation. How the inclination to have intimate relations with people of one's own sex is expressed is limited and directed to some extent by social constraints and cultural conventions. (See Weinrich, 1990, ch. 8.)

It is rationally appropriate to consider those states and events by which we explain patterns of behaviour as being real. (This was explained at some length in Chapter 1.) To say someone has a certain disposition, be it a belief, value, atti-tude or sexual orientation, is to say that they are inclined to behave in certain circumstances in certain ways. This is a lawlike fact about their nature, at least for a certain period of time. For instance, to say someone believes in God implies that that person is disposed to say yes when asked whether they believe in God, to worship God from time to time, to pray to God when they or their friends need help, and so on. The evidence for a person's dispositions lies in their pat-terns of behaviour, but it is the disposition which explains that behaviour. We say that the disposition is real because it explains so much.

The contrast between public and private assertions and attitudes, mentioned in Chapter 2, can only be explained by contrasting apparent beliefs and attitudes with 'real' ones, those which one would 'sincerely' avow and 'prudently' act upon. The contrast between patterns of behaviour and real dispositions is very clear in cases of deception. When people deceive others, they know one thing but say another. So the concept of deception requires belief in real mental states as opposed to publicly perceived patterns of behaviour.

Geoff Baldwin has noted that in the late Renaissance authors contrasted the creation of a public self, or *persona*, through certain patterns of behaviour, and one's private convictions, which one was reluctant to express in public. He writes: 'The negotiation of the boundary between public *persona* and private self had become apparent as one of the criticisms of the functioning of a traditional rhetorical humanism.' The writers recommended a certain personal detachment from the public role one was obliged to live (Baldwin, 2001, p. 347). The concept of a private self which one refuses to display also implies a contrast between real mental states and patterns of behaviour.

Once you acknowledge that there are competing discourses in society, some recommending one set of values and practices (e.g. the pursuit of wealth and power), others pointing in another direction (e.g. the pursuit of justice and compassion), there is a need to explain why people choose to follow one discourse rather than another. Foucault does not offer an explanation, being content simply to point out the implications of the discourses they do adopt. His work suggests, however, that people will choose that discourse which most increases their power. But that is not how people experience their choices. They experience them as the result of a process of deliberation.

Christopher Norris has made a similar point in his critique of postmodern theory. This theory, says Norris, suggests that when people decide what to do there is 'a conflictual process that is somehow carried on in the absence of anything – reasons, values, principles, or justifying grounds – which could make sense of that process in humanly intelligible terms.' The theory cannot allow that people consider all the possibilities and decide between them in the light of their beliefs and interests, because for postmodernism a person capable of doing these things does not exist. In postmodern theory, Norris says, the human subject 'is so completely "decentred" – so much a plaything of linguistic structures beyond its utmost powers of reflective grasp – that it becomes simply a product of discursive definition, a word . . . lacking any real explanatory power but employed to balance the equations' (Norris, 1996, pp. 19–20).

Although discourses influence people's patterns of thought, to explain how people decide what to do it is reasonable to adopt something like the classical commonsense theory of human nature, which sees people as capable of forming rational judgements and intentions. It is important to distinguish discourses, which are abstracted fields of words and meanings, and the particular sets of beliefs and ways of thinking which inform particular agents in history. In fact it is the latter which are important in explaining actions, for it is their individual patterns of ideas which enable people to interpret their situation and to imagine how it could be changed. People's individual framework of belief is informed by discourses available in their community, but does not correspond precisely to any one of those realms of discourse. The important point historians have learned from the study of discourse, is that very often, how people respond to a situation does not depend simply upon the nature of that situation, but upon how they perceive it. (Jay M. Smith has argued and illustrated this point very clearly. See Smith, 2001.) It is also important to remember the ability of people to deceive themselves about their real reasons for acting, be they for material advantage, for sexual satisfaction, or for an increase in power. The thoughts which justify an action do not always cause it. Some actions are better explained in terms of unconscious dispositions, rather than the reasons which agents produce for what they do.

Then what is reliable evidence of a person's real dispositions? Is private behaviour a better guide? For instance, would a private, sincere confession of beliefs, values and attitudes be reliable? Historians sometimes have the private diary of a person to consult, as well as records of their public statements and behaviour. Generally private confessions would be more reliable, since in these circumstances there is generally no reason to dissimulate. Occasionally, however, even in private one is motivated to present beliefs, values and attitudes of which one can be proud, and to ignore others of which one might be ashamed. Self-deception can be quite profound.

In the end, we take all of a person's behaviour as evidence of their mind and character, what they say and do, in public and in private. The account we give of their beliefs and attitudes is then the best explanation we can reach of all the relevant evidence available to us. We assert them to be real, because their presence helps to explain the patterns of behaviour which are otherwise a matter of chance.

Cultural and social causes of human actions

People's behaviour is not only a product of their state of mind; it is also influenced by the culture and society in which they are placed. If people's lives are shaped by the discourses they adopt, then their actions are largely directed by their culture. Discourses help to define social practices and roles, as well as justify (or criticize) them. People can also identify practices and roles by observing regular patterns of behaviour in those around them. Historians are increasingly interested in these cultural and social causes of human actions.

Social practices

The culture of a society includes both its discourses and its practices, and these do not always reflect one another. Joseph Margolis describes the culture of a community as everything in it which is intentional, which includes the things people say and make and do, including their common practices (Margolis, 1999, p. 75). Roger Chartier has insisted that cultural history examine not just the discourses of a community, but its practices as well. He writes: 'That practices, articulated with but not homologous to discourses, are not reducible to discourses can be considered the fundamental partitioning principle in all cultural history' (Chartier, 1997, p. 69; and cf. 1991, p. 18).

It is quite difficult to define a practice. A practice is a regular pattern of response to a certain kind of situation adopted by an individual and perhaps by many members of a community. The way we dress, eat, communicate . . . all these are common practices. What explains people's regular behaviour, however, is really the habit they have acquired of behaving as they do. A habit is a disposition to respond in the same way to the same circumstances. Habits produce practices. That is why Pierre Bourdieu called the collection of habits which produce the practices of an individual or a group their 'habitus'. He wrote: 'the habitus, the product of history, produces individual and collective practices, and hence history, in accordance with the schemes engendered by history' (Bourdieu, 1977, p. 82). Whether a person's habitus is a disposition of their body, or of their unconscious or conscious mind, is hard to say. What we do know is that such behaviour seems to be fairly automatic, and that it has generally been induced by social training.

While some social habits are deliberately taught and instilled, mostly to children, others are acquired by imitation. The importance of imitation as a cause of common forms of human behaviour has been emphasized recently by Susan Blackmore in her book *The Meme Machine* (1999). The *Oxford English Dictionary* defines a meme as: 'An element of a culture that may be considered to be passed on by non-genetic means, esp. imitation' (ibid., p. viii). Just as genes are transmitted from body to body, so Dawkins has written of memes being transmitted from brain to brain (ibid., p. 6). Blackmore explains:

> Everything that is passed from person to person in this way is a meme. This includes all the words in your vocabulary, the stories you know, the skills and habits you have picked up from others and the games you like to play. It includes the songs you sing and the rules you obey. (p. 7)

> We humans, because of our powers of imitation, have become just the physical 'hosts' needed for the memes to get around. (p. 8)

It is amazing just how much human behaviour conforms to social practices. They are most regimented, often backed by written rules, in institutions such as parliaments, churches and courts of law, as well as in games people play. They are also at work in less formal settings, in businesses and colleges, and as we saw, even at home.

The concept of a role overlaps the concept of a practice, because most social roles involve the adoption of a range of practices. But roles also involve responsibilities which people sometimes fulfil with careful thought, at times in a novel way. Individuals fulfil a number of roles, and are expected to conform to a variety of practices. In fact so prevalent are these constraints upon people's behaviour, that some writers have thought individuals spend their lives negotiating the scripts written by the various roles and practices society prescribes, so to speak. Elizabeth Deeds Ermarth, for example, has learned to think of herself

> as a moving site of discursive specification, a subject position or, more accurately, a simultaneous plurality of subject positions because I inhabit semiotic systems in multiples simultaneously, not one at a time; I am indistinguishably teacher, thinker, musician, colleague, parent, scholar, friend, driver, voter and so on. . . .
>
> I am invited . . . to recognize the obligation for constant negotiation among the many semiotic systems or discourses that constitute my context of meaning and value as a sort of environmental possibility. In such ideas the semiotic complexity of my day begins to find an intellectual model adequate to it.
>
> (Ermarth, 2001, p. 210)

If someone deliberately follows a written or spoken rule, then their behaviour can be explained in terms of their conscious beliefs about what they ought to do. It is the more or less automatic employment of common practices which is being discussed here.

As well as individual practices, there are collective ones, in which people act together in a conventional way to achieve an outcome that all members of the group desire. Charles Tilly, for example, has seen many forms of collective protest as following conventional forms of practice:

> Hijacking, mutiny, machine breaking, charivaris, village fights, tax rebellions, food riots, collective self-immolation, lynching, vendetta have all belonged to the standard collective-action repertoire of some group at some time. People have at sometime recognized every one of them as a legitimate, feasible way of acting on an unsatisfied grievance or aspiration.
>
> (Tilly, 1978, p. 153)

The fact that a practice is widespread in a community does not mean everyone follows it. Often it is followed by an identifiable sub-group in the community, as we shall see. It is important for historians to take care in defining the scope of a practice as precisely as possible, that is, the precise group of people who conform to the practice, and the place, time and conditions of its existence.

Even within a designated group, practices are not always followed in a perfectly regular manner. A practice has been analysed as a pattern of habitual behaviour, which has been instilled by observation and imitation, frequently through the encouragement of parents and teachers, and often reinforced by rewards and punishments. However people do not always follow the practices they have been taught. Bourdieu recognized that people act in a social context, or 'field' as he called it, and use conventional patterns of behaviour to further their goals within it, adopting 'strategies' for achieving the outcomes they desire.

He was unclear as to precisely how conscious people were of the process of forming strategies, or to what degree they modified the practices they had been taught to achieve the results they wanted. For example, if one person were offended by another, instead of objecting he might overlook the offence and behave amicably in the hope of winning the cooperation of the other for some purpose. Or, if he decided to fight the other, he might introduce new methods of fighting, such a head butting or kicking, which had not been adopted before. Practices, and the habitus that drives them, are best thought of as a common repertoire of responses rather than as a collection of entirely automatic responses to various situations.

Practices can be difficult to identify. Some are so complex that it is difficult to capture them precisely, as anthropologists and cultural historians are only too aware. Even those who follow a practice cannot always state it. For example, people who know how to speak a language correctly are often unable to state the rules of language they are following. Even when the conventions are not as difficult as this to state, for example conventions governing table manners, it can be hard to describe them accurately. In Western countries today one generally eats meat with a knife and fork, or if the meat is in small pieces (how small?) with a fork alone, but sometimes it is permissible to pick up and gnaw a bone (when exactly?).

Ideally, one can identify a practice by observing the regularity of certain patterns of behaviour, and the prevalence of those patterns in the community. Historians seldom have enough data to do this. There are fairly detailed and complete records of the proceedings of parliament, of law courts, of committees, and sometimes of patient care in hospitals. So practices in institutions such as these can be discovered. But where such records are not available, historians have to rely upon the reports of witnesses. Thus Rhys Isaac has recorded the customs of fighting in the taverns of Virginia during the eighteenth century.

> The causes for which Virginia males could come to blows were recorded by a visitor to the country. It might be that one 'has in a merry hour called [another] a *Lubber* . . . or a *Buckskin*, or a *Scotchman* . . . or offered him a dram without first wiping the mouth of the Bottle.' Custom permitted the fight to be carried on with 'Kicking, Scratching . . . Biting . . . Throttling, Gouging [the eyes], Dismembering [the genitals],' all of which 'generally is attended with a crowd of People.' An Englishman, commenting with distaste, remarked that a code of honor applied nonetheless. It was common for contestants to agree in advance whether to limit modes of attack, and 'that whatever terms are specified . . . let the conflict be ever so severe, they never infringe [their agreement].'
>
> (Isaac, 1982, pp. 95, 98)

Presumably the writers quoted in this passage had observed a number of fights, or talked to locals about them, but it is difficult to know just how conventional

these patterns of behaviour were. How common were the patterns of provoca-
tion and response, indeed how common did they have to be to constitute a
practice? The concept of a practice is rather vague in this respect.

Lawrence W. Levine devotes most of his book *Black Culture and Black Consciousness* (1977) to an analysis of Black beliefs and attitudes, but he also describes
a number of their cultural practices, for example the practices in which Negro
spirituals were created. Note his concern throughout this passage to justify his
descriptions as derived from a large number of reports.

> The contemporary accounts of one observer after another make it indis-
> putably clear that during the period when the spirituals were being forged
> . . . black men and women, slave and free, were commonly present at reli-
> gious revivals and regular church services alongside whites throughout the
> South, and that the contributions of the black singers were often distinctive
> enough to be noted.
>
> (p. 21)

[This] account of the creation of a spiritual is typical and important:

> We'd all be at the 'prayer house' de Lord's day, and de white preacher
> he'd splain de word and read whar Ezekial done say –
> Dry bones gwine ter lib ergin.
> And, honey, de Lord would come a'shinin' thoo dem pages and revive
> dis ole nigger's heart, and I'd jump up dar and den and holler and shout
> and sing and pat, and dey would all cotch de words and I'd sing it to
> some ole shout song I'd heard 'em sing from Africa, and dey'd all take it
> up and keep at it, and keep a'addin' to it, and den it would be a spiritual.

This 'internal' account has been verified again and again by the descriptions
of observers, many of whom were witnessing not slave services but religious
meetings of rural southern Negroes long after emancipation. The essential
continuity of the Negro folk process in the more isolated sections of the
rural South through the early decades of the twentieth century makes these
accounts relevant for the slave period [prior to 1862] as well.

> (p. 26)

Levine went on to quote descriptions of how everyone in the church, black and
white alike, would be moved by the passion and excitement of the singing.

> The similarity of these accounts, not only in their details but in their very
> language, is impressive. They make it clear that even outsiders had difficulty
> resisting the centripetal pull of black religious services and song. Created
> within this atmosphere, spirituals both during and after slavery were the
> product of an improvisational communal consciousness. They were not, as

some observers thought, totally new creations, but were forged out of many pre-existing bits of old songs mixed together with snatches of new tunes and lyrics and fit into a fairly traditional but never wholly static metrical pattern.

(p. 29)

It is interesting to note that the spirituals themselves were constructed largely from traditional words and music, used in a slightly novel way. The practice of creating spirituals and using them in worship was an important element of Black culture, from the eighteenth to the twentieth century.

One could regard descriptions of common practices as generalizations of a special kind: not merely summative but regulative, because the practice explains most of the instances of it as well as describing them. Seeing practices as generalizations draws attention to the problem of verification they have in common: the need to establish how representative the sample of cases they examined was of the whole community. As was said before, some practices are uniform among a subset of a community, rather than among all members of it. Levine gives us no idea how many churches produced spirituals in the manner he described, or indeed how many blacks attended Christian churches at all. John B. Boles has written that 'Blacks worshiped in a variety of ways, and some did not participate in any Christian worship, for, especially in the colonial period, a smattering of blacks practiced Islam and others clung tenaciously to traditional African religions' (Boles, 1988, p. 2).

Social roles

When historians write about social roles, they can be referring to one of two things. First, a social role is commonly defined as a set of social responsibilities a person is expected to fulfil, often with rules and practices to guide them. Sometimes such roles are specified by people of authority in an institution; and sometimes they are traditional, learned by observing others in a similar social position, and noticing what others expect them to do. For example, the duties and responsibilities of officers in an army are probably specified by those in authority; whereas most of the duties and responsibilities of a father or mother are not, but have been agreed informally between them. The second sense in which historians write of the social role of a person is that which refers to their social function, a function which no-one may have authorized, and of which even the agent may have remained ignorant.

Defined responsibilities

Another distinction which it is important to note is that between social roles as defined by those in authority, and the roles actually adopted by those fulfilling them. In a fascinating discussion of the roles of masters, overseers, slave drivers and slaves on Southern plantations in North America, John W. Blassingame explains that these roles were defined 'in contracts and numerous essays on plan-tation management' (Blassingame, 1979, p. 238). For example, an overseer's responsibility was to supervise the day-to-day operation of a plantation. This meant directing and controlling the slaves from dawn to dusk to ensure that the plantation was profitable. In addition, he was expected to 'keep a daily record of plantation events, see that the slave's food was properly prepared, and maintain fences and tools in good repair' (p. 240). In practice, however, overseers inter-preted their role to suit themselves. In large plantations they could not supervise all the slaves all the time; and some left the plantation periodically to seek re-creation (p. 276). The ideal and the actual role did not precisely coincide.

Roles differ from simple practices in that there is much more discretion left to agents as to how they will fulfil them. Some planters were cruel in enforcing their will, others kind and many were in between (pp. 261–5). Blassingame com-ments: 'In spite of the institutionally defined roles, the treatment of slaves varied from plantation to plantation. Differences in family life, childhood experiences, and religious beliefs caused the planters to treat their slaves in a great variety of ways' (p. 265).

In the case of slaves, the difference between their defined role and their actual role was more subtle. In theory slaves were expected to act with deference and respect towards their social superiors, as well as obey their orders, but in practice that deference and respect was often lacking. Blassingame summarized the ideal role of a slave thus:

> Planters and overseers defined the role of the slave in very explicit terms. The institutionally defined role of the slave required him to identify with his master's interest, to be healthy, clean, humble, honest, sober, cheerful, indus-trious, even-tempered, patient, respectful, trustworthy, and hard-working. . . . Systematic labor, implicit obedience, and unconditional submission (as child to parent or soldier to general) were expected of slaves.
>
> (p. 242)

What was the reality? Blassingame notes that in literature slaves were portrayed as cheerful and compliant, if somewhat childish and lazy, having what he calls a Sambo personality (p. 227). He explains that, although slaves did not generally have such a personality, writers were motivated to present them thus 'to prove that slavery was not an unmitigated evil' (p. 230). The planters, on the other hand, feared that their slaves were hostile and rebellious, and were constantly worried about keeping them under control (pp. 231–8). In fact, Blassingame says, slaves did not accept the roles given them by their masters, but had to be goaded into obedience. 'It is obvious from the writings of the planters that the slaves did not internalize the roles and automatically submit unconditionally to their masters. Consequently, the primary guarantee of obedience was the lash' (p. 244).

So although slaves were compelled to fulfil the roles assigned to them, the best explanation of their behaviour is that they did so, not because they had personally accepted those roles, but because their overseers and slave drivers made them act as their role required. They functioned as if they had internalized their roles, when in fact they had not done so. They fulfilled the function of a slave without have accepted that role. They conformed from a desire to escape the lash (pp. 295–6).

Despite his sensitive analysis of the roles of those on plantations, Blassingame is quite unconcerned about problems of generalization. Did not the treatment of slaves, and the role of overseer and driver, vary significantly in plantations of different size, and in plantations cultivating different crops? According to Kenneth M. Stampp, it certainly did (Stampp, 1965, ch. 2). The smaller the farm, the closer the planter was to the slaves. Only planters with large farms working thirty slaves or more could afford an overseer to supervise them, enabling the planter to enjoy a more leisured life. Only on such large farms did one find slaves specializing in various occupations, rather than being required to do many of them. Furthermore, the role of slave drivers varied depending upon the kind of crop being grown. Cotton planters used gangs of slaves, and it was the drivers' job to make the gang work hard all day. However those who grew rice in fields divided into segments by ditches, gave slaves a daily task to be completed in their own time, and the driver's role was to allocate the work to each individual and ensure it was done properly. Many plantations used both systems: 'Cotton planters often worked plow-hands in gangs but gave hoe-hands specific tasks of a certain number of cotton rows to hoe each day' (ibid., p. 55). Stampp notes that as well as cotton and rice, different districts grew sugar, tobacco and hemp, each requiring different patterns of work. Furthermore, by 1860, Stampp says, 'probably a half million bondsmen lived in southern cities and towns' doing a great range of more or less skilled work (p. 60).

Not only is Stampp sensitive to the way roles varied with types of plantation and occupation, but he is also conscious of the need to specify the period of time during which these roles existed as he describes them. In fact, he says, the roles did not change much during the period that interests him, from 1830–60. He writes:

> The rigid and static nature of ante-bellum slavery, 1830–1860, makes it possible to examine it institutionally with only slight regard for chronology. The important variations in detail . . . were not evidences of progressive changes in the nature of southern bondage. Rather, they were evidences of regional variations within the South itself and of natural variations among individual masters and slaves.
>
> (p. 28)

Social roles can explain a variety of historical facts. Clearly social roles explain many features of the behaviour of individuals who have adopted them. In many cases, such as these, they also explain the fact that so many individuals in certain places and times behaved in a similar way in similar circumstances. They explain patterns of behaviour of individuals by pointing out that they fulfil, more or less, the socially identified roles which there is reason to believe the individual has adopted. And they explain the prevalence of such patterns of behaviour in a society by showing that such roles were commonly enforced and had been widely adopted.

Social functions

In some cases, when historians say that a person fulfilled a certain role in an organization, they are referring to a regular function that they performed, not to a set of responsibilities they had adopted. This is called 'a functional role', and it does not explain their behaviour but describes its regular effect.

There has been much discussion among historians about Hitler's role in the government of Germany. Ian Kershaw has summarized and commented upon this debate very authoritatively in his book *The Nazi Dictatorship. Problems and Perspectives of Interpretation* (1989). He introduces his chapter on this topic thus: 'Locating Hitler's role and function within the Nazi system of rule is less straightforward than initially it may seem' (p. 61). Later he refers to Hitler's 'functional role within a multi-dimensional (polycratic) system of rule' (p. 70). It becomes clear as the chapter proceeds that the debate is about Hitler's function in government, not about his idea of his role, far less about a widely shared concept of a Führer's role of the kind we have just been examining.

The use of the word 'role' in the following extracts confirms this impression. The first describes Martin Broszat's view of Hitler's role in government, presented in his book *The Hitler State*.

> Hitler is seen by Broszat as tending more to *sanction* pressures operating from different forces within the regime rather than creating policy: the symbolic Führer authority is more important than the direct governing will of the person of Hitler. . . . In this rather complex argument, Hitler is certainly accorded a vital role in shaping the course of the Third Reich, but not in so simple and straightforward a fashion as the ideological 'intentionalists' would have it.
>
> (Kershaw, 1989, p. 67)

Hans Mommsen similarly denied that Hitler produced clear policy directives, but saw his role as one of inspiring other officials through his speeches. Kershaw writes:

> Two issues lie at the forefront of Mommsen's concern: the absence of clear planning and consistent direction from Hitler; and the complicity of the German élites in Nazi policy. . . . In a recent, particularly clear statement of his interpretation, Mommsen summed up: 'Hitler's role as a driving force . . .

should not be under-estimated. On the other hand, it must also be recognized that the Dictator was only the extreme exponent of a chain of antihumanitarian impulses set free by the lapse of all institutional, legal, and moral barriers, and, once set in motion, regenerating themselves in magnified form.' . . . the role and complicity of the dominant élites . . . must be the subject of special concern.

(ibid., pp. 68–9)

Similar views are expressed about Hitler's role in the persecution and elimination of the Jews. Kershaw says: 'His major role consisted of setting the vicious tone within which the persecution took place and providing the sanction and legitimation of initiatives which came mainly from others' (p. 105).

It is not difficult to detect a connection between unique social functions, such as these historians have been discussing, and common social roles. All social roles describe social functions, the part a person should play in a social context. In the case of common social roles, this part is both generally recognized and personally accepted by people who adopt them. In unique social roles, the function of the agent is sometimes not recognized, either by the agent or members of the society in which the agent functions, nor in most cases has it been deliberately adopted. It was left to historians to work out what Hitler's role in German government had been.

Why do people adopt social roles and practices?

It is interesting to ask why people adopt social roles and practices, especially those which are to their disadvantage. Many social practices have the effect of keeping one group of people subordinate to another. Judith M. Bennett has listed some of the practices which kept women subordinate in preindustrial England.

> In the world of preindustrial England, all people – men as well as women – worked hard, long, and in difficult circumstances, but the working status of women – compared to that of men – was consistently lower: they received less training, they worked at less desirable tasks, they enjoyed less occupational stability and a weaker work identity, they received lower wages.
>
> (Bennett, 1994, p. 64)

As Ava Baron writes: 'a key ingredient in the making of a gendered working-class history is exploring how meanings of masculinity as well as femininity are constructed and naturalized and then structured into the fabric of social relations and institutions' (Baron, 1994, p. 148).

Why do people adopt roles and practices which make them subordinate to others? There are three common reasons for doing so, which recur again and again. People are commonly influenced by those who impress them, those who entice them and those who threaten them. Those who impress them include those whose authority or superiority they respect. Thus young people might adopt roles indicated by parents, teachers or priests out of respect for their wisdom and authority over them. Even adults sometimes respect the wisdom and integrity of their leaders. Those who entice people are those who offer people a reward of some kind for complying with their wishes. The reward might be promotion within a firm, admission to a select group, or public recognition of some kind. Those who threaten, are people who have it in their power to harm those who refuse to conform to their wishes: parents; police and judges; employers; and competitors of various kinds.

For people to be able to entice and threaten others, they must have the right and power to do so. This is usually given to them by systems of rules and practices, which enable them to reward and punish others in various ways. And they also need physical resources to do so, such as available money to reward the compliant, and strong police to arrest offenders, and jails in which to incarcerate them. It is clear, then, that the structures of society in which people live and work exert a tremendous influence upon their behaviour. Responsible historians should make this influence quite clear to their readers, to help them recognize its importance and value.

The classic explanation of the subordination of women until fairly recently, presented by Betty Friedan (1963) and restated by Shulamith Firestone (1970), illustrates the influence of society very well. The subordination of women to men was largely a function of the practice of excluding women from any employment bringing social status and economic independence. Fifty years ago women found it easy to become nurses or teachers, shop assistants or waitresses, but they were largely excluded from the professions of law, medicine and engineering, and from management positions in business or industry. They were expected to get married and fulfil the roles of lover, housewife and mother instead.

Some women agreed with those in authority who suggested that these were roles for which they were by nature best suited, and adopted the roles with enthusiasm. There were, in addition, rewards that could be hoped for. Women who married well acquired some of the social status of their husband, sharing some of the respect others gave him, being admitted to the circles in which he moved. In addition to social status, there were material rewards: a man could earn much more than a woman, and a wealthy husband could provide comforts and a life-style which no woman could hope to enjoy on the low levels of pay available to female employees. With any luck, there was also emotional security in marriage, achieving a sense of worth and identity by becoming precious in one's husband's eyes. The final force driving women to marriage was fear of remaining a spinster. Not only did spinsters lack the status, wealth and identity of married women, but they were regarded by society as something of a failure for not having married as they should. Friedan wrote: 'For the woman who lives according to the feminine mystique, there is no road to achievement, or status, or identity, except the sexual one: the achievement of sexual conquest, status as a desirable sex object, identity as a sexually successful wife and mother' (Friedan,

1963, p. 255.) It was only by changing the social prohibition of admitting women to better paid jobs that women became liberated from the need to marry and to remain compliant within marriage.

Here is another historical case of one social group agreeing to subordinate itself to another. Some had thought that the German army might have resisted the Nazi Party and protected Germany from its rule. In fact, however, the army accepted the authority of the party by and large, and certainly did not prevent it from ruling Germany. What drove the army to that position? Robert J. O'Neill explains how the army was incorporated into the Nazi state in his book *The German Army and the Nazi Party, 1933–1939* (1968). O'Neill's thesis is that 'the army was subject to an overwhelming number of influences which combined on many levels to make it subservient to its political master' (p. 175). He sums up several of these in the Conclusion of his book.

First, members of the army were impressed with Hitler's leadership. Under his rule the army increased in size and efficiency. 'The greater availability . . . of materials, men, and finance, the improved conditions of service, the moderniza-tion of the army, the fascination of new work and the emphasis on professional proficiency were associated in the minds of many soldiers, and with considerable justification, with the National-Socialist government' (p. 174). Hitler's success in the Rhineland and Czechoslovakia contributed to 'the myth of his military invincibility and political infallibility' (p. 174). So out of respect for Hitler's gov-ernment, they were willing to comply with its wishes. Further, they acknowledged a duty to do so. On the death of President Hindenburg in August 1934, soldiers had been required to swear allegiance to Hitler, and their honour required that they respect his authority (p. 173).

Second, after 1935 recruits to the army were drawn from the Hitler Youth Movement, and were enthusiastic supporters of the new regime. To obtain their co-operation, officers had to express their support as well. So the compliance of officers was rewarded with the loyalty of their troops (p. 173). Doubtless it impressed the government as well, and made promotion more likely.

Third, at all levels of the army there were men who sought favour with the party by exposing any members of the army who were not very enthusiastic about Hitler and his rule. O'Neill says that 'the mere presence of these men was a pow-erful coercive force' on any who resisted Nazi rule, as was the knowledge that Hitler was willing to replace malcontents with his supporters (p. 172). The replacement of General Fritsch and others early in 1938 for being too reactionary was typical of the treatment suffered by those officers whose enthusiasm was doubted.

The reality of social causes

Whereas Foucault was content to discuss the social contexts in which discourses are used, some have gone so far as to deny that these contexts are anything more than texts themselves. This radical idea arises from a belief that descriptions of the world acquire their meaning from their relation to other words and discourses, and not from the world itself. To say that a certain description is indeed of reality is just another way of talking about it, they say. Gabrielle M. Spiegel has noted the consequences of this move for historical explanation.

> If the imaginary is real and the real imaginary and there are no epistemological grounds for distinguishing between them, then it is impossible to create an explanatory hierarchy that establishes a causal relationship between history and literature, life and thought, matter and meaning. The context in which a text is situated is itself composed of constituted meanings, as 'texts of everyday life,' so to speak, and the connections between them are essentially intertextual. It becomes impossible, on this basis, to identify aspects of social, political, or economic life which somehow stand apart from or make up a 'reality' independent of the cultural constructions which historically conditioned discourses generate; text and context are collapsed into one broad vein of discursive production.
>
> (Spiegel, 1990, p. 68)

You might think that scientists can prove certain descriptions of the world true, but, Lyotard and others maintain their standards of proof are simply part of an inherited discourse, and the validity of their conclusions cannot be proved. To present a description of the world as 'scientific' is an attempt to impose it on others, Lyotard says, an exercise in power. (See extracts from Lyotard's *The Postmodern Condition* in Seidman, 1994. The essays by Seidman and Richard Harvey Brown support this view.)

The question of whether the social context of a text or an action can be real was raised in Chapter 2. Here I would simply stress that the main reason for insisting upon the reality of social relations and cultural influences is their explanatory value. My vice-chancellor has the authority and power to sack me for gross misconduct, and it would be foolish of me to suppose that that authority and power does not really exist. Its existence explains why staff are occasionally compelled to leave the university and are not reinstated. Similarly the culture of a society has real influence, chiefly through discourses which even postmodernists allow to be real and influential. These convey beliefs, values and attitudes which constrain and direct so much of our behaviour. Once again, the reality of culture has important explanatory value. The fact that neither authority, power, ideas nor values are physical things which can be seen and touched is not enough reason for denying their reality. There is no reason to confine reality to the physical; indeed it would be disastrous to do so.

It is tempting to say that social realities are no more than concepts which people have about such things as authority and power, concepts which they have acquired from common discourse about society, and which influence their behaviour. Indeed all descriptions of society, such as Weber's analysis of legal, traditional and charismatic authority, can be regarded as referring to nothing real at all, even though they sometimes have great explanatory power, for example in explaining the authority of a leader. At this point it is important to recall why we assume physical things exist in the world. We have no more than ideas about the physical things that exist. We believe they exist, however, to account for our perceptions of them. Similarly, it is convenient to believe the vice-chancellor has authority to account for people's willingness to obey him. We believe in the reality of things because it is convenient to do so, especially when they are capable of affecting our experiences.

It is also worth noting here that our beliefs about the structures of the world make repeated use of the relationship of supervenience. For instance we think of particles making atoms, and atoms making molecules, and molecules making compounds; then we think of collections of iron molecules making, say, steel, and steel being used to make a knife. In every case the relationship is one of supervenience: in which the more complex thing exists in virtue of features of the simpler things which compose it. The same is true of the organic world of proteins, genes, cells, organs and organisms. We are happy to believe that all of these exist because each of these has properties peculiar to itself, which are not properties of the things which constitute it. The most discussed example of supervenience is that of the mind upon the brain, and here it is easy to see that properties of the mind, such as colour, sound and odour are not properties of the brain, which is a physical object. It is reasonable to think of the social world as supervening upon the activities of individuals and the material goods they employ. Thus the authority of a vice-chancellor depends upon the laws and regulations that people have passed defining his authority; traditions of the respect given to vice-chancellors within the culture; as well as the personal charisma of the particular vice-chancellor in question. But the vice-chancellor's authority can increase and diminish, and can cause regular patterns of deferential response. It is convenient to assume that it is real.

It is important for historians to distinguish historians' own analysis of past societies from the beliefs about a past society held by its members. An historian might write of the charismatic authority of a leader, whereas the leader's followers were conscious simply of his traditional authority to lead them. As was pointed out above, ethnographic historians often fail to make such distinctions carefully. That is not to say that historians should refrain from using modern concepts when describing the past. There were undoubtedly classes in feudal society, for example, whether they were conscious of the concept of class or not. Marc Bloch, careful as ever, wrote of the feudal nobles for example as 'a de facto class' (Bloch, 1965, vol. 2, p. 283). Confusion becomes more likely when the same word is used today in one sense and previously in quite another. He points out that serfs regarded as unfree in the Middle Ages have been regarded as 'half-free' by modern writers, using their own sense of the word (Bloch, 1954, p. 173; see Bloch, 1965, vol. 1, p. 161). In exasperation he adds: 'A nomenclature which is thrust upon the past will always end by distorting it, whether by design or simply as a consequence of equating its categories with our own, raised, for the moment, to the level of the eternal' (ibid., pp. 173–4). He obviously forgot this when he wrote of feudal classes!

To learn how people viewed their societies in the past, historians must examine their discourses about it. But to provide a modern analysis of past societies, it is better to study their practices. For example, when Henri Pirenne wrote: 'In its essentials the medieval craft may be defined as an industrial corporation enjoying the monopoly of practising a particular profession, in accordance with regulations sanctioned by public authority' (Pirenne, 1936, p. 184), he was clearly using modern concepts, and he justified this description by describing how the urban artisans formed fraternities from the end of the eleventh century in Europe, and how they soon became regulated by municipal authorities in the towns.

Conclusion

In this chapter we have considered a range of mental and social states which historians commonly assume could have caused people's actions in the past.

When historians use these assumptions to create a hypothesis about the causes of an act which produced a piece of evidence available to them, they often do not provide a complete explanation of that act. Rather, they focus upon just those parts of the explanation which interest them. Thus the various hypotheses about Abelard's reasons for writing his History were formulated to produce different possible accounts of what he truly believed about the seduction of Heloise, in particular whether he might have exaggerated her innocence in the matter. Similarly historians allow for bias in reports of events in letters, newspapers and official documents, always looking for corroboration before accepting what they say as an accurate account of events.

Once historians have arrived at a credible account of particular events, their search for causes often goes on, revealing more information about the past. For example, Collingwood was certain that Romans had built the wall in northern England, but then wanted to know their intention in doing so. He was not interested in precisely who built it, and how the building was organized. He simply wanted to know why it was built, how it was intended to be used, so that was the only part of the explanation he thoroughly investigated. Similarly, when Goldhagen had collected evidence of atrocious acts against the Jews in Nazi Germany, he wanted to discover the motives of those who perpetrated them, to judge the importance of anti-Semitic attitudes and propaganda within the German state. He did not pay much attention to the bureaucratic methods of implementing the policy of Jewish imprisonment and extermination, because they were not of much interest to him.

Occasionally historians want a comprehensive explanation of the events they have discovered. In that case they will draw attention to all the causes which they judge to have been significant. To conclude this chapter, here is an example of an historian, Timothy Tackett, explaining the origins of the reign of terror which occurred during the French Revolution between 1792 and 1794, in which many people were imprisoned and executed on suspicion of opposition to the newly established republic. What sparked this behaviour were rumours of conspiracies, both at home and abroad, to abolish the Assembly. Tackett writes:

> a consuming fear of the presence of conspiracy, or a small group of perpetrators or even a single master conspirator, wilfully seeking to destroy the revolution and the revolutionaries through secret action, beset much of France's political élite between the spring of 1792 and the summer of 1794. During this period, over 90 percent of judicially ordered executions were against individuals accused of various forms of sedition or collusion with enemies of the republic. An obsession with plots was clearly part and parcel of the political culture of the Reign of Terror.
>
> (Tackett, 2000, p. 692)

Once fear of conspiracy was established, it became the motive for searching out and executing likely enemies of the revolution. To prevent the destruction of the revolution and the revolutionaries it was necessary to destroy anyone who might be an agent of such destruction. This rational explanation is neat and simple. It was most fully defended by François Furet, who argued that commitment to the ideology of Jean-Jacques Rousseau was important, as radicals worked to achieve a united society based upon popular sovereignty, assuming that their decisions embodied a 'general will'.

But this explanation is clearly not enough. Why did the revolutionaries fear defeat, and why did they execute so many so irrationally? Arno J. Mayer observes that 'there was something distinctly wild and blind about the slaughter of defenceless prisoners [in September 1792] who were presumed to embody a ubiquitous domestic enemy with close ties to the *émigrés* and European powers. Even more terrible than the scale of the killings were the furious and primitive ways in which they were carried out' (Mayer, 2000, pp. 178–9). Mayer attributes the irrational ferocity of the terrorists to a motive for 'vengeance' (ibid., ch. 5), presumably against anyone who dared oppose them, but he does so without any particular theoretical support.

Tackett's paper offers an explanation of the fear of conspiracy. He notes that there was evidence of counter-revolutionary activity throughout the revolution, but it was not enough to explain the degree of anxiety which motivated the reign of terror. Tackett offers three explanations of that, one rational, one socio/cultural and the other psychological . The radical Jacobins, he said, had 'a deeply held sentiment that their version of democratic egalitarianism was profoundly true and right'. . . . 'It was only one step further to the assumption that all who disagreed with the Jacobins' positions must of necessity be fools, dupes, or conspirators. In this sense, the Jacobins' paranoid style was linked to the intensity of their convictions' (Tackett, 2000, p. 705). In other words, so passionately were the Jacobins committed to the revolution, that anyone suspected of subverting it would be attacked zealously, often without good reason. Thus the Jacobins' values provide an explanation of their fear and hatred of conspiracy.

Second, Tackett notes that many of the deputies in the second Assembly came from 'more mediocre social positions and from smaller communities, [and] felt less social distance from the popular classes than had their predecessors. Possibly, for that very reason, they were in closer contact with a popular culture permeated with fears of plots and conspiracies and less touched by the rational skepticism of the Enlightenment' (p. 709). If the deputies did acquire their fear of conspiracy from their local communities, that just shifts the question to ask why those communities held such fear.

His final explanation, the psychological one, is built upon a theory of individual paranoia. Psychologists say that individual paranoia 'is often characterized not only by a deep mistrust of others but by a mistrust of oneself: a weak and unstable sense of autonomy and an exceptionally frail sense of identity' (p. 712). Tackett explains that the revolution had radically disrupted normal government in France, and raised enemies abroad against the new regime. The flight of King Louis XVI to Varennes in 1791 added enormously to people's sense of insecurity: 'there was an increasing fluidity of identity, a growing uncertainty as to who one was, what one could rely on, and whom one could trust. The ambiguity of one's own collective identity reverberated in uncertainty and mistrust of others – specially those others perceived as outsiders or potential outsiders to the revolutionary community' (p. 713).

Tackett has not confined his explanation to just one source of motivation, but has dug out every kind he can. When available rational and cultural explanations did not seem to account for the strength of feeling involved in the reign of terror, he sought a psychological explanation to supplement them, using a psychological theory which seemed relevant.

Chapter 5

Types of historical narrative

Historical investigations may begin with a question about the past, or a doubt about a recent interpretation of some historical event. They usually involve an extensive search for materials relevant to the initial concern, and the gradual development of ideas about the subject. Eventually the time comes to assemble the information and ideas and to present them to the public. There are several ways of doing this. Intellectual historians will set out to analyse an author's ideas; cultural historians will describe a range of symbols and practices, and what they meant in the society that produced them. Two of the more common forms of historical synthesis take the form of historical narratives and historical explanations. This chapter is about narratives, and Chapter 8 will examine explanations. Often narratives are designed to provide explanations, combining the two forms in one, but it remains useful to consider them separately.

While a lot has been written about the structures of historical explanations, remarkably little has been said about the structures of historical narratives. Debates about historical narratives usually focus upon their credibility and fairness, as we shall see. But to understand the point of these debates, it is necessary to identify the kinds of narrative they are about. It is useful to contrast three different kinds of historical narrative: commonsense structures; colligatory patterns; and summary interpretations. There is a fourth, namely genetic explanations, but these will be discussed in Chapter 8.

There are two very common ways for historians to produce narratives that will be strongly criticized. The first is to structure their narrative according to some preconception of the nature of the subject without checking whether it accurately represents the detailed information known about the subject. I call this 'top-down' history, history written to illustrate existing convictions about the subject, and more often than not it proves to be incorrect. 'Bottom-up' history is written to do justice to the particular facts believed true of the subject, even if this means overthrowing currently respected general interpretations of it.

The second common way of producing bad history is to focus on just a part of an historical subject, thereby giving a misleading impression of the whole. This is often done for moral or political reasons. For example, Australian aboriginal children were housed, fed and educated by the Australian government early in

the last century, to give them the best chance in life. To implement this programme, the children were taken from their families, often against the will of
their parents, and housed together in hostels in cities. Those in favour of the
programme emphasized its educational benefits; those opposed to it focussed on
the psychological and social damage it did. To obtain a fair impression of it, both
aspects need to be considered. If historians want to present just part of the
history of a subject, they should say that is what they are doing, so that readers
will not assume they are presenting a fair account of it as a whole.

What complicates matters is that excellent historical narratives draw upon
preconceptions about the nature of their historical subject, and select only those
aspects of their history which they find to be of interest. So it looks as though all
histories must be equally unsatisfactory! In describing the different kinds of
historical narrative, it will be important to distinguish those ways of drawing
upon preconceptions that are acceptable, and those that are not; and to contrast
those criteria of selection which will avoid obvious bias with those which regularly produce it.

In centuries past, historians looked for a pattern of change in the whole of
Western history, and then wrote history to illustrate the pattern they had found.
Jean-François Lyotard called these patterns 'metanarratives', and he is famous for
having condemned them (in Lyotard, 1984). Lyotard knew that historical metanarratives had been used down the ages to justify oppression, torture and
executions, and so he understandably condemned them. The metanarratives he
referred to were very general accounts of historical change, which placed the
present within a continuing story. They described how people should behave if
the story was to achieve the happy ending envisaged. Let me sketch some of the
more influential metanarratives of Western history.

The Christian metanarrative, which dominated Western culture for almost a
thousand years prior to the Renaissance of classical learning around the fifteenth
century, presented history in terms of Christian theology as found in the Bible,
interpreted by the Church. The Bible said that God had chosen to reveal himself
to the Jews, and had given them his law (including the Ten Commandments),
which they had often failed to keep. God had then visited his people in the
person of Jesus, whose sacrifice on the cross paid the price of salvation from
eternal punishment for all who accept and follow him. Since his death, we wait
for his second coming, which will be when everyone will be judged, and the faithful saved. To ensure salvation, people should obey God's ministers, especially the
Pope and the Emperor and those in authority under them. Thus the history legitimated obedience towards the authorities of Church and state in medieval Europe.

The Enlightenment of the seventeenth and eighteenth centuries brought
another metanarrative, this time about the freedom which would be brought to
those who pursued science, both of nature and of society. The use of reason had
revealed laws of nature and of society which can be used to regulate each, in the
interests of all. Furthermore, by using their reason, people had developed
new means of production, which steadily improved people's standard of living.

Freedom from poverty and disease, and from injustice and immorality were promised consequences of the application of reason. It was important, therefore, that people conform to those laws of the land which promoted justice and morality, so that the peace and freedom of all could be ensured. Unjust feudal institutions should be overthrown in the interests of liberty, equality and fraternity. And new, rational laws should be strictly followed instead. The interests of the individual lay in conformity with the demands of the state.

In the mid-nineteenth century Marx taught people to see history as determined by the means by which people produced the goods they needed. The means of production, he said, determined the relations of production. The class system of a society was one which suited the means of production it employed. In ancient times, the division was between masters and slaves; in feudal times, between lords and serfs; and in modern times, capitalism required capitalists who owned the means of production and workers whom they employed to work in their factories. The final stage, according to Marx, would be one in which the working class, realizing how much they were being exploited by the capitalists, seized control of the means of production for themselves and established a classless society. Everyone would then be able to share in the profits fairly. This history was used in the nineteenth century to legitimate appeals to the working class to realize their situation and revolt against the capitalists who enslaved them. In the twentieth century it legitimated the absolute government of Lenin and Stalin, and other communist regimes, which claimed to be defending a new socialist society.

Nazi racist theories of history developed in the twentieth century are almost too dreadful to be told. The German people became convinced that they lost the First World War because of the Jews in their midst, a race which Nazi propaganda said had exploited the German people, that is the Aryan people, for their own advantage. Germany would be great again, Hitler argued, if the Jews could be isolated, and if the kind of selfishness they displayed could be replaced with commitment to the German motherland, especially to the Führer who would lead the people to restore its glory.

In each of these examples, the metanarrative in fact legitimated a reign of terror so dreadful that Lyotard said such metanarratives should never be believed again. Christians held inquisitions and burned heretics at the stake; during the French Revolution, the revolutionary government used the guillotine to execute enemies of the state; the ways in which Lenin and Stalin hunted down opponents and killed or banished them is well known, as are the incredible attacks by Nazis upon Jews and others.

The metanarratives of today have yielded less horror, perhaps because they have not been embraced wholeheartedly by those in power. These are the stories of the oppression of blacks, women, the poor and homosexuals; and stories about the exploitation of nature. They are told in the hope of encouraging governments to pass laws to relieve the plight of the oppressed, and to conserve the benefits and beauty of nature. Once again, their purpose is to legitimate something held to be of great value. One could add to the list metanarratives about the growth and effects of economic globalization; and about the gradual disappearance of a sense of civic responsibility.

Lyotard hated metanarratives for legitimating terror. 'The nineteenth and twentieth centuries have given us as much terror as we can take', he wrote (Lyotard, 1984, p. 81). He also objected to them for failing to capture the truth about the past. In particular, they ignore the specific details of history, always describing general processes of historical change instead. Strictly speaking, the particular events of history cannot be truly represented in all their detail: one can only try to indicate what they are. Lyotard writes of things being 'sublime' in that they cannot be adequately captured in prose or paint; such detail, he said, is 'unpresentable'. The attempt to present them in all their detail results in a 'nostalgia' for the thing in itself, which is absent (ibid.). In modern art and prose we see attempts to capture the particular, which really only point to it.

There is no denying that many historical narratives have been written in conformity to metanarratives, either deliberately or unconsciously. Early histories of Australia used to begin with its discovery by brave white European males, and continue to describe its settlement and civilization by agents of the imperial British government and by other white settlers, using convict labour for some of its roads and fine stone buildings, and clearing away any aborigines who obstructed their progress. Thus the British Empire brought civilization to Australia. Today the histories are written with special focus upon the disadvantaged, women, blacks and convicts. Soon no doubt there will be histories about the decline of civic responsibility under capitalism and its governments, and on the degradation of the environment.

The problem with top-down history, written in conformity with a prevailing metanarrative, is that it is generally insensitive to exceptions and to alternative readings of the relevant evidence and the facts about the past that can be inferred from the evidence. Top-down history promotes the metanarrative on which it is based. Responsible historians will try to be fairer in their consideration of evidence and historical facts, so as not to mislead people about what happened. We now know that while some white Australians treated the aborigines cruelly, others did not. We also know that some famous explorers were not simply heroes opening up the wilderness, but were motivated by the hope of material reward for the new pastures they hoped to discover. The truth is often more complicated than metanarratives would have us believe.

Responsible history is bottom-up history, in which historians begin by assembling as much information about their chosen topic as they can, and then consider its general significance. Some of the recent metanarratives mentioned above have indeed been reached by this bottom-up approach, which is why they are widely respected. But they should never be used to impose an interpretation on an historical topic, just in case the topic provides an exception to them.

In order to judge the credibility, fairness and intelligibility of an historical narrative, it is necessary to identify the type of narrative it is intended to be. The most important distinction to note is that between narratives which are intended to provide a comprehensive account of a designated subject, and those which simply point out features of the past which are of interest. Comprehensive narratives are expected to provide accounts of their subjects which are not only credible and intelligible but fair. Partial narratives, on the other hand, while they are expected to be credible and intelligible, are not expected to be fair. (This distinction is discussed in McCullagh, 2004, forthcoming.)

To judge the credibility and intelligibility of historical narratives, it is useful to note the different ways in which they are structured. To highlight some of these differences, I propose three ideal types of narrative, which I call 'commonsense structures', 'colligatory patterns', and 'summary interpretations'. In practice the distinctions between these are not always clear, as we will see, but there are enough differences between these three types of narratives to justify characterizing them separately.

Commonsense narratives

Commonsense narratives use everyday concepts to identify the subjects of the narrative, and everyday beliefs about the causes of actions and events to explain what happened. They do not employ concepts and explanatory theories drawn from specialized social sciences, as do colligatory patterns and summary interpretations. The dividing line between commonsense theories and specialized theories is not entirely clear. I would regard almost all the explanatory theories discussed in the previous chapter as commonsense ones, the exceptions being some sophisticated modern psychological theories of behaviour. Theories about the importance of human interests and natural instincts in motivating people's behaviour have become so commonly accepted as to be regarded today as commonsense.

There are several common forms of commonsense narratives.

(1) Some trace the history of a continuous historical subject, for instance a person or an institution. Biographies are often good instances of commonsense history, telling the story of someone's life along general lines that are familiar to all. Individuals in the past had unique ambitions, and shared beliefs and values which are not commonsense today. But the structure of a life, the general ways in which family, education, employment and faith can influence a life are fairly well known.

Should historians employ their own beliefs about the causes of past events? In doing so, will they not be misrepresenting the past? The alternative is to present an account of past events which would have been given by those involved in them. Some who have written about historical narratives have recommended that historians describe events from the perspective of the agents, though not exclusively from that perspective. F.A. Olafson, for example, has declared that historical narratives are structured in such a way as to present a sequence of human actions, and

it is a condition of grasping this kind of action-based continuity of historical narrative that the actions themselves be identified by the historian under the descriptions which the agent may be supposed to have used as well as those used by those who were in some way affected by those actions.

(Olafson, 1979, p. 151)

Olafson thinks that an historical narrative will describe agents' appraisal of a situation, their deliberation about it, their forming an intention and their response to it, all from their point of view. David Carr has provided some support for this analysis, by pointing out that people experience their lives in narrative form.

> In action we are always in the midst of something, caught in the suspense of contingency which is supposed to find its resolution in the completion of our project. . . . The actions and sufferings of life can be viewed as a process of telling ourselves stories, listening to those stories, acting them out, or living them through. . . . The retrospective view of the narrator . . . is not in irreconcilable opposition to the agent's view but is an extension and refinement of a viewpoint inherent in action itself.
>
> (Carr, 1986, pp. 122, 126)

The 'first-order narratives' historians tell, says Carr, reflect the experiences of the people whose activities they narrate.

While it is true that we often view our own lives in such narrative terms as Carr describes, it is virtually never the case that historical narratives are confined to the story that some historical agent told about their life. To begin with, most historical narratives involve several people interacting with one another, often producing outcomes which none foresaw. Second, agents are often mistaken about their situation, and historians need to correct their misapprehensions in order to account for the often unexpected outcomes of their actions. Third, as Carr has admitted more recently, historical narratives are highly selective and abbreviated accounts of what happened (Carr, 1991, p. 165). To follow the trials and ruminations of real life as experienced by historical agents would be unacceptably lengthy and tedious. So historical narratives do not mirror the experiences of life. The events they record have been carefully selected.

In fact historians often have a lot more information about past events than contemporaries had, and are in a better position to provide an accurate account of them. To present the views of the agents without comment, knowing them to be mistaken, would be to mislead the reader and to provide a history whose credibility could not be rationally justified. For history to be credible, it must employ the best explanatory theories available to the historian, such as those listed in the previous chapter.

Another worry about biographies is that historians commonly dwell upon events in the lives of their subjects which are of present interest, and so fail to provide a fair account of the lives as a whole.

It is important to acknowledge that selection does not necessarily produce an unfair history. So long as historians maintain a consistent level of generality in describing a subject, and a consistent level of detail in selecting the events to be described, they can produce histories which are brief but fair. Some biographies are huge, describing lots of events in great detail, and some are much briefer, picking out just the important ones, and providing a summary account of them. Both can present a fair portrait of the subject.

What is worrying is the habit of paying much attention to events of interest to the reader, and skipping over other parts of the subject's life quite quickly. Does this practice necessarily result in misleading accounts of the subject? Consider, for example, biographies of Winston Churchill. Churchill had a long political career, but by far the most important part of it was his years as Prime Minister of Britain during the Second World War. Churchill had served during the First World War as Home Secretary, and then as First Lord of the Admiralty. His resignation from the Admiralty in 1915, after the failure of his policy on the Dardanelles, and the loss of his seat among the Liberals in parliament in 1922, seemed to mark the end of his political career. But he rejoined the Conservative Party and served in Cabinet between 1924 and 1929, and then in opposition until he joined the War Cabinet in 1939, replacing Chamberlain as Prime Minister in May 1940. His fame rests upon his leadership of Britain during the Second World War, from 1940 to 1945, when, after peace was declared, he was defeated in a general election. The commonsense narratives of his life, therefore, devote far more pages to each of those war years than to any other years of his life. The number of significant decisions he made during his period as Prime Minister far exceeds the number made in previous years. That is why they take much more space to describe. Clive Ponting, for example, in his biography of Churchill allowed about 40 pages a year to those war years, and only six or seven pages a year on average for the years preceding them (Ponting, 1994). Similarly, John Charmley (1993) devoted about 270 pages of his biography to those five war years, and 355 pages to the 65 years preceding it. It is interesting, by the way, to note how both these authors found they had to set aside the public image of Churchill as a great man in order to write his biography, and address the evidence of his life as impartially as they could. As Charmley writes: 'It became a matter of getting the icon off the shelf and of trying to discern the lineaments of the living man' (ibid., p. 2).

The practice of devoting much more space to events of public interest does not result in an unfair portrait of a subject so long as the main features of the whole life have been described in a consistent, balanced manner. If, however, the less interesting years are ignored altogether, or scarcely acknowledged, the reader might well be left with an impression of the subject that is quite mistaken. For example, Churchill's leadership and popularity during the war years were not typical of his life as a whole. This is perfectly obvious in the biographies just mentioned, because they do give a fair account of his life as a whole. Magnifying those events of particular interest does not obscure the other aspects of his life, or prevent the reader from obtaining a fair impression of it as a whole.

The temptation to write a biased biography is greatest when the historian admires or detests the subject, and so is prone to omit the bad or the good aspects of the subject's life. J.R. Jones mentions such motivated misrepresentation of an historical subject in the introduction to his biography of Churchill's forebear, the first Duke of Marlborough (1650–1722). A charming courtier and an outstanding general, who led an alliance which defeated the French and their allies at Blenheim (1704) and Ramillies (1706), Marlborough was showered with wealth and honours by Queen Anne, though he kept rather aloof from British politics. In the nineteenth century, Whig historians Henry Hallam and T.B. Macaulay wrote to demolish his reputation. Macaulay thought of Marlborough

> as a courtier and patronage broker [who] belonged to an evil system, the Old Corruption whose remains liberal Whigs were eradicating. As a soldier-politician Marlborough disquietingly resembled Wellington, the arch-reactionary, and it was contrary to the principles of reformed representative government for the entire destiny of the nation to lie in the hands of a single man, and particularly a soldier.
>
> (Jones, 1993, pp. 2–3)

With this presupposition about Marlborough, and attitude towards him, Macaulay 'unsparingly caricatured [him] as an odious careerist driven by ambition, avarice and an unbalanced wife who manipulated Anne without mercy' (p. 5). Jones says that 'Macaulay's artful selection of evidence to fit his case was exposed in devastating detail by John Paget', in a piece published in the mid-nineteenth century in *Blackwood's Magazine*. Between 1933 and 1938 Winston Churchill published a four-volume biography to re-establish his reputation. (Winston S. Churchill, *Marlborough: His Life and Times*. Jones notes that Churchill's biography is a bit biased too: see Jones, 1993, pp. 228–9.)

If historians wish to focus upon just one or two aspects of a person's life, they can avoid giving a misleading impression of the subject by clearly stating that their history is not intended to be comprehensive. Jones's own biography of Marlborough is a case in point. He declared that he would focus upon Marlborough's 'military and diplomatic genius for the simple reason that he altered the history of Europe and Britain by his achievements during the War of the Spanish Succession. Anything else would be perverse and unbalanced' (Jones, 1993, p. 6). Clearly Jones believes that one should study the historically significant achievements of great men and women, and not, for example, those personal or domestic affairs which were of little lasting consequence. The latter are of interest only in as much as they explain the former. For instance, Jones said that Marlborough's modesty and calm confidence were maintained 'by his practice of frequently retiring into privacy' (p. 8). Jones's decision to portray Marlborough's military and diplomatic skills is clearly reflected in the structure of his book. A long first chapter explains each step of his rise to seniority in the army, the result very largely of his service to King James II and King William III. The bulk of the book, however, provides a quite detailed account of Marlborough's European wars, of the strategy which brought him success, and of the diplomatic negotiations which accompanied them.

Commonsense histories of continuing institutions are more complicated than histories of individuals. Unlike individuals, they have more or less complex structures, structures in which there are several different sources of initiative. One has only to think of some familiar institutions, be they legal, educational, medical, industrial, commercial, military or whatever, to recognize that this is so. Historians are interested in how they served society and how they were affected by changes in society, but they are also interested in significant changes to their internal structure, and how the various parts of the organization related to one another and contributed to its output.

(2) Many commonsense narratives study the relations between two or more groups of people. They are often competing for something: for victory in war, for markets, for votes in an electorate, for a greater share of a firm's income, and so on. Occasionally the relationship is cooperative, as between government and industry, or between judicial and welfare organizations.

Just as there are common beliefs about what influences a person's life, so too there are common beliefs about what influences the fortunes of war, and about what helps to enlarge or diminish a market for goods, and about why some candidates win elections and other lose. Some of these beliefs were originally developed in theories of war, economics or politics, but they have become common knowledge now.

The temptation when describing competitive relations is for historians to feel more sympathy for one side than the other, and consequently to misrepresent the interests of each, favouring one and denigrating the other. A fair history is not misleading, so historians have to be very careful to search for all the reasons people on each side had for the activities they undertook. If they decide to write the history of only one side of a conflict, that is fine so long as they do not offer unsubstantiated opinions about the other side. Such a history is less intelligible than a more balanced account, because it leaves the actions of the other side unexplained.

(3) Some commonsense histories describe and explain the events which brought about a particular change of some kind, for example a constitutional change from absolute monarchy to democracy, or an economic change from poverty to prosperity, or a change of technology from spears to guns to rockets. The range of examples is endless.

Narratives of this sort usually describe events which destroyed one state of affairs, and events which created the new state of affairs that replaced it. For the history of the change to be fair, all the important stages must be described, at a chosen degree of detail and level of generality.

(4) Finally, some commonsense histories describe the causes of a major event. They do so by describing the prior events which significantly increased or decreased the probability of such an outcome in the circumstances. Teleological

narratives, which describe how people achieved a great ambition, can be particularly enthralling.

For a genetic narrative of this kind to be fair, it must include all the causes down to a chosen level of significance. In a brief history, only those causes which did a lot to increase the probability of the outcome will be described, whereas a longer history would be able to include lesser causes as well.

Commonsense narratives not only describe the histories of their subjects, but are designed to make them intelligible. They usually do this by setting the historical scene at the start, and by then adding further bits of information as necessary to make each major stage of the story intelligible. A chronicle would simply list the changes in chronological order without explanation. Narratives go further, by explaining the major events they describe. The continuity of their central subject also provides them with a thematic unity which chronicles normally lack.

The explanations provided in basic narratives remain at what might be called an everyday, commonsense level, and are not particularly profound. They will provide immediate reasons for actions, but not investigate deeper motives and more remote causes. These are provided by profound explanations once the basic narrative is complete.

Even everyday explanations, however, draw upon general theories, for example about the influence of beliefs and desires upon human behaviour. So are basic narratives instances of top-down history after all? Up to a point they are. The important difference which this chapter is designed to emphasize is this. Historians know a whole range of possible reasons and causes for most events, and the history they write records all that they find to have been influential, down to a certain chosen level of importance. Top-down history begins with a preconception of which among all the possible reasons and causes were influential, and confines itself to describing just those.

Colligatory patterns

Historians often find patterns in the past, or more strictly, in the information about the past they have acquired after studying available evidence. These are patterns formed by actions and events, and often represent changes of a certain kind. Descriptions of these patterns provide new information about the past, about the way in which actions and events related to one another.

The concepts used to describe these patterns are not everyday concepts, but are concepts developed from the study of history, such as 'renaissance' and 'revolution'. They name types of pattern quite often found in history. Generally, as will be seen, they have not been defined very precisely, so the same term is sometimes used to refer to patterns of somewhat different kinds.

The word 'colligation' is derived from the Latin word *colligere*, meaning to bring things together. Some colligatory words and phrases name unique patterns, in the same way as proper names refer to unique people or places; and some colligatory words name common patterns, just as common nouns can refer to many things (philosophers say they name classes of things). The phrase 'the French Revolution' refers to just one pattern of events, whereas the word 'revolution' is a common noun, which can be used to refer to a whole range of revolutions. I will describe some unique colligatory concepts first, and then some common ones.

W.H. Walsh was the first to apply the word 'colligation' to history (Walsh, 1958, pp. 59–64), when he pointed out that historians often make actions and other events intelligible by showing them to be part of a pattern. His first example was one in which several events were described as the means by which Hitler carried out his policy 'of German self-assertion and expansion'.

> Hitler's reoccupation of the Rhineland in 1936 might be elucidated by reference to the general policy of German self-assertion and expansion which Hitler pursued from the time of his accession to power. Mention of this policy, and specification of earlier and later steps in carrying it out, such as the repudiation of unilateral disarmament, the German withdrawal from the League of Nations, the absorption of Austria and the incorporation of the Sudetenland, do in fact serve to render the isolated action from which we started more intelligible.
>
> (ibid., p. 59)

All the events picked out by Walsh have this in common: they help to fulfil Hitler's wish to increase the extent of Germany's power. Even if others have longed to increase Germany's power, so that the policy is not entirely unique in its content, what makes it unique in this case is that it is held by Hitler. These events are all in fulfilment of his wishes.

The pattern in this case is a rational one: the events can all be related to a common purpose. This is perhaps the most common form of historical interpretation: historians often pick out and arrange actions that were performed to achieve someone's particular purpose. Walsh adds that sometimes people can be seen to follow a policy which they have not consciously formulated. The example he gives is of Britain's idea of its 'imperial mission'. He says that in the late nineteenth century '[t]here was, in fact, a recognizable imperialist phase in British political history, even though the policy of imperialism was not consciously accepted or deliberately pursued by the majority of those in power at the time' (ibid., pp. 61–2).

There is another rational pattern of events which Walsh touched upon. These are cases in which a variety of activities can be colligated under the concept of a movement which has not got a particular goal, but shares particular ideas and values. The movements Walsh mentions are 'the Enlightenment, the Romantic movement, the age of reform in nineteenth-century England, [and] the rise of monopoly capitalism' (p. 60). Once again, events gathered under these names can all be related to a common set of ideas, which is why the pattern is rational.

Another group of patterns which historians often detect are patterns of change, named by words such as 'growth' and 'decline', 'evolution' and 'revolution', 'polarization' and 'conflict'. I call these 'formal' concepts (McCullagh, 1978, p. 272) because they describe forms of change. Sometimes these terms are qualified, as in 'economic growth', 'political decline', 'cultural evolution' and 'scientific revolution'. The qualifications add a lot more content to the concepts. Economic growth must refer to a growth in wealth, often the result of increased productivity; political decline must refer to a decline in power relative to the power of others in a society; cultural evolution must refer to an evolution of beliefs, values and practices; and scientific revolution must refer to a sudden change of scientific world view. I say 'must' to emphasize that these terms have a common meaning in our language, and are not attached to any particular paradigm cases.

Having said that, however, historians sometimes want to fill out the characteristics of these patterns of change in quite a lot of detail, drawing upon examples with which they are familiar. Historians who do this often end up disagreeing with one another. Lawrence Stone reviews the major modern theories of revolution in a long introductory chapter to his book *The Causes of the English Revolution. 1529–1642* (1972). (See also Richardson, 1998, ch. 7.) Stone particularly admires a typology of political revolution produced by Chalmers Johnson which identifies six types

> identified by the targets selected for attack, whether the government personnel, the political regime, or the community as a social unit; by the nature of the carriers of revolution, whether a mass or an élite; and particularly by the goals and the ideologies, whether reformist, eschatological, nostalgic, nation-forming, élitist or nationalist.
>
> (ibid., p. 6)

For example, 'the *jacquerie*, is a spontaneous mass peasant rising, usually carried out in the name of the traditional authorities, Church and king, and with the limited aims of purging the local or national élites.' The *'millenarian rebellion*, is similar to the [*jacquerie*] but with the added feature of a utopian dream, inspired by a living messiah' (p. 6). And so on (see pp. 7–8). In the end Stone opts for an analysis of political revolution by Rex D. Hopper which outlines four stages of revolution. The first stage is one in which people are dissatisfied with traditional values; the second stage is one in which the intellectuals and others define the goals of an opposition to the current regime; the third sees a revolutionary movement in action, with moderates giving way to radicals; and the fourth sees a new regime legalized (Stone, 1972, pp. 21–2).

The formal colligatory concepts just mentioned can describe more than one instance. They are really general ideal types of historical change. To identify a particular set of events as a political revolution, for example, is to classify it, to say that it fits the general model which the formal term, political revolution, names. That being the case, it makes sense to ask whether the description of a set of events as constituting a revolution is true or not. If the events do fit the pattern, then the description is true; if they do not, it is false.

Interestingly enough, some particular cultural movements, like the Renaissance and the Enlightenment, have essential features which can be found on other occasions in history as well. C.H. Haskins, for example, found several characteristics of the Renaissance of the fourteenth to the sixteenth centuries in other periods of European history. These characteristics, he said, were 'revival of the Latin classics and of jurisprudence, the extension of knowledge by the absorption of ancient learning and by observation, and . . . creative work . . . in poetry and in art' (Haskins, 1957, p. 4). Such values, said Haskins, were manifest in the renaissance of the twelfth century, and also in the Ottonian Renaissance under the German Emperor Otto III (994–1002) and the Carolingian Renaissance under Charlemagne around 800 (p. 5). Similarly George Holmes wrote a book called *The Florentine Enlightenment 1400–1450* (1969) in which he argued that the culture of Florence in the first half of the fifteenth century resembled that of the European Enlightenment. In his book, he said, 'its resemblance to some of the attitudes commonly regarded as characteristic of the Enlightenment of the seventeenth and eighteenth centuries has been stressed: the preference for a common-sense approach in philosophy, indifference or hostility to traditional religion and metaphysics [and] artistic realism' (Holmes, 1969, p. 266). Leonardo Bruni's writing, he said, reflects a thoroughly secular outlook on both history and the state; and the work of Alberti and Donatello manifests an interest in realism in art (p. xix).

In practice, given the relative vagueness of the meaning of colligatory terms, their application can be uncertain. For example, historians disagree about which events, if any, in English political history in the 1640s, constituted a revolution. Brian Manning has summarized a few opinions with these words:

> David Underdown says that there were two revolutions in mid-seventeenth-century England: '. . . the moderate constitutional one of 1640–2; the more violent one of 1648–9 in which Parliament was purged and the King executed . . .' Conrad Russell also discerns two revolutions: the first in 1642–6 was 'the revolution of Parliament' and the second in 1647–9 was 'the revolution of the army'. But he adds that the former should be characterised rather as a 'rebellion', while the latter was 'a revolution in the full sense of the term'. . . . [O]ther historians date the 'real revolution' from the autumn of 1648. 'It was not till after the Second Civil War . . . that the whole New Model Army became authentically revolutionary', writes Ian Gentles.
>
> (Manning, 1992, p. 13)

Manning prefers to see the events of December–January 1648–9, when the New Model Army occupied London, purged the parliament and tried and executed the King, as 'the climax and watershed of the revolution and not the whole of the revolution', which he would date from the collapse of royal government in 1640 to its restoration with limited powers in 1660 (p. 14). He prefers to call the events of 1648–9 'a military *coup d'état*' of a revolutionary nature (p. 15).

In particular historical situations, such as England between 1640 and 1660, movements and processes of change have a number of peculiar characteristics. In England, for example, the monarchy and aristocracy were toppled from political power and parliamentary government established for a short while, but the revolution was driven by Cromwell who constantly appealed to God's will for vindication of his deeds. In other words, the ideas which drove this revolution were unique to its place and time. The concept of a political revolution provides a useful general concept for colligating a lot of events, namely the events which brought the revolution about. But it does not really explain them at all. To do that historians must look to the ideas which motivated them, the people who led them, and the means by which they were accomplished. And these are what make particular revolutions unique, unique instances of a general kind.

Once a colligatory word or phrase has been accepted, historians often disagree as to what it really refers to, and whether its use in reference to a particular pattern of historical change is warranted or not. Until a colligatory phrase has been defined, it is impossible to decide whether its use is warranted. These points are clearly illustrated by Joel Mokyr's discussion of the question whether there was an industrial revolution in Britain between 1760 and 1830 (in Mokyr, 1999). To put it briefly, striking industrial innovation occurred in only a few sectors of the British economy during this period, so he questions whether the whole period is adequately colligated as an industrial revolution. And second, the changes, while impressive, did take several decades to accomplish, so he wonders whether the word 'revolution' is really applicable.

Mokyr points out that historians have in fact referred to quite different patterns of change in the British economy during this period as constituting the Industrial Revolution. He describes four different accounts of the Industrial Revolution. 'The Social Change School' sees it as 'a change in the way economic transactions between people took place. The emergence of formal, competitive, and impersonal markets in goods and factors of production is the basis of this view' (Mokyr, 1999, p. 7). 'The Industrial Organization School' emphasizes 'the structure and scale of the firm . . . the rise of capitalist employment and eventually the factory system' (ibid.). 'The Macroeconomic School' notes 'aggregate variables, such as the growth of national income, the rate of capital formation or the aggregate investment ratio, or the growth and composition of the labor force' (p. 8). And finally, 'the Technological School' takes changes in technology to be fundamental to all other changes. Technology is not confined to new industrial techniques, but also includes 'techniques used for the organization of labor, consumer manipulation, marketing and distribution techniques, and so forth' (p. 8).

Mokyr himself seems to adopt a macroeconomic approach. He justifies calling this period of history an Industrial Revolution by remarking: 'The annual rate of change of practically any economic variable one chooses is far higher between

1760 and 1830 than in any period since the Black Death [1348]' (p. 3). But he is worried by the fact that the most striking innovation and growth was confined to just a few sectors such as cotton, wool, iron and machinery. Is it correct to say that there was a revolution in the whole industrial economy of Britain? Traditional sectors, such as agriculture, construction and many trades seemed to change little. Mokyr answers this objection by observing that the modern sector increased in size during the revolution, and gradually affected the traditional sector, resulting in its modernization (p. 15). He does admit, however, that the 'Industrial Revolution was, above all, a regional affair, affecting Lancashire and parts of the adjoining counties and the Scottish Lowlands but leaving most of the rest of the country without visible marks. As late as 1851, only about 27 percent of the British labor force worked in the industries that were *directly* affected by the Industrial Revolution, although almost everyone had been touched by it indirectly as consumer, user, or spectator' (pp. 4–5). Perhaps it would be more accurate to say that a revolution took place in parts of the British economy during this period, and not characterize the whole economy as undergoing such a revolution. As Mokyr said: 'What took place was a series of events, in a certain span of time, in known localities, which subsequent historians found convenient to bless with a name' (p. 2).

Mokyr also queries whether the rate of change in the economy was great enough to justify calling it revolutionary. 'Revolutions do suppose an acceleration of the rate of change,' Mokyr writes, 'but how much does the rate have to change in order for it to qualify' (p. 3)? Seventy years is quite a long time for a change to be accomplished. 'Economic change is rarely dramatic, sudden, or heroic. Consequently, some scholars have found the revolutionary aspects difficult to stomach' (p. 3). Mokyr is happy to call the changes revolutionary because they were profound and lasting (p. 5) – but evolutionary changes can be profound and lasting as well!

Narratives can be structured to present a colligatory pattern. If the pattern is referred to by a colligatory term, then the term describes it credibly if the conditions which warrant its application were present. To know what those conditions had to be, the historian must define the term as clearly as possible.

The patterns which enable historians to colligate events are not meant to represent some historical subject in a fair way, though sometimes they are taken to do so. There was an Industrial Revolution in Britain between 1760 and 1830, even if this pattern does not adequately represent the whole of the British economy during that period. Because colligatory patterns do not represent any particular subject, they should not be judged for their fairness – unless they are mistakenly taken to represent some subject as a whole.

There is sometimes a temptation to characterize an historical subject as whole by referring to just a part of it, in order to present it in a certain light. The relationship between the governments of the United States of America and the Union of Soviet Socialist Republics after Germany's defeat in 1945 until the collapse of the communist government of the USSR in 1989 has often been referred to as a relationship of Cold War. The war was cold because it did not involve shooting between the two great powers. It was called a war by western powers because the USSR was thought to be working for a communist overthrow of capitalism, and the USA responded to those intentions by building up its military, economic and international political power to such an extent as to make the USSR refrain from attacking it with weapons, and to contain the spread of communism to a very large extent. (See Hunter, 1998, Introduction.) Historians have subsequently referred to this version of events as the bi-polar view of hardline realists.

This account of the Cold War was the official view of the US government. In 1990 President George Bush said: 'For more than forty years, America and its allies held communism in check and ensured that democracy would continue to exist' (quoted in ibid., p. 3). This simple description of the relationship between America and its allies and the Soviet Bloc was designed to present it in a good light.

If historians had assumed that this colligatory pattern correctly represented the relationship between the super-powers, they would have written a narrative of that relationship simply to illustrate it. When they examined the relationship in detail, however, they found that it was much more complicated than the official description suggested. Early revisionists found evidence that US foreign policy was designed to promote domestic economic interests, as well as national security (Hunter, pp. 8–11). In 1984 Melvyn P. Leffler, with access to government documents, wrote: 'Economic considerations also made defence officials determined to retain American access to Eurasia as well as to deny Soviet predominance over it. . . . [Government officials agreed] that long-term American prosperity required open markets, unhindered access to raw materials, and the rehabilitation of much – if not all – of Eurasia along liberal capitalist lines' (Leffler, 1994, p. 24). Indeed, the more closely historians examined the relations between the USA and the Soviet Union, the more complex they discovered them to be. As Leffler and Painter write: 'To portray the Cold War in all its complexity scholars now realize that they must analyze the interconnections between the rivalry of the United States and the Soviet Union and the unfolding of internal developments elsewhere. To do this effectively they have to integrate the geopolitical, strategic, and ideological competition of the Great Powers with local and regional socioeconomic trends and political struggles' (Leffler and Painter, 1994, p. 11).

In fact relations between the United States and the Soviet Union after the Second World War were so complex, that they cannot be confined to the straitjacket of the official version of the Cold War. That concept is no longer useful as a summary of those relations. It is better regarded as a concept used by world leaders for their own purposes, but one which did not correctly represent the relations to which it referred. As Leffler has written recently, given the complexity of those relations, 'the Cold War will defy any single master narrative' (Leffler, 1999, p. 502).

The history of the historiography of the Cold War shows how top-down history was gradually revised in the light of detailed information about the relations between the superpowers, and how the complexity of those relations was finally acknowledged. The official version had been designed to justify US military and foreign policy, as a cold war against communism, whereas in fact US objectives were much more varied and complex. Now the US is conducting a somewhat hotter world-wide war against terrorism. Responsible historians will watch the detail rather than the official line.

Summary interpretations

Once historians have written a commonsense narrative history of an historical subject, they often look back at that history to see whether it is possible to sum up, in general terms, what has been described. They want a summary which is both credible and fair, and if possible intelligible.

Sometimes the summary interpretation is simply added on to the common-sense narrative, as a reflection upon what has been said. For instance, R.B. Woods wrote a long detailed biography of Senator J.W. Fulbright (Woods, 1995), and towards the end of it he reflected on the character of Fulbright as a way of summing up, and to some extent explaining, what had been said. According to Woods, commentators have found it difficult to make sense of Ful-bright's character, for sometimes he behaved like a liberal and sometimes like an arch-conservative. Immediately after the Second World War, Fulbright was keen that America contain communism by strengthening Europe, through the Mar-shall Plan, and by giving military aid to Greece and Turkey. At home, in America, he supported the War on Poverty, he attacked 'rabid anticommunists [McCarthyites], white supremacists, and religious zealots of various sorts' (Woods, 1995, p. 692). He established an international academic exchange pro-gramme, the Fulbright Scholarship Scheme, 'to break down the barriers of ignorance, nationalism, and xenophobia' (p. 691). But besides the liberal, there was Fulbright the conservative. He consistently opposed any legislation aimed at integrating the black and white communities in the South. And in foreign affairs, after 1965 he opposed American involvement in overseas countries, par-ticularly in Vietnam, and was anxious to give the Soviet Union and other countries a chance to reform. How could these apparently inconsistent attitudes be reconciled?

In his biography, Woods finds a characteristic of Fulbright which enables him to make sense of all his policies. This was his conviction that people would progress if given the opportunity to develop their understanding of the world, and the freedom to act rationally within it. He was not committed to particular rules or religious convictions, but tested every policy to see whether it would contribute to progress or not. He believed that since most Americans were ratio-nal, they would see the error of racism and discrimination in time, and move away from it. He thought that presidents Lyndon Johnson and Richard Nixon 'had become prisoner of the radical right, the military-industrial complex' (p. 695), and that their policies, clouded in secrecy, were contrary to the interests of both America and the overseas countries with which they were involved. He did not want the Northern States to impose their mores upon the South; nor did he want America to impose its democratic institutions upon Vietnam. Both should be left free to develop the institutions they judged best. So the theme which makes sense of Fulbright's life is a commitment to informed, rational self-determination, as the surest path to progress. In Woods's opinion, 'whatever his errors and misperceptions, America was well served by J. William Fulbright, this rational man combating an irrational and immoral world' (pp. 697–8).

Woods is aware of alternative explanations of some of Fulbright's behaviour. Being from Arkansas in the South, his continued opposition to legislation for racial integration might have had cultural and social roots (p. 331). And some have suggested that Fulbright's opposition to President Johnson's policies in Vietnam might have been a reaction to the President's not making him a secretary of state. But Woods shows that 'there was more to the Arkansan's dissent than resentment over thwarted ambition' (p. 694). Woods's general interpretation of Fulbright's character remains convincing.

Instead of adding a general interpretation of an historical subject to a commonsense narrative of it, historians frequently use such an interpretation to provide the structure of their narrative. A general interpretation of the events which made up the English Revolution between 1640 and 1660 would look for ways of summing up the groups involved, and the reasons for their behaviour towards one another. Here is an example of a general summary interpretation of the politics of this period. It is a statement of the thesis of David Underdown's book *A Freeborn People. Politics and the Nation in Seventeenth-Century England* (1996). Underdown begins by identifying two political cultures in seventeenth-century England, which he names 'élite' and 'popular', and following Disraeli he calls these 'two nations'.

> When I use the term 'élite' I shall be talking about the nobility, the courtiers, the country gentry: those who participated in, or directly influenced, the government of shire and kingdom. When I use the term 'popular' I shall be talking about people of lower status: yeomen, husbandmen, craftsmen, small urban householders. All these lesser people were owners of property, and were thus part of the political nation in ways that the increasingly numerous vagrants and landless poor were not.
>
> (ibid., p. 10)

He then proceeds to state his general thesis:

> In this book . . . I shall argue that the political cultures of the two nations were much closer to each other than is commonly supposed, particularly in the first part of the seventeenth century. During and after the civil wars this

began to change. The radical forces unleashed by the war destroyed the gentry's confidence that their inferiors shared their priorities. There was a sharper separation between the two political cultures: this process might be seen as part of the more general polarisation of élite and popular cultures that some historians have observed in these years.

(p. 10)

Thus Underdown describes a kind of change, namely the separation of the cultures of the two groups, and a kind of causal process at work, describing this separation as a result of radicalism 'unleashed by the war'. By means of this general account of what happened, he is able to draw together a host of discrete facts. He notes a number of events in the 1620s, prior to the war, which were supported by both groups (pp. 50–1); several complaints made by both groups and some political beliefs that they shared (p. 52). He later describes how the war turned many gentry away from popular culture to become royalists (p. 78ff), how parliamentarians displaced them in local government, how the demands of the invading Scots annoyed them, and how the threat of lawlessness made them yearn for a strong central government again (p. 108).

> Before the civil war the gentry had assumed that the common people shared their priorities – the freeborn Englishman's agenda of liberty, property, and anti-popery . . . They then took fright when it became clear that many of the lower orders wanted something more than the limited changes their leaders had secured for them in 1641, or even than the more drastic ones a minority had imposed on them in 1648–9. Memories of New Model agitators [demanding pay and indemnity], of Diggers on St George's Hill [where they established colonies], of mechanic and women preachers, of Quakers refusing their betters the elementary marks of subservience like hat-honour, of Ranters flamboyantly drinking and fornicating, and all the other wild excesses of the 1650s, convinced them that the people were not to be trusted after all.
>
> (p. 112)

This interpretation clearly accommodates a large number of facts in the political history of the period and is probably as comprehensive as one could hope for. In fact there were so many groups in so many places involved in the conflicts of the period that a truly comprehensive summary of them is well nigh impossible. In that case, it is perhaps better to call Underdown's thesis a general account of just one of the processes at work at the time. It is always important to identify the subject of a generalization as accurately as possible, to prevent readers from supposing it describes more than it really does. When judging a summary interpretation of an historical subject, it is important to discover whether it is intended to be comprehensive or not.

Historians often use general terms found in social sciences such as politics and economics when summarizing the history of an historical subject. It is always important to define those words as precisely as possible in order to judge their applicability.

Once again, the ever present danger for historians is that they will adopt general interpretations which are fashionable, without checking their credibility, fairness and intelligibility. Brian Manning has written a history of the period 1640–1660 in England, in which he comments upon two traditional interpretations and their shortcomings.

Traditionally, says Manning, historians have seen the English revolution 'as arising from divisions within the ruling class. Although true up to a point, this does not justify historians studying only the nobility and gentry, and perhaps the clergy, lawyers and merchants, to explain these events . . . as if the other 97 per cent of the population did not exist or did not matter' (Manning, 1996, p. 1). Recent studies, especially of local history, show that others, known as 'middle sort of people', played an important part in many of the events of that time. These he describes as 'a substantial middle rank in the population between the wealthy aristocrats and the impoverished masses' (p. 4). A civil war clearly requires followers as well as leaders, and to understand it historians should consider why so many were willing to fight it. Manning writes:

> It is not plausible that a country could be plunged into two decades of turmoil, upheaval and violent conflicts, without divisions running wide and deep, and active partisans on both sides would soon have been contained and neutralized if they had not been nourished by very large numbers of less active people who in varying degrees sympathised with their causes. (p. 71)

> In discounting the importance of popular opinions and actions historians have overlooked the nature of the phenomenon they are studying, which is that civil wars spring from deep divisions in a society. Recognition of this allows the traditional picture of the English Civil War to be enlarged, so that it does not arise only from within the ruling class but also wells up from below. (p. 55)

The second fashionable reading of the period which Manning wants to qualify is the assumption that divisions were not class divisions but were over religious matters. Christopher Hill's early Marxist interpretation of the period, which saw it as a conflict between the feudal aristocracy and the rising capitalist middle classes (Hill, 1955), was soon set aside, as it was apparent that aristocrats fought on both sides. Historians then focussed upon the religious and constitutional matters which were fiercely debated by royalists and parliamentarians. What Manning has found, however, is that groups in the middle and lower classes were concerned about how different forms of government could promote their socioeconomic interests, indeed their class interests. Manning writes:

Out of the diversity of the 'middle sort' there emerged elements that, without being exactly the same as the growing capitalist or bourgeois tendency, became conscious of the difference between their economic and ideological position and that of others, and found themselves united to defend it against the party which they identified with the aristocracy or ruling class. Thus they reached a level of both radicalism and class consciousness.

(p. 71)

Under Cromwell, Manning says, 'A new ruling class emerged, selected from among minor gentry, yeomen, merchants, army officers and radical clergy, and it governed the country effectively in the 1650s, but it lacked the economic power and social base to sustain its position permanently' (p. 115).

On the basis of these findings, Manning corrects the traditional rather narrow interpretation of the issues involved.

It is a false dichotomy in conservative historiography to set an interpretation in terms of religion against one in terms of class, and to regard religious explanation of the conflict as an alternative to social explanation. While it is clear that religious issues were very important, they do not explain everything, for religious conflicts coexisted with political, social and economic conflicts, and each influenced the other.

(p. 4)

Perez Zagorin has made the same point against the view that the Civil War was fought over religious issues. He says that one cannot ignore social concerns entirely, for that renders a number of events unintelligible.

Confined to their standpoint, we either answer inadequately, or do not answer at all, many questions of importance: why, for example, Puritanism was more prevalent in the towns, why the clothing districts supported Parliament, why Parliament abolished feudal tenures but left base tenures intact, why the radical movement appeared and made the sort of protest they did.

(Zagorin, 1998, p. 31)

In 1649 a group known as the Diggers

protested against private property, the market economy and waged labour. They tried to establish communes on the uncultivated common and wastelands as models of a society in which there would be no landlords, no rents to pay, no one would have to work for wages, but all would own land in common, cultivate it together and share equitably its produce.

(Manning, 1996, p. 116)

The motives of the Diggers in supporting the revolution were clearly not religious, but economic.

Conclusion

At the beginning of this chapter I remarked that historical narratives are often criticized for following a preconceived notion of their subject which does not do justice to the evidence, and for presenting only part of the story, thereby giving a false impression of the subject as a whole. In each section we have seen how 'top-down' histories, written according to preconceptions of the subject, have been criticized as inadequate in the light of detailed information about it. And we have noted how partial histories can sometimes give a misleading impression of their subject as a whole.

We have also admitted, however, that the detailed information about historical subjects of the kind found in commonsense narratives, upon which critics rely, is itself structured according to everyday beliefs about general causal processes, of the kind described in the previous chapter. Why are commonsense narratives written in conformity with preconceptions of their subject acceptable, while other narratives often are not? The reason is that the everyday beliefs about general causal processes upon which commonsense narratives depend are so well established that there is no need to query them seriously. General theories about the nature of certain kinds of historical change, however, such as theories about the causes of political and industrial revolutions, are much less certain, and certainly cannot be relied upon to identify the causes of such events accurately. The examples given above illustrate this point vividly.

Turning to the second problem, when historians narrate just part of the history of an historical subject, or just one of the possible patterns they can find in an historical period, do they necessarily give a biased, misleading impression of the subject or period as a whole? They do not, if they admit that they have no intention of describing the subject or period as a whole. The problem arises when they make no such admission, and readers assume they intend to provide a comprehensive account of the subject or period, and so read the partial account as representing the whole. Historians are not always as careful about the fairness of their narratives as they should be.

But even narratives that present a comprehensive account of an historical subject are selective. Biographies of Winston Churchill, for example, focus upon his political activities and his literary achievements, but say little about his personal life, the minute details of which would be very boring. Perhaps we should say that the subject of such biographies is not his life as a whole, but his public life. However, even narratives more or less confined to the public life of Churchill will not be exhaustive, selecting the more important events in that life, and not recording every tiny detail of his political and literary moves. Selection of this kind is not misleading so long as the historian maintains a consistent degree of detail and level of generality, as was explained above.

Chapter 6

Judging historical interpretations

Historians often structure their narratives about the past to illustrate a colligatory or general interpretation of the events they describe. Examples of this practice were examined in the previous chapter. All such interpretations are expected to be credible, fair and intelligible.

The credibility of historical interpretations

The reading public expect historians' descriptions of the past to be credible. That means that there is good reason for believing them to be true. As was explained in Chapters 1 and 3, we cannot prove that any descriptions of the world are necessarily true, for we cannot prove what an ideal explanatory theory of all possible perceptual experiences would be. But when a description of the world is strongly supported by other beliefs, and there is no good reason for believing it false, then it is usually reasonable to believe that it is true.

There are several different kinds of description of the past which are expected to be credible. These include commonsense descriptions of past events and causal relations, descriptions of colligatory patterns discerned among past events, and summary descriptions of historical subjects. Ways of justifying several of these were discussed in Chapter 3. Here I want to consider some objections to the possibility of establishing the credibility of colligatory and summary descriptions of the past. Some of these have been touched upon elsewhere, but it is useful to consider them together here. There are four main lines of criticism about the credibility of these kinds of historical interpretation, which will be discussed in turn.

Hermeneutical circles

Colligatory and summary interpretations of the past which use well-defined words are judged to be true if the particular events to which they refer warrant the use of those words and descriptions. For instance, if a political revolution is a sudden, often violent change in the government and the constitution of a country, then clearly there was a political revolution in England in 1648, in

France in 1789 and in Russia in 1917. In each case royal government was effectively abolished and replaced by a republican one.

The first objection is that the particular facts which warrant a general interpretation are in fact understood in the light of that interpretation. In recent years this objection has been made by Robert Berkhofer. In his book *Beyond the Great Story*, Berkhofer emphasizes the point that particular facts of history acquire their meaning by being placed in an historical context. 'The problem with historical facts', he writes, 'as with histories themselves, is that they are constructions and interpretations of the past. Evidence is not fact until given meaning in accordance with some framework or perspective' (Berkhofer, 1995, p. 53). So the facts have no independent existence outside the context in which they are placed. Berkhofer is aware that historians normally defend their interpretations by appeal to the facts, as we have seen above, but he dismisses such arguments as nothing more than empty rhetoric: 'modern rhetorical analysis, as it did classically, treats both the logic and the stylistics of argument as parts of a presentation meant to persuade its hearers or readers' (ibid., p. 80; and see p. 101).

The mistake in this argument lies in the assumption that because historical events acquire meaning from their context, the context must be that of the general interpretation they are used to support. If it were, we would indeed have a case of hermeneutical circles: the plausibility of the general interpretation depending upon that of the events it interprets, and the plausibility of descriptions of those events depending upon that of the general interpretation to which they contribute. In fact, however, the meaning of commonsense events is normally given by their commonsense, everyday context, quite independently of the general interpretation they are later used to support. Their credibility is not a function of that of the interpretation in which they occur.

Just occasionally the significance of a piece of historical evidence does depend on a complex interpretation of which it is a part. This is sometimes true of descriptions of people's intentions, which are decided by judging which account of them fits best with the actions performed by the agent, in the context in which the actions occurred. Most often, however, historical facts are established independently of the complex interpretations of which they are a part.

The subjectivity of historians' perspectives

There are two versions of this objection, neither of which is at all impressive.

The first depends upon a contrast between observable, material things in the world, such as people and their activities, and historians' ideas about the patterns which those activities form. Descriptions of people and their activities can be true or false, because they can have happened in the world. But historians' ideas about the patterns formed by those activities seem to exist in the historians' heads alone. So it seems that descriptions of them cannot refer to anything real in the world. They are just expressions of how the events seem to the historians. As

F.R. Ankersmit put it: 'Generalizations do not express any truths on the nature of (socio-historical) *reality*; they only reflect regularities in how we have actually *decided* to conceptualize reality' (Ankersmit, 1983, p. 160). He says that 'the past itself has no narrative pattern or structure' (ibid., p. 110). According to Ankersmit, 'the "historical landscape" is not *given* to the historian; he has to *construct* it. . . . The structure of the narratio [narrative] is a structure *lent* to or *pressed* on the past and not the reflection of a kindred structure objectively present in the past itself' (ibid., p. 86).

Ankersmit no longer insists upon this point, and indeed seems to deny it (see McCullagh, 2000, pp. 57–9). There are many social facts which supervene upon particular actions, yet are regarded as real just the same. For example, a game of football depends upon a lot of particulars, people behaving according to certain rules in a certain physical context, yet no-one would deny that the game actually occurred. Similarly, an election depends upon voters registering their preferences through particular actions, but the election is real enough. Likewise, a revolution depends upon a pattern of particular actions, but can be said to exist because those actions occurred. Certainly general colligatory concepts exist in the minds of historians, but the events they describe can be quite real.

The second form of this objection denies the objectivity of colligatory and general patterns of events on the grounds that historians always represent the past in ways which accord with their interests and values, as can be seen by studying their writing on any particular topic. Consequently it is naïve and mistaken to suppose that any general interpretation of the past could be objective and so credible. This is the argument presented by Peter Novick in the introduction to his massive history of American historiography entitled *That Noble Dream* (Novick, 1988). There he wrote that the concept of objective history 'promotes an unreal and misleading invidious distinction between, on the one hand, historical accounts "distorted" by ideological assumptions and purposes; on the other, history free of these taints' (ibid., p. 6).

There is no doubt that historians often draw attention to patterns in the past which interest them. But that does not mean their descriptions cannot be rationally justified, as Novick seems to assume. Those few who write 'top-down' history often impose a pattern on the past that suits their interests. But most historians are careful to check their general interpretations against the known facts, to ensure that they are warranted. If they make a mistake, their colleagues will usually point it out, as we have seen.

Most historical generalizations are false

This objection applies particularly to general summary interpretations of the past, which can provide the structure of historical narratives. It is almost always the case that generalizations about the past are strictly false, in that there are some exceptions to them. This is a particular problem for very general summary interpretations, as their scope is often great and the opportunities for exceptions are numerous. Those general interpretations which are meant to be comprehensive, to give an accurate and fair impression of a subject, are frequently criticized for overlooking important exceptions.

In a paper on interpretations of the motives for the American Revolution, T.H. Breen has drawn attention to the inadequacies of some well known accounts of it. Traditionally the dispute between the Americans and the British has been presented as one over taxation without representation, but he said that this would scarcely account for 'the shrill, even paranoid, tone of public discourse in the colonies' (Breen, 1997, p. 31). Bernard Bailyn had suggested that Americans were passionately concerned about the possibility of royal despotism and government by a corrupt court, and saw British taxes as evidence of this. But this interpretation, said Breen, 'does not seem sufficient to account for the sudden sense of personal humiliation. The extraordinary bitterness and acrimony of colonial rhetoric requires us to consider the popular fear that the English were systematically relegating Americans to second-class standing within the empire.' The complaint of Americans that their 'British Brothers' were treating them like 'negroes' 'cannot be easily explained as an American echo of English political opposition' (ibid., pp. 31–2). Here are features of the motives for the American Revolution that Breen believed previous general interpretations cannot accommodate.

Breen offers his own interpretation of the American motives. It is quite interesting, but its generalizations are so sweeping that one must suspect that it too is inaccurate. His interpretation can be summarized thus. Before the 1760s, Americans considered themselves to be British, of equal standing with the English. 'They believed that the English accepted them as full partners in the British Empire, allies in the continuing wars against France, devout defenders of Protestantism, and eager participants in an expanding world of commerce' (p. 27). With the imposition of the Stamp Act, Breen says, Americans suddenly discovered that the English did not regard them as equals at all. 'The source of anger was not so much parliamentary taxation without representation as it was the sudden realization that the British really regarded white colonial Americans as second-class beings, indeed as persons so inferior from the metropolitan perspective that they somehow deserved a lesser measure of freedom' (p. 29). After their intense loyalty during the Seven Years' War, 'the colonists felt badly betrayed' (p. 31). Their response was to seek independence, so as to restore their dignity, and to this end they 'took up the language of natural rights liberalism with unprecedented fervor' (p. 34). Before the 1760s they were not much interested in that political theory, but after the Stamp Act they found it 'emotionally compelling' (p. 35). Liberal theory 'owed much of its initial popularity to its effectiveness as a rhetorical strategy' (p. 37). It legitimated the declaration and war of independence which followed. And the new nation gave the people a new American identity.

Should we accept Breen's interpretation? Breen argues that his interpretation captures more features of the revolution than others have. There are some reasons for questioning it, however. Consider three questions which responsible historians will ask of all such general interpretations. First, one can ask whether all Americans shared the characteristics attributed to them. In this case that means asking whether all Americans involved in the war against Britain were strongly motivated by a sense of betrayal and humiliation. Second, one can query whether this motive was indeed the strongest motive activating them. I agree with Breen that explanations confined to theories of natural rights scarcely account for the passion of the revolutionaries. But that passion could be explained as resentment towards Britain for draining the wealth of Americans without consultation, a resentment based not simply on the judgement that doing so was unjust, but on natural self-interest. People readily become passionate about others taking their money. One must allow for complexity of motivation: passion and conviction both play a part in producing most actions. Finally, one can examine each of the major stages of a conflict to see whether the Americans really did hold the attitudes Breen ascribes to them, and whether their actions had other important motives as well. It is disconcerting to find that Breen does not consider these questions in presenting his interpretation. I doubt that the kind of resentment he describes was felt by all Americans, and that it was the most important reason for their revolution. I suspect Breen is fond of the psychological theory which explains actions as expressions of emotion, and simply wants to apply it to this period of history.

Lyotard's attack upon the grand narrative schemes of history was extended to all generalizations, indiscriminately (see McCullagh, 1998, pp. 298–302). Rather than generalize about the past, Lyotard recommended that historians confine themselves to little stories of particular events, not necessarily of any general consequence. I suspect that he did so because he believed generalizations are always produced in order to legitimate the oppressive use of power. My present concern is that they are almost always slightly inaccurate, and therefore perhaps unworthy of belief. Why should we accord them the credibility that we normally do?

The summary generalizations in question are not lawlike, and so are not used in drawing inferences from evidence or in explaining actions and events in the past. But they draw attention to relationships which might have wider significance. If many Americans resented being treated as inferior to Englishmen so much as to rebel against their rule, this fact might be relevant to other governments that treat one section of their empire as inferior to others. Similarly, if religious concerns motivated the English Revolution against royal government, such concerns could motivate rebellions in other countries. We ignore such historical information at our peril. The fact that not all Americans resented Britain, and not all of the English rebels fought for religious freedom does not diminish the significance of the generalizations. It is enough that a very large number did, for the generalization to be significant. Nevertheless, historians still have a duty to make their generalizations as accurate as they can, at their chosen level of generality to avoid being misleading.

Historical interpretations are commonly contested

Historians often make their reputations by attacking previous interpretations of an historical subject and proposing a new interpretation in its place. We have just seen an example of that with Breen's discussion of the motivation of the American Revolution. There is no doubt that many historical interpretations are soon superseded, so is it not unreasonable to believe any of them to be true? This is the most telling objection to the credibility of historical interpretations

There are three common reasons for proposing a new interpretation of an historical subject or period. The first is that new evidence is examined, yielding information that requires a change in previously reasonable accounts of the subject. The second is that historians find significance in aspects of the subject which previous historians had overlooked. And the third is that historians adopt an explanatory theory, rather as Breen did, which has been scarcely noticed in the past.

The effect of new evidence upon an historical interpretation can vary. Often it modifies part of a commonsense narrative of a subject, leaving much of the account as credible as ever. But new information can wreak havoc upon generalizations in history. Evidence of this is to be found in economic history, where statistical methods of the 'new economic history' have led to discoveries which severely qualify old generalizations. John A. Davis reports that W.W. Rostow's model of economic take-off, in his book *The Stages of Economic Growth: A Non-Communist Manifesto* (1960), generated a lot of research which cast doubt on the validity of the model.

> As the empirical evidence generated by . . . research agendas built up, so too did the doubts over the validity of the theories that inspired them. Rather than demonstrating the validity of the concept of a sudden 'take-off', for example, research has tended to suggest that relatively slow, often lumpy and even discontinuous processes of economic development and industrialization were most generally the case.
>
> (Davis, 1989, p. 47)

Responsible historians will know whether the instances of generalizations they have studied constitute a significant, representative sample or not (see McCullagh, 1984, pp. 144–9). If they do not, they should warn readers of this, so that they can treat the generalization with the degree of scepticism it deserves. Impressionistic history, which has no statistical basis, is the most unreliable of all. Lack of adequate data is the most important reason for doubting historical generalizations.

A second reason for changes in summary interpretations of the past lies in changes in the sort of thing historians are interested in. This is particularly evident in general causal explanations of major events. Over the past century or so, historians were first interested in the role of the ideology of leaders in bringing those changes about, then in the economic interests of the leaders and their followers, following Marx in seeing ideology as mere justification for the pursuit of economic interests, and finally in the motivation of the mass of people who followed the leaders, particularly in the discourse and symbols which moved them. One can trace these shifts in the historiography of the English, American and French revolutions, for example, without difficulty.

Accompanying these changes of interest went a change in the popularity of general theories of historical change, from Whig to Marxist to Postmodern. In fact, as was said in Chapter 3, people are moved by ideas, and interests and discourses. All three can influence human behaviour. Some historians give more weight to one of these causes than to others, but there is little theoretical justification for doing so. Nevertheless the uncertainty about their relative importance is a source of instability among historical explanations.

In the light of these facts, historians should be sceptical of summary generalizations which have an inadequate statistical basis, or which emphasize some of the range of relevant causes while ignoring others. Conscientious historians will be careful to inform readers when these conditions obtain, and warn them that acceptance of the generalization must be tentative. Note that one does not have to wait for a generalization to be disconfirmed before doubting its validity. Insufficient evidence in support of it is reason enough. And the worry remains that a new explanatory theory might be discovered which makes previous explanations inadequate.

Fairness

When a commonsense narrative, a colligatory narrative or a summary interpretation is presented as a comprehensive account of a designated historical subject, it is expected to provide not only a credible but also a fair account of that subject. A partial account can be credible without being fair, describing the good features of a person, for example, but ignoring the bad. There might be good reason to believe the good features did exist, but if no mention is made of the bad, then the overall impression of the person's character given by the history will be misleading.

There are three common ways in which histories can be unfair and so misleading. One is of the kind just described, where an historian correctly describes part of a subject, thereby giving a false impression of the whole. A second is when an historian picks out some of the important causes of an event, but does not mention them all. And third, partial histories can give a misleading impression of who were responsible for certain important historical events. Historians' concern for each of these forms of fairness is evident in their comments upon Conrad Russell's explanation of the English Civil War (in Russell, 1990). So to illustrate them, let me describe Russell's interpretation and report the criticisms made of it.

The fairness of historical descriptions

General causal interpretations of history always include general descriptions of certain states of affairs. The first way in which such interpretations can be criticized for lack of fairness concerns the fairness of such descriptions. As we have just seen, they are misleading when the description they offer, while correctly describing part of a subject, gives a false impression of the whole. Often there are some minor exceptions to historical generalizations, but when there are many exceptions, then a responsible historian will admit as much, and qualify the generalization accordingly. Admittedly there is room for subjective judgement here in deciding how many exceptions are tolerable. I suspect that the degree of accuracy depends in part upon the purpose for which the generalization is offered. If the discussion is a statistical one, then an accurate percentage might be required. If a general impression is all that is required, there is more room for latitude, but a careful historian will acknowledge the exceptions, especially when to ignore them results in a misunderstanding.

Russell begins his account of the causes of the English Civil War by describing relations between king and parliament under James I and Charles I until the 1630s. He presents parliament as generally supportive of the crown, with parliamentarians believing this to be their loyal duty. Critics have objected that this picture is somewhat misleading, for it ignores quite serious disagreements between the king and parliament. Richard Cust and Ann Hughes have explained the objection. Russell, they say, has

> stressed the desire for unity and harmony in early Stuart politics and denied the existence of any fundamental ideological cleavages between king and parliament that would have predisposed them to conflict. . . .
>
> These views on the structure and ideology of English politics and the nature of parliaments have proved controversial. At the level of political ideas, Johann Sommerville has argued that there were fundamental differences over issues such as the degree of consent that was required before the king could levy taxes, the extent to which his freedom of action was circumscribed by law and the scope of parliament's role as king's adviser and representative of the people. Spokesmen for the royal prerogative tended to advance an absolutist interpretation of such matters, arguing that ultimately the king was answerable only to God, while proponents of the common law and government by consent insisted that the king's powers were limited.
>
> (Cust and Hughes, 1997, pp. 5–6)

Russell went on to say that much of the tension which arose between the court and the parliament was caused by parliamentarians putting local interests and concerns ahead of national ones, and failing in their duty to support the crown by authorizing the taxes needed for good government. In particular this left the king with inadequate forces to defeat the Scots in 1639–40. Critics have found two parts of this interpretation to be misleading. First, 'a growing body of work . . . has argued that local inhabitants were much less self-contained and inward looking' than Russell assumed (ibid., p. 15). Clive Holmes has found that many 'were well informed and deeply concerned about national religious and constitutional issues . . . [and] participated in a national political culture' (quoted ibid., p. 16). Hughes concludes that 'the opposition to Charles was not particularist, concerned only with a variety of local or privileged interests, but general, concerned with the nature and direction of one central government' (Hughes, 1998, p. 57). There was undoubtedly some concern with local issues among the MPs, but it is misleading to suggest that this was their only concern, or even their major one.

Second, Russell's assertion that parliament would not raise taxes for the crown is also misleading. As Hughes puts it: 'Russell's picture of a House of Commons simply avoiding unpleasant realities is partial' (ibid., p. 27). Certainly it was not enthusiastic about raising taxes, but it did so in May and June 1641. (And see Cust and Hughes, 1989, p. 30.) So here is another description of the past which is thought to be unfair.

The fairness of causal explanations

The second way in which general causal interpretations can be unfair is that they might identify some important causes of the event being explained, but not all. Once historians have chosen a form of causal explanation, they are expected to include all the relevant causes, at the appropriate level of generality and at the appropriate degree of detail. The level of generality and degree of detail relevant to this judgement are those generally adopted in the book or paper in which the interpretation occurs. Brief books usually describe only the major causes, that is, those which substantially increased the probability of the outcome in the circumstances. Books of greater detail supply minor causes as well. Again, there is room for personal judgement here, but critics are sure to object when major causes of an event are ignored.

Russell was inclined to blame the breakdown in relations between king and parliament, and the final war between them, on failures of royal administration. He explains how the Civil War came about by identifying seven important causes in the events leading up to it. First are the Bishops' Wars against the Scottish Covenanters, which broke out in 1639. Russell writes that 'there is no doubt that they started the immediate sequence of events which led to the English Civil War . . . and . . . without them, it could not have happened in the way it did' (Russell, 1990, p. 11). The English were defeated, and the king would normally have arranged a political settlement bringing peace between the Scots and English. The failure to make such a settlement is Russell's second important cause of the English Civil War, for the continuing demands of the Scots provided a focus for opposition activity. The third was the king's failure to dissolve or prorogue the parliament in 1641. 'A dissolution or prorogation would have left the King, even if badly shaken, still in possession of the field, and would therefore have left a very different power structure from the one which ultimately resulted' (p. 16). Next came the division of parliament and the nation into two roughly equal parties. Russell points out that the differences between them were of long standing, and by themselves did not produce war (p. 19). In the Lords, the opposition came from those who thought 'that politics was too important to be left to kings', and wanted the king to take parliament's advice. In the Commons, the opposition was largely from men who desired 'further reformation' along Calvinist lines (p. 20). In this they reflected the opinion of many towns and counties in the country. Russell's sixth cause of the war was the failure of the opposed parties to negotiate a peaceful resolution of their differences, which he explains as the result of both sides 'concentrating on trying to win support in Scotland which might have made their opponents afraid to fight' (p. 22). His seventh and final cause is the king's 'diminished majesty', that is his failure to command respect and obedience, especially in parliament.

This is a very idiosyncratic list of the causes of the Civil War. One would have expected it to include the challenge to royal authority presented by the Irish rebellion in October 1641, the Grand Remonstrance, a list of objections to royal rule presented by the Commons in November 1641, King Charles's impeachment of five leading members of the House of Commons in January 1642, and parliament's raising an army under the Earl of Essex in July. But Russell is more impressed by the failure of the king to maintain order than by the development of ideological opposition to royal autocracy as the cause of the war.

There is strong evidence, however, of several passionately held objections to Charles I's government, which motivated hostility towards him. Sommerville, for example, defends his claim that parliament opposed the crown for ideological reasons by quoting its Declaration of August 1642, 'setting forth the grounds and reasons that necessitate them at this time to take up defensive arms for the preservation of his majesty's person, the maintenance of true religion, the laws and liberties of this kingdom, and the power and privilege of Parliament' (Sommerville, 1989, p. 47). He also quotes statements by Henry Parker, John Pym, William Prynne and others, giving similar reasons for opposing the crown. He concludes:

> So there is good contemporary evidence for supposing that many Parliamentarians in the 1640s believed they were fighting against the attempts of the King or his evil counsellors to subvert the English system of government and to introduce 'arbitrary' power. There is evidence, too, that they believed these attempts dated back at least to 1625. Yet, in much recent writing on the origins of the Civil War, this type of explanation has been given short shrift, and the suggestion has been advanced that the war had few if any long-term origins.
>
> (ibid., pp. 48–9)

Sommerville goes on to elaborate the evidence for political debates over royal prerogative, and in a final section examines the arguments presented by revisionists such as Russell for their view that consensus prevailed. He points out that although some defended the crown's rights, for example to tax without consent, others denied them. And even after the concessions made by the king to parliament in 1641–2 (see Hughes, 1998, pp. 160–1), many did not trust him to respect parliamentary rights in the future.

Another to object to revisionist explanations of the war is John Morrill. He adduces evidence for the importance of objections to the king's policy on religion as an important reason for attacks upon his government. He writes 'that the localist and legal-constitutionalist perceptions of misgovernment lacked the momentum, the passion, to bring about the kind of civil war which England experienced after 1642', and that 'it was the force of religion that drove minorities to fight, and forced majorities to make reluctant choices' (Morrill, 1997, p. 161). The evidence on which he bases his case is the behaviour of the Long Parliament during its first session. It was slow to pass statutes limiting royal powers, or to penalize those who had enforced royal policies (p. 164); whereas it was quick to condemn Laud's programme of Arminian teaching (against predestination, and in favour of salvation through the sacraments) and (popish) practices in the church. 'From the outset, the reform of the church was more contentious, more impulsive, and more divisive . . .' (p. 167). Clerics were judged and punished for Arminian tendencies (p. 168). Also, a vast literature appeared on religious matters, but very little on constitutional concerns (p. 170). There were passionate debates for and against episcopacy, and it was this issue which drove people to war (pp. 175–6). Clearly the Civil War was not simply the result of poor administration by the crown.

The fairness of ascriptions of responsibility

The third common way in which historical interpretations are often judged to be unfair is in their attribution of responsibility for historical events. It comes as no surprise to learn that at the time of the Civil War, the royalists blamed the Puritans and the Puritans blamed the royalists. Ann Hughes writes: 'there existed two rival conspiracy theories which explained religious and political conflict; both were rational and each reinforced the other' (Hughes, 1998, p. 113). The king and his supporters feared 'the incipient egalitarianism of Calvinism' (p. 109); and others linked the court's imposition of Arminian observances with a plot to restore papal authority in Britain (p. 112). Each side blamed the other for the conflict, claiming that it was defending its traditional rights against attack from the other.

Historians are expected to be much less biased in their judgements of responsibility. Of course both sides were partially responsible for the English Civil War. Judgements of responsibility are based upon an analysis of the causes of an event, and so vary with that analysis. Causal responsibility is not enough for moral responsibility, however. To be morally responsible for an event, people must not only help to bring it about, but do so knowingly and freely, or, if they act blindly, be responsible for their blindness. Furthermore, to be praised or blamed for their actions they must be judged against certain standards which it was reasonable to expect them to uphold. This is where difficulties arise, for who should decide the standard which it is reasonable to expect people to uphold? The king and the parliament clearly held different standards of royal behaviour.

Conrad Russell, for example, regarded the royal expenses as normal, whereas others sometimes regarded them as excessive (Hughes, 1998, pp. 25–6); and Russell considered parliament's reluctance to sanction the taxes requested by the crown as irresponsible, whereas others argued that it was justified in order to the win the just concessions they sought. As Hughes remarks: 'Much of Conrad Russell's analysis of the "functional breakdown" is from the monarch's point of view: their financial problems were intractable and the failure to solve them is attributed mainly to the localism and irresponsibility of members of the House of Commons' (ibid., p. 25).

I suggest that it is so difficult for historians to decide what standards people can reasonably be expected to have maintained, that they should not attempt to praise or blame people for what they did in the past. They can, however, often make a reasonable judgement about the degree to which people acted freely and knowingly in bringing about certain events. They often know what pressures were being brought to bear on agents, and whether or not agents could have predicted the outcome of their actions. In short, historians can often hold people morally responsible for their behaviour, without praising or blaming them for what happened. A fair interpretation will mention all the actions, at the appropriate level of generality and degree of detail, which people performed knowing they could well lead to the event which is being explained. Charles I could have anticipated popular objection to his expenditure on the court and on wars with Spain, and also objection to his promotion of Armenian church-manship. It was harder, I suspect, for the Puritans to anticipate the amount of support the king would receive, once they made their demands plain. It would be interesting to examine the evidence of their deliberations with this question in mind.

Clearly, it is sometimes difficult to decide whether or not people were respon-sible for events which their actions brought about. But it can often be quite clear that certain people knew the consequences of their actions, and deliberately brought them about. A fair history is one in which all those who are clearly morally responsible for an event are identified, relative to the appropriate level of generality and degree of detail.

Conrad Russell's general interpretation of the causes of the English Civil War has thus been criticized as unfair in each of the three ways I have mentioned. It includes unfair descriptions; its account of the causes of the war is unfair; and its claim that the war was the result of the irresponsibility of the members of the House of Commons, together with some foolish mistakes by the king, is unfair as well. Russell's colleagues were able to point out these inadequacies and to some extent correct them.

How fair is the corrected account of the Civil War? There is so much documentary evidence of the time, and the conflicts were so numerous and complex, that it is very difficult indeed to be sure that any account of it is entirely fair. Here one must rely on successive generations of historians gradually improving on the accounts that have gone before.

The idea of an historical interpretation being largely right but capable of improvement is one that deserves attention. In science the analogy is with theories which are largely accepted as a sort of paradigm, but are modified and improved with further inquiry. Perhaps there are degrees of fairness.

In practice historians judge the fairness of an interpretation in relation to the evidence relating to it of which they are aware. Their aim, however, is to produce an account of an historical subject which is fair relative to all possible evidence of the subject. Once again the question of the degree to which available evidence represents all possible evidence becomes an important question. For example, if historians have studied a large and varied, representative sample of the pamphlets produced during the English Revolution, then they might reasonably claim to have a fair idea of the views they all expressed. When there is a mass of evidence, as in this case, the chance of new evidence making much difference to the significance of what is already at hand is quite slight. On other topics, for which little evidence is available, this might not be the case. On the basis of little evidence historians can seldom be very confident that they have a fair idea of their subject.

The intelligibility of historical interpretations

Colligatory and summary interpretations of historical events make the events they interpret intelligible by drawing attention to important goals which those events were intended to achieve, important values which they expressed, or important outcomes which they in fact brought about. In these ways they display patterns of significance which would not be noticed if the events they interpret were considered in isolation. Often these patterns themselves become the subjects of further historical inquiry.

Examples of colligatory and summary interpretations presented in the previous chapter illustrate these points well. Walsh gave examples of colligatory interpretations, one of which showed how many acts of German foreign policy could be related to Hitler's policy 'of German self-assertion and expansion'. He also explained how certain values characterized those activities colligated as the Enlightenment, the Romantic movement, the age of reform in nineteenth-century England and the rise of monopoly capitalism. Formal colligatory terms on the other hand, identifying types of change such as growths and declines, revolutions and evolutions, do not help us understand why the changes they refer to occurred, though they do supply interesting information about kinds of change that occurred that might not otherwise have been noticed.

Similarly, some summary interpretations add to the intelligibility of the events they describe and others simply sum up their structure. When Woods summed up the life of Senator Fulbright as one dedicated to encouraging people and states to pursue informed, rational self-determination as the best basis for personal and national progress, he contributed significantly to our understanding of the man. Summary interpretations of the English Civil War attempted to identify the main groups involved in the conflict and describe the values which united them. So, while providing a summary of the structure of that conflict, they also added to our understanding of the motives which produced it.

Sometimes an historical interpretation makes a set of events intelligible in all three ways mentioned above. An interpretation of the French Revolution, for example, would normally describe the goals of its leaders to which their decisions and actions could be related, the groups involved and the values that moved people to support them, and the stages by which the revolution was so quickly accomplished.

Once a general pattern of events has been identified, such as a cultural movement, a civil war or a political revolution, historians often consider it to be an event in its own right, and discuss why it occurred as and when it did, and what effects it had.

Although colligatory and summary interpretations contribute to the intelligibility of the events they colligate or summarize, they inevitably do so in a very general way, pointing to general goals that many actions were designed to achieve, or general values that were manifest in many cultural and political pursuits. The individual events they interpret are made more intelligible within the body of the narrative, where their occurrence is explained in detail. However, colligatory and summary interpretations often identify general underlying aspirations and values that individual explanations ignore. In effect they help to provide a slightly more profound explanation of the events they refer to than is provided by the narrative itself.

Chapter 7

Causes and conditions in history

Historians study causes all the time: what caused their evidence to have the features it has; what caused people to hold and express the beliefs that they did; what caused people to act as they did; what caused certain changes to occur in society; and so on. Causes have a dynamic function: they bring about changes. Conditions are the circumstances in which changes occur. Some are necessary for the changes to occur, and historians take most of these for granted. Others are comparative states of affairs, which can explain why one effect occurred rather than another.

For an event to be correctly identified as a cause of a certain effect, it must satisfy certain logical and scientific conditions. Most causes are necessary for the occurrence of their effect, in the circumstances; and all increase the probability of that effect. These are logical conditions they must satisfy. Furthermore, judgements about the necessity and sufficiency of causes for their effects depend upon previous observations of such events, more or less scientific inquiry. For historians to know whether they have correctly identified causes and conditions in history, it will help if they know what they are like. This chapter will begin by describing causes and conditions in history, and then devote a few sections to methods of checking them out.

The nature of causes and conditions in history

Once you look for references to causes in historical narratives, you find them everywhere. Here is a simple example from James M. McPherson's history of the American Civil War. In May 1862, a Northern Republican army under General McClellan threatened the Southern Confederate forces under General Johnston and was about to attack the town of Richmond in Virginia. McPherson says that the Southern general, Johnston, moved his Confederate forces south, closer to Richmond, in order to defend it. McPherson comments: 'While perhaps prudent militarily, this retreat had adverse political consequences. Coming amid other Confederate reverses, it added to the depression of public morale' (McPherson, 1988, p. 423). The Northern attack under McClellan proceeded slowly. 'Frequent rains had impeded operations during April; even heavier rains bogged down the armies during May.' A flotilla of Northern gunboats on the James

River, which hoped to sail up the river and bombard Richmond, was stopped by Confederate batteries of guns mounted on a bank high above the river, which the gunboats were unable to dislodge. The ships' guns 'could not be elevated enough to hit the batteries on the ninety-foot bluff' (p. 427). Richmond was safe, and did not fall until 1865.

This is a typical historical narrative, full of causal statements as you can see. Johnston's movement of his forces south *caused* public morale in the South to fall further. Frequent rains *caused* the armies to move slowly and finally *caused* them to be bogged down, stuck in the mud. The Confederate batteries of guns *caused* the Northern flotilla of ships to stop sailing up to Richmond.

When you examine the causal statements provided by historians, you find that every one of them, both simple and complex, has two dimensions. One can call these 'logical' and 'scientific'. Every relation is of a certain logical kind. For instance, the occurrence of causes is usually necessary in the circumstances for the occurrence of their effects. (When there is more than one sufficient cause for an effect, the causes are jointly, but not individually, necessary for their effect in the circumstances.) And all causes are sufficient to increase the probability of such an effect. As was mentioned before, these are the logical characteristics of causes. To identify particular causes, historians have to draw upon general knowledge of the world, which is more or less scientifically based. To identify the cause of a disease, for example, an historian needs medical knowledge. That is clearly the product of science. To find the reason for an action, however, an historian must use a commonsense theory of mind, relating beliefs, values, attitudes and intentions to actions. Such theories have been refined through careful observation, as studies of emotion, for example, reveal. However, often historians draw upon commonsense theories of human nature which they have not acquired from specialized scientific studies. The commonsense theories are scientific in that they have succeeded in making sense of masses of observable behaviour. But they have not always been rigorously tested. (Several theories about the motivation of human behaviour were discussed in Chapter 4.)

Let me illustrate the logical and scientific features of causal statements by discussing some of the examples provided by McPherson's narrative.

(1) Causes are events whose occurrence was necessary for the occurrence of their effects, in the circumstances. That means, if the cause had not occurred, the effect would not have been the same. All the causes mentioned in this passage were necessary for their effects. If Johnston had not retreated, public morale would not have fallen as it did. If it had not rained heavily, then the armies would not have been impeded and finally bogged. If the Confederate guns had not protected Richmond so well, the flotilla of gunboats on the James River would probably have taken the city.

Notice that causes in history are not universally necessary for their effects, they are only necessary for them in the circumstances. For instance, in the circumstances it was Johnston's apparent retreat towards Richmond which depressed Southern morale further. That was not the only thing which could depress

Southern morale. Humiliating defeats in battle had depressed the South before. But at the time in question, the further drop in morale would not have occurred if Johnston had not led his forces south. It was necessary for that event, in the circumstances.

Sometimes several different causes contribute to an outcome, usually in such a way that the outcome would have been different at least in degree had any one of those causes been absent. As I said, the movement of Johnston's troops was not the only event which lowered morale in the South. The loss of two forts to Northern troops shortly before, Fort Henry and Fort Donelson, was largely responsible for its demoralization. The withdrawal of Johnston's troops just deepened their depression.

Occasionally there are several causes of an event, each of which was sufficient to produce it. For instance, if several soldiers in a firing squad shot a man through the heart, any one of those bullets would have killed him. In these cases we say the effect was 'overdetermined' by its causes. Now you can argue that no single bullet wound was necessary for the victim's death, for if it had not existed the man would still have died from the other bullets entering his heart. All we can say is that if none of the bullets had done so, he would not have died as he did. So in cases of such simultaneous overdetermination, we cannot isolate any cause as particularly important. We can only say that the collection of causes produced the outcome. Cases like this are very rare, however. Generally there are several causes of historical events, each of which made a discernible difference. Thus several events lowered Southern morale, each driving it lower than before.

(2) Causes are events which tend to produce certain outcomes, but this tendency can be offset by other tendencies at work in the situation. The decision to send gunships up the river to bombard Richmond was an event which, if unimpeded, would probably have resulted in the destruction of much of Richmond; but that tendency was impeded by the Southern guns, which fired down on the ships from cliffs, so that the original plan was abandoned.

So causes do not always produce their customary effects. Rather, they increase the probability of those effects occurring in the circumstances, so long as no other tendencies impede them. (Philosophers say that causes increase 'the objective chance' of their effects occurring (Paul Humphreys, 1989) or that they increase 'the propensity' of their effects' occurrence (Hugh Mellor, 1995).) The actual outcome of a causal process is a function of the various tendencies at work, furthering or impeding a certain kind of effect. Quite literally, for example, the progress of the Northern army was a function of the power of the horses and men to go forward and the power of the mud to restrain them. As the rains persisted, the power of the mud finally prevailed.

Sometimes an event makes a consequence very probable without actually causing it. Thus a drop in a barometer makes it very probable that there will be a storm, but it would not cause the storm. The drop in the barometer was merely a symptom of the real cause, which was a sudden fall in air pressure. To exclude cases like this, we require that causes not only increase the probability of their effects, but have been necessary for their occurrence as well. The change in the barometer was clearly not necessary for the occurrence of the storm, which would have occurred had there been no barometer at all.

(3) Some philosophers are content to rest their analysis of causation at this point, but I think causal processes can be analysed in more detail. Causes are events of a special kind. One could say that a cause is a process in which an event triggers a disposition in something to produce a tendency to bring about a certain kind of effect. Thus rain triggers the disposition of soil to turn into mud, so that it in fact tends to become mud. And mud has a disposition to retard the wheels of heavily laden wagons and heavy guns, and when the Northern army's wagons and guns encountered the mud, that disposition was triggered, and the mud tended to slow them down. Things can have dispositions which are never triggered: if it never rained, the disposition of soil to turn to mud would never be triggered; and if wagons and guns never entered a muddy field, its disposition to retard them would never be activated.

Very often the disposition of things to behave in certain ways is a function of their microstructure. Thus soil turns to mud when wet, whereas gravel does not, because of its microstructure. One way of explaining a causal reaction is to describe the microprocess which produces it. For example, water tends to rust iron, and it does so because oxygen in the water binds with the iron to form iron oxide. The iron atoms release electrons to the oxygen, so that the oxygen atoms become negatively charged and the iron atoms positively charged, and the two bond loosely together, leaving hydrogen as a residue. We say that the macro-process 'supervenes' upon the relatively small microprocess. This is an example from chemistry, but the same occurs frequently in social science. Social changes can often be explained as a function of the individual actions upon which they supervene. It is only the dispositions of fundamental particles which cannot be explained in this way.

The third important feature of causes, then, is that they are processes in which events trigger dispositions to produce tendencies of a certain kind. The trigger event alone does not produce the tendency for an effect to occur in a regular manner; only the triggering of a certain disposition does that. That is why the trigger event alone is not the cause of the consequent tendency.

(4) Particular causal relations are always instances of general laws. Causal relations between natural events are instances of universal laws of nature, like the laws of physics and chemistry. Causal relations involving human behaviour are often instances of laws of psychology, economics and perhaps other social sciences. These, like the laws of nature, represent ideal situations which are seldom perfectly instantiated in history.

Reference to general laws is necessary in order to distinguish accidental sequences of events from genuine causal relations. For a cause to be necessary in the circumstances for a certain effect, so that the latter would not have been the same without it, there must have been a set of conditions necessary for its occurrence including the cause in question. It sometimes takes scientific inquiry to distinguish the symptom of a cause, which is not necessary for an effect, from the cause itself. Similarly, for a cause to increase the probability of an effect, it must be the case that such causes regularly do so.

In centuries past, people connected illness with sinful behaviour, regarding the former as a punishment for the latter. Today, thanks to scientific investigation, we recognize that there is no lawlike relation between many illnesses and wicked deeds; rather we relate them to bacteria and viruses and other physical causes. I am not denying that psychological states can cause physical trauma, but many illnesses have no mental cause at all.

It is important to recall that the general laws which underlie causal relations are laws relating certain kinds of events, the causes, with certain tendencies (objective chances, or propensities) for a certain kind of event to occur. The actual effect which occurs is normally the product of several tendencies at work in the situation. The general law does not relate causes of a certain kind with actual effects of a certain kind, only with tendencies to produce effects of a certain kind, tendencies which might be offset by other tendencies in particular situations. Thus a person might normally stop their car at red traffic lights, but drive through one in an emergency. The fact that they drove through the red light would not imply that they lacked a disposition to stop. It would only mean that it was overridden by an urgent need.

Given this analysis of causes, what method should historians adopt for discovering the causes of an event? Here are a few hints.

To check that the cause you suspect to have brought about an event was indeed necessary in the circumstances for that event's occurrence, you have to use what Michael Scriven once called 'backward-looking generalizations', which are generalizations about all the possible causes of events like the one in question (Scriven, 1966). Suppose you were interested to discover why a gun carriage being pulled by a horse stopped moving towards the enemy. You immediately imagine the range of things which might have stopped it. Perhaps the soldiers decided to stop and go no further; perhaps the horse dropped with exhaustion; perhaps a wheel fell off the carriage; and perhaps the wheels got bogged in mud. These are all things you know that can stop a gun carriage proceeding, and to find the cause of a particular instance of such an event, you will check to see which of them produced it. If you find only one possible cause present, you can say its occurrence was necessary in the circumstances for the effect to occur. In the extract above, if the wheels of the Northern carts and guns had not become bogged, they would not have stopped.

Notice a couple of additional points here. First, there are sometimes causes at work which you have not thought of. These can sometimes be detected by studying the events leading up to the effect in detail. For instance, suppose someone had released the horse from the gun carriage and sent it away, then that would obviously stop it proceeding, yet it was not something you had thought of. So to be sure you have detected the causes at work, you have to examine the preceding events carefully. They sometimes suggest possible causes you had forgotten about.

Second, sometimes there is more than one cause at work, in which case all must be mentioned. Suppose the carriage stuck in the mud just at the time the horse became exhausted. It might be that each of these events was sufficient to stop the carriage, in which case you cannot say which caused that to happen. You can only say that if neither had happened, the carriage would not have stopped.

In case you doubt that we do use general knowledge of causes in order to detect them, just think of events whose causes you do not understand. Suppose, for example, you developed a rash on your skin. What caused it? You know where you have been, what you have eaten, what soap and lotion you used on your skin, but can you pick out the cause of the rash? Not unless you have general knowledge of the kinds of thing that can cause such a rash. We take our general knowledge of everyday events for granted, but it is essential for identifying causes just the same.

Historians take an interest in conditions when events occur which were not expected to occur in the circumstances. The conditions which explain the unexpected can be the absence of states of affairs which had been assumed to exist, and whose absence reduced the probability of the expected outcome. For instance, if the muddy fields had been frozen hard, the Northern army would not have been impeded by a sticky quagmire as it was. Then again, the explanatory conditions are sometimes additional states of affairs which increase the probability of the unexpected outcome. For example, the retirement of Confederate forces to Richmond depressed morale in the South, coming amid other reverses. If it had not done so, historians would wonder what circumstances could account for such an unexpected response. Perhaps few knew of the event, or they believed that reinforcements were on the way. Conditions are states of affairs which account for one thing occurring in circumstances where another was expected.

Indeed, historical conditions can explain why one event occurred rather than another even when neither was particularly expected. 'Why did the North win the American Civil War rather than the South?' This is to ask for a contrastive explanation. It appeals to general knowledge of the conditions which give victory to one side rather than another. Historians who have asked this question have pointed to a variety of factors: the superior resources of the North in money, equipment and personnel; the superior political leadership of Abraham Lincoln, as opposed to Jefferson Davis in the South; superior military leadership; and greater unity of purpose, for the South was often torn by disputes over States' rights. These are picked out because it is generally known that the side with greater resources, better leadership and greater unity is more likely to win a war. But notice that each of these is a state of affairs, indeed a comparative state of affairs. It was not just that the North had a lot of supplies, but that they had roughly twice the resources of the South. It was not just that the North had Lincoln, but that he was much shrewder and more decisive than Davis. (This example is discussed in detail later in this chapter.)

If one defined a cause as a condition which was necessary for a certain outcome, and which significantly increased the probability of that outcome, then these explanatory conditions could be called 'causes'. Such a definition would cover dynamic causes as well. But I think the dynamic element is essential to our common understanding of cause, and for that reason I am unwilling to call mere explanatory conditions causes, even though some historians do so. Causes are events which help to bring about changes.

Checking out particular causes and conditions

Checking causal claims

When historians judge causal statements, they consider several things about them: (i) they check whether it is reasonable to believe that the events referred to in the causal statement really occurred; (ii) they consider whether the logical features of the causal claim can be justified: was the cause necessary for the effect in the circumstances, i.e. would the effect have been different without it; and (iii) did the cause increase the probability of the effect?; (iv) to decide whether these logical requirements have been met, historians look for general laws of the relevant kind which would justify them. Often this general knowledge is of a common, everyday sort; occasionally it is specialized historical or scientific knowledge. Quite often a general law is established by discovering the relatively microlaws which make it true. The importance of these conditions in judging causal explanations is evident in the following examples.

Niall Ferguson has discussed three popular explanations of the outbreak of the First World War (1914–18) in his book *The Pity of War* (1998), showing how inadequate they are, and in the process revealing how professional historians judge causal claims.

Marxist historians have said that capitalist economies, to secure more markets and raw materials, inevitably seek an overseas empire, and in the pursuit of colonies they are bound to clash and to fight one another (Ferguson, 1998, p. 31). Many have attributed the First World War to competition between great imperial powers, particularly between Britain and Germany. Ferguson criticizes this explanation by first of all objecting to the general theory upon which it rests. He argues at length that, although capitalist countries did compete for empire, that competition was not sufficient to produce war. They were often able to settle their differences peacefully. 'If there was a war which imperialism should have caused it was the war between Britain and Russia which failed to break out in the 1870s and 1880s; or the war between Britain and France which failed to break out in the 1880s or 1890s' (p. 39). So the Marxist theory is mistaken. He then considers whether there was, in fact, a vigorous competition for colonies between Britain and Germany driving them to the war. On the contrary, he said, the capitalists in Britain and Germany prior to the war did not want a war to break out (pp. 32–3). Furthermore, so great was the wealth of Great Britain, that in fact it had no quarrel with Germany, whom it regarded as posing no threat to its interests (pp. 35–53). The cause proposed by Marxist theory, namely imperial conflict between Britain and Germany, did not even exist.

Ferguson produces similar criticisms of another explanation, namely that an arms race, particularly between the German and British navies, led to the outbreak of war. First he criticizes the theory that arms races are sufficient to cause war, by pointing out that during the Cold War after 1945, an arms race between the USSR and the West maintained the peace (pp. 82–3). Next he denies that there was an arms race, explaining that British naval superiority was so great that neither side imagined Germany could match it. Likewise, the combined armies of Britain, France and Russia, which formed a Triple Entente, far outnumbered those of Germany, Austria and Italy, the Triple Alliance (pp. 83–92). Finally, far from German confidence in their armed forces causing the war, Ferguson argues that it was their fear of losing the arms race in the long run, because of their limited access to finance (ch. 5), which moved the military leaders to persuade the German Government to launch a pre-emptive strike against the Triple Entente (p. 83, 98–9). He is able to establish this explanation from a close study of the particular events leading up to the outbreak of war. Once again, the proposed explanation fails.

A third explanation Ferguson considers is that provided by Fritz Fischer (see Fischer, 1967) and his pupils, that Germany's aim in declaring war was control of Europe, 'through annexations of French, Belgian and possibly Russian territory, the founding of a Central European customs union and the creation of new Polish and Baltic states directly or indirectly under German control. In addition, Germany was to acquire new territory in Africa, so that her colonial possessions could be consolidated as a continuous Central African area' (Ferguson, p. 169). In other words, Germany's aim was conquest. Once again, the explanation collapses for lack of evidence: 'no evidence has ever been found by Fischer and his pupils that these objectives existed *before* Britain's entry into the war' (ibid.). He admits that the Kaiser sometimes 'fantasized' about an empire, but says that he did not do so consistently, nor did he have very much influence over the government (p. 170).

General theories about the causes of kinds of historical events and trends can be useful in suggesting possible causes, but to discover which of those possibilities was operative in a particular case, historians need much detailed information about the particular event in question. Critical historians keep the general theories they have learned in mind, but survey the detailed events leading up to the one they wish to explain to see whether any of them are relevant. If not, they look for other causes at work.

From a close study of the particular events leading to the outbreak of war, Ferguson notes that

> it was the German military which ultimately secured, by a combination of persuasion and defiance, the mobilization orders, the ultimata and declarations of war which unleashed the conflict.
>
> (p. 149)

> The evidence points . . . to a military 'first strike', designed to pre-empt a
> deterioration in Germany's military position – though this is by no means
> incompatible with the idea that the outcome of such a strike, if successful,
> would have been German hegemony in Europe.
>
> (p. 153)

The immediate explanation, then, is a rational one. But what was the situation
which worried the German military? Ferguson provides a profound explanation
of their decision by giving a detailed analysis of the relative strengths of the
German and Alliances' armed forces and sources of revenue, and a lot of evidence of German concerns over these. What is rather less well explained is why
the German military and government were so concerned about their relative
military inferiority. Perhaps the desire for a European customs union and concern
over the arms race were, after all, more important than Ferguson had allowed as
motives for war in this case (see N. Stone, 1999, pp. 246–56).

The points made about explanations of large-scale events apply also to explanations of large-scale trends. When economic historians want to explain a very
large-scale trend, such as the period of growth in the British economy between
1951 and 1973, you might think that they would simply draw upon a well-
established economic theory to tell them what the main causes of such growth in
such an economy must have been. In fact, however, the economic theories available to them are not nearly powerful enough to do that. The most they do is
suggest some general kinds of causes which must be investigated. R. Floud and
D. McCloskey, for example, begin their inquiry by noting

> three sets of determinants. First, the supply of the primary factors of produc-
> tion, labour and capital . . . Secondly, it is necessary to consider the
> demand-side effects, and in particular the exogenous influences on demand
> stemming from Britain's international economic transactions. Thirdly, there
> are exogenous influences on the trends in productivity, such as technologi-
> cal innovations, and these constitute an independent contribution to the
> growth of output. The full story is inevitably more complex than this simple
> listing of separate factors indicates.
>
> (Floud and McCloskey, 1994, p. 104)

With this list in mind, the historians examine details of British economic history
during this period, to see whether instances of these causes of prosperity can be
found. Not only does it prove difficult to identify them, but there is also considerable doubt about their causal significance. Consider, for example, whether an
increase in the amount and flexibility of labour contributed to the post-war prosperity of Britain. B.W.E. Alford notes that the war broke up traditional patterns
of employment, increasing labour mobility (Alford, 1996, p. 248). That might
have helped. On the other hand Floud and McCloskey note that these years saw
full employment and a shortage of labour, and a reduction in the length of the

working week from an average of 45.6 hours in 1951 to 41.4 in 1973 (Floud and McCloskey, 1994, pp. 104–5). According to standard economic theory, the shortage of labour and reduction in working hours would have limited economic growth. Floud and McCloskey support this conclusion by noting how countries with reserves of labour grew more rapidly: 'The implicit counter-factual proposition – that Britain could have grown more rapidly if there had been a more elastic supply of labour – gains support from the fact that this was the case in other countries which enjoyed more rapid growth in this period' (p. 105). But perhaps there were compensating forces at work in the British economy, so that the shortage of labour was not significant. Perhaps firms invested more in machinery to compensate for scarcity of labour. The authors consider this theoretical possibility but doubt that such investment would have been sufficient 'to compensate for the constraining effects of the diminishing supply of labour' (ibid.). Alford does not believe there was a shortage of labour: 'rapid economic growth was accompanied by the rapid growth and redistribution of the labour force' (p. 248), but he does question whether the growth of the labour force was a cause or an effect of economic growth: 'it is by no means clear that these were causative conditions. For one thing, there is much evidence to suggest that, given demand, labour supply expands relatively easily as, for example, part-time, female and foreign workers are drawn into the labour force' (Alford, 1996, pp. 248–9; and see p. 258).

If an increase in the labour force did not produce the prosperity, did an increase in capital do so? Floud and McCloskey certainly think it did. They point out that fixed capital increased in Britain at an average of four per cent per year between 1951 and 1973, and a lot of this incorporated modern technology which contributed to economic growth. Furthermore, the demand for new plant itself stimulated economic growth (Floud and McCloskey, 1994, pp. 105–6). Alford, however, suspects that this increase in capital was a consequence, not a cause, of economic growth. He attributes growth much more to public expenditure by governments at home, which rose to almost 43 per cent by 1973 (Alford, 1996, p. 248), and to the growth of overseas markets, attributed in part to post-war reconstruction programmes (p. 247). Floud and McCloskey point out, however, that government expenditure was of money already in the economy, raised by taxes, and that indeed governments maintained significant savings throughout the period (Floud and McCloskey, 1994, p. 107). They agree, however, that overseas demand did contribute significantly to the growth of the British economy.

Sometimes detailed study of particular events yields insights which theory would never provide. For example, there was a marked decline in the mortality of slaves on British ships after 1750, and historians studying the changing circumstances of the slave trade have noted several different possible causes of this trend.

They include increased immunity gained by African populations to a variety of new diseases following the gradual merging of epidemiological regions,

improved economic and health conditions within Africa, and the introduction of new ships designed to carry, and to collect (from rainfall), greater
volumes of water. Another important innovation from the 1760s was the
coppering of hulls which may have resulted not only in faster voyages, but
in a reduction in shipworm and thus in dampness below decks . . . [D]rier
decks were conducive to better health. The decline in death rates in the
1790s may also have been associated with a marked decline in the volume
of slaves transported.

(Haines and Shlomowitz, 2000, pp. 262–3)

I suggest that no theory would have suggested the coppering of ships' hulls as a
cause of improvement in the health of their passengers. Haines and Shlomowitz
offer yet another cause to explain the trend, namely 'gradual improvements in
empirical knowledge related to disease prevention' (p. 264), which enabled sur-
geons on board ships to improve hygiene and health conditions is such a way as
to reduce mortality. This is a simple example of the way in which many different
causes of an historical trend can be discovered by close examination of the particular circumstances in which it occurred. The identification of these causes
depends upon general knowledge of the causes of disease, but the discovery of
which were present was the result of a careful study of the particular circumstances of the trend of reduced mortality among the slaves.

Checking contrastive explanations

Contrastive explanations identify causes or conditions which made it more probable that an event of one kind would occur rather than another. Floud and
McCloskey, for example, move on to consider why the British economy did not
perform as well as some others during the same period (1951–73) (Floud and
McCloskey, 1994, pp. 115 ff). The cost of production in Britain was higher than
that of several of her competitors, so that she exported less and imported more
than they did; so the British produced less than the others did, and made smaller
profits. Consequently investment in British industry fell, and new technology
was not adopted, whereas the opposite was true of her competitors, such as
Japan, Germany, France and Italy, giving them an advantage. To explain why
Britain performed less successfully than these others, Floud and McCloskey refer
to detailed studies of development (ibid., p. 118), and write with much more
authority than before. They show that other countries were much less prosperous
than Britain in 1948, and so had a greater incentive to modernize and work hard
to repair the damage of war. In the process, they were able to borrow the most
advanced technology, organization and practices, giving them an advantage.
Finally, they had more surplus labour, particularly agricultural labour, which
could be transferred to high-productivity branches of the economy (pp. 118–20).
Clearly theory informs this contrastive explanation, suggesting relevant differences which have been found to exist in fact. Note that the second part of this

explanation is a profound explanation for the first, in particular for the higher costs of production in Britain which was the root cause of her relative inferiority.

To identify a cause or condition (C) for an event of one kind (E1) occurring rather than another (E2), historians must check (i) that C actually occurred or existed; (ii) that C was necessary for the occurrence of E1; (iii) that C was sufficient to make the occurrence of E1 more probable than E2; and (iv) there was no other cause or condition which would counteract or balance the influence of C in the circumstances, i.e. which would prevent it making E1 more probable than E2, or which would make E1 just as probable as E2. An excellent example of historical judgement based upon these requirements is provided by an essay written by J.M. McPherson considering a range of explanations which historians have given of why the Union forces of the North won the American Civil War instead of the Southern Confederacy (McPherson, 1992). I shall summarize his arguments, to show how they relate to the conditions just listed.

The first explanation of why the North won instead of the South is that the North had overwhelmingly more men and resources. McPherson denies that this is sufficient to ensure victory (i.e. condition iii is not satisfied), noting several occasions on which victory went to the side with inferior resources, such as the victory of America over Britain in the war of independence. He agrees that superior men and resources were necessary for the Northern victory, for it would not have happened otherwise (condition ii was satisfied), but it does not suffice to explain it.

Second, McPherson considers the view that 'the Confederacy lost because it was plagued by dissent and divisions that undercut the strong and united effort necessary to win the war' (p. 23). He finds three flaws in this explanation. First, the effect of opposition in the South was *offset* by the enthusiasm of state governors mobilizing and supplying troops, and by Confederate government decrees conscripting troops and suppressing dissent (condition iv was not satisfied). Second, opposition to the war was even 'more powerful and effective in the North than in the South' (p. 25), so that its effects in the South were more than *balanced* by the effects of those in the North. (Again, condition iv is not satisfied.) Third, McPherson says that internal opposition to a war is not sufficient to ensure defeat, as 'Americans in the war of 1776 were more divided than Southerners in the war of 1861' (p. 26), yet they were not defeated. (Condition iii is not satisfied.)

The third possible explanation McPherson presents is that the South lost because two major groups of its population, namely the non-slaveholding whites and the slaves, were not committed to the war, or became alienated from it. The whites sometimes deserted back home to look after their families, and the blacks deserted to join Northern armies. McPherson remarks that such alienation is not sufficient to produce defeat, once again citing the experience of the American Revolution. (So condition iii is not satisfied.) But even more important, there was an enormous amount of alienation in the North which 'weakened and at times threatened to paralyze the Union war effort' (p. 28), so the effect of alienation in the South was *balanced* by its effect in the North (condition iv not satisfied).

The fourth explanation is that Southerners lacked the will to fight, unlike the Unionists, and so lost the war. McPherson notes three versions of this explanation. The first suggests that the South lacked a sense of patriotism or nationalism. This is just false, McPherson says, for the Confederate government believed it was defending the nation and its constitution from the Yankees, who would corrupt it. (Condition i does not obtain.) Indeed they suffered more than the Unionists in defending their cause, showing no lack of will. The second version of this explanation also rests upon false assumptions. It is that Southerners lacked the will to fight because they felt guilty over the institution of slavery. This is just false, McPherson says, for most Southerners thought slavery was good for the blacks, an excellent form of labour, and a fine way of settling relations between superior and inferior races. (Condition i is not satisfied.) The third version of the explanation is that Southerners' morale fell with defeats, so that they began to doubt whether God was on their side. McPherson observes that in this case 'military defeat caused loss of will, not vice versa' (p. 34). In which case, loss of will was not necessary for defeat (condition ii does not obtain), but a consequence of it.

The fifth explanation focusses upon leadership. It also has three versions. The first is that Northern generals were superior to Southern ones, which is why they won the war. McPherson admits that they were superior during the last year or two of the war, when Grant and Sherman devastated the South, but denies that all were so brilliant. 'On more than one occasion the outcome seemed to hang in the balance because of *incompetent* Northern military leadership' (p. 38). So he denies that their superiority was sufficient to ensure victory (condition iii does not apply). The second version of this explanation attributes Northern success to its superior skills in the management of money, supplies and troops. McPherson thinks Northern strength in this area was to some extent *balanced* by the ability of several Southern administrators, who kept the war going with quite limited resources. (Condition iv does not apply.) Third, some ascribe Northern victory to the leadership of President Lincoln, who was a superior statesman to Confederate President Davis in the South. McPherson argues that without Sherman's military success just prior to his re-election in November 1864, Lincoln would have been defeated and the Union forces would have failed. Victory was a product, not of Lincoln's ability, but the turn of a battle. (Condition iii is not satisfied.)

McPherson would attribute the outcome of the Civil War almost entirely to 'contingencies'. In the context, this seems to mean that the outcome was not made probable by any event or state of affairs prior to the last shot being fired, so to speak. He writes in conclusion: 'To understand why the South lost, in the end, we must turn from large generalizations that imply inevitability and study instead the contingency that hung over each military campaign, each battle, each election, each decision during the war' (p. 42). This is a disappointing conclusion.

Large generalizations do not 'imply inevitability': they help identify causes which simply increased the probability of certain outcomes. Furthermore, this conclusion ignores what McPherson had admitted earlier on, that superior resources of men and materials, superior generals and statesmen contributed significantly to the Northern victory. It also plays down the significance of Southern demoralization, which was not just a consequence of some defeats in battle and Sherman's raids in the South, but also of Lincoln's reelection, of his determination to win the war, and of his having the resources to do so. (See A. Jones, 1992, pp. 43–78, 73–4.)

Checking necessary and sufficient conditions by judging generalizations

Most causes and conditions are *necessary in the circumstances* for their effects, such that if the cause or condition had been absent the effect would have been different. And all causes are *sufficient* to increase the probability of their effect. To judge these logical relations between causes and their effects, historians have to consult general knowledge about the relations between events like the causes and effects.

Often this general knowledge is accepted common sense. Sometimes it has been established in a scientific way by psychologists, sociologists, economists and political scientists among others. Occasionally the required general knowledge is the result of historical inquiry, acquired by comparing a range of similar cases.

The relation between causes and conditions and their effects is a lawlike relation. So not only do events like designated causes and conditions generally produce events like the designated effect, but if the effect were to occur, so would the causes and conditions (in the circumstances). Lawlike generalizations and their justification were discussed in Chapter 3. Here is it enough to note that one way of testing assumed lawlike generalizations relating causes or conditions to effects is by looking for exceptions to them. If exceptions can be found, which cannot be explained away, then they constitute good reason for doubting the truth of the lawlike generalization. In some of the examples which follow, hypotheses about causes and conditions are refuted by showing that the generalizations they assume are not universally true.

Checking necessary conditions

To know that a particular cause, C, was necessary in the circumstances for its effect, E, historians must know that E is always produced by a range of events including events like C, and that no other instances of that range of events was present in the circumstances besides C.

Historians sometimes have an idea that a certain event or state of affairs was necessary for a certain outcome, but to check that it was they compare similar situations to see whether the outcome could occur without it. For example, some have thought that for international peace to exist between nations, they must enjoy a balance of power. There must also be a degree of mutual good will, or at least respect, but the basis of the stability, they hold, is a balance of power. However Geoffrey Blainey (1973) has argued that lasting peace has been achieved between nations whose power was not equal, but quite unequal. The defeat of Napoleon's army in 1815 inaugurated a period of lasting peace between Britain and France, and the defeat of the French by Bismarck in 1871 produced a long period of peace between Germany and France. Similarly, the defeat of German armies in 1918 and more particularly 1945 produced lasting peace between Germany and other European countries. 'Those years of extreme imbalance marked the first stage of perhaps the most pronounced periods of peace known to Europe in the last three or more centuries' (p. 113).

Clearly a balance of power is not a universally necessary condition of peace. But nor is a striking inequality of the kinds Blainey mentions. It seems that the peace maintained between the USA and the USSR in the second half of the twentieth century rested largely upon a perceived balance of power. Perhaps for peace to continue between two nations it must be the case that neither can see any advantage in fighting the other. That condition is satisfied (i) when there is a perceived balance of power between them, or (ii) when one is so much stronger than the other that the weaker of the two would never contemplate attacking the other. In that case, there could be cases in which peace is preserved by condition (i), a balance of power, and other cases in which it is preserved by condition (ii), a greater inequality of power. Certainly (i) is not universally necessary, but it could be necessary in certain circumstances, namely when (ii) is absent.

Checking the necessity and sufficiency of causes and conditions

Causes and conditions are always necessary for their effects, in the circumstances. Causes also increase the probability of their effect.

To check whether a cause is necessary for an effect, as we have just seen, historians study comparable cases, and if the effect occurs without the cause then they conclude it was not necessary for that effect. If on the other hand the cause occurs without the effect, then the cause is not generally sufficient for the effect. In fact it is absurd to regard causes in history as universally sufficient for their effects, for all can have their effect offset by other forces at work in the situation. Still, if a cause is frequently accompanied by a certain subsequent event, and if exceptions to this can be explained by the presence of other forces at work, then it is reasonable to suppose the cause is indeed sufficient to make the subsequent event highly probable.

A really neat example of an historian checking whether a cause is necessary and sufficient for a kind of event is provided by Stanley Elkins (1968, chs. 2 and 3). Elkins believed that many slaves in the southern states of America had a childlike personality, which he called a 'Sambo' personality. Recall how the masters of adult slaves called them 'boy' and how anxious the slaves seemed to be to please their masters. Elkins considered that this behaviour was caused by the slaves living in a tightly closed society, the plantation, where their life and well-being depended totally upon the whim of their owner.

To show that this condition was necessary for the Sambo personality of slaves, Elkins compared the slaves of the South with those in Latin America. The latter, he argued, had a freer existence with their families and priests, and did not have such a subservient manner. If total dependence were *necessary* for a Sambo personality, then the absence of that dependence would result in a different personality. So the South American finding confirmed his hypothesis (pp. 84–5). It also disproved an old theory that the Sambo personality was a racial characteristic of African slaves, for African slaves in South America did not manifest it (pp. 82–4).

To show that total dependence was *sufficient* for a Sambo personality, Elkins looked for similar cases of total dependence to see whether such personalities existed with them or not. He found these in German concentration camps. 'The concentration camp was not only a perverted slave system; it was also – what is less obvious but even more to the point – a perverted patriarchy' (p. 104). The well-being, indeed the life, of inmates depended upon absolute obedience to the prison authorities (p. 107). The older prisoners were observed to have adopted childlike characteristics (pp. 111–13). So it seems that such conditions of total dependence are sufficient to produce a Sambo personality.

There is always a slight worry about observed correlations between different characteristics, and the worry is that the correlation might be quite accidental. The chance of this diminishes as the number and variety of comparisons increases, but it remains a worry just the same. Elkins was able to find support for his hypothesis from several psychological theories. Freudians, for example, have a theory of infantile regression, which involves identification with the authority who threatens one's existence (pp. 116–18). Such theories suggest that the process Elkins had observed is indeed a natural one for everyone in such situations.

Critics of Elkins' theory doubted whether Southern slaves all had the Sambo personality that Elkins had described. Elkins, in reply, was willing to allow 'degrees' of childishness (Elkins, 1971, p. 350), 'a wider range of slave behavior, embracing various forms of independence and non-cooperation with the slave-holding regime' (p. 353). The interesting question this objection raises is how many exceptions can a hypothesis tolerate before it is abandoned. Rather than abandon it, Elkins agreed to modify it. He agreed that other 'total institutions' besides concentration camps would serve as appropriate comparisons, namely asylums and prisons (p. 353), and he adopted Erving Goffman's catalogue of common responses: '(1) situational withdrawal (apathy); (2) colonization (a kind of practical adjustment to the world of the total institution; (3) conversion (internalization of the institution's definition of him); and (4) intransigence (a . . . personal . . . rejection of the institution)' (pp. 353–4). He also agreed to distinguish slaves' official role and behaviour, demanded by the institution, from their other roles within the slave community, tolerated by the plantation system (pp. 354–5). He even allows 'that Sambo was a product of role-playing rather than a true internalization of the master class's picture of him' (p. 356, and see p. 359). Still, thus modified, Elkins stands by his hypothesis (p. 358).

Here is another example which illustrates the importance of establishing the necessary and sufficient conditions of an event in order to identify its causes, and to show how hypotheses can be checked by comparative methods. Prior to the Industrial Revolution in Britain (1760–1830), a lot of work was done in people's homes. Spinning and weaving, for example, were cottage industries which had met the demand for cloth for many centuries. Why did this change? What caused industrialists to establish factories? J. Mokyr has considered several possible causes. First, new technology produced large pieces of machinery which could not be accommodated in cottages: 'iron puddling furnaces and rollers, steam and water engines, silk-throwing mills, chemical and gas works' for example (Mokyr, 1999, p. 104). But critics have pointed out that the operation of such machinery was *not necessary* for the establishment of factories. Factories were established before much of it was invented; and anyway, many of the factories at first used techniques similar to those used in cottages (ibid.). I suspect that the use of large machines consolidated the use of factories, but it did not always cause it. A second possible explanation is that factory owners wanted to discipline their workers more effectively, and could do so if they were all together in one place. At first, however, discipline in the factories was very slack. Workers were paid by the piece, and more or less left to their own devices (p. 105). So once again, the proposed cause, a desire to improve discipline, was *not necessary*: factories existed without it. The third possibility is that factories were created to improve quality control and prevent theft of raw materials, because the control of inputs and outputs was much easier in a factory than in a number of cottages. But, remarks Mokyr, these were old problems which had not been sufficient to stimulate the creation of factories in the past. So clearly the need to control production was *not sufficient* to drive manufacturers to form factories (pp. 105–6). A fourth explanation which has received quite a lot of support is that factories made possible division of labour, which has many advantages. It develops expertise in workers which enhances their productivity, both in quantity and quality; workers can be given tasks which match their ability; and workers can be taught their job quite quickly. Once again, however, these advantages were *not sufficient* to explain the existence of factories, for they could be achieved in cottage industries: 'division of labor did not require factories. Domestic industries practiced it, and a large part of the function of the merchant entrepreneur was to shuttle goods in process from one cottage to another' (p. 108).

Notice the way in which Mokyr checks whether the suggested causes were indeed necessary and sufficient for the effect. To check whether they were necessary, he asks whether the effect would have occurred as it did without them. In other words, he looks for cases in which the effect occurs in the absence of the proposed cause. When he finds cases like this, he knows that the proposed cause was not always necessary for the effect. To check whether a possible cause was sufficient to make an event like the effect probable, he looks for cases in which the cause existed but the effect did not follow. When he finds these, he knows the proposed cause was not sufficient to produce the effect (assuming there were no other tendencies at work, counteracting the tendency of the proposed cause to produce such an effect).

The explanation Mokyr finally approves is that factories reduced the cost of production. 'As the division of labor became finer, the final products more complex, and the equipment more expensive, the costs of geographical dispersion rose, and firms switched from decentralized to centralized production' (ibid.). Mokyr not only identifies this cause of the development of factories, but offers a more complex explanation in terms of a general process of change.

> Technological progress led to lower prices and better or new products, which increased demand and thus expanded the market; and increase in the extent of the market further led to a finer division of labor which increased productivity further and led to changes in industrial organization. This kind of positive feedback process serves as a good illustration how the Industrial Revolution can be seen as a self-reinforcing process.
>
> (p. 109)

This theory is offered without defence. It seems to appeal to elementary economic theory, that when the price of a good falls and its quality improves, demand for it will grow. And when demand grows, that stimulates an increase in productivity and supply. Elsewhere in his book, Mokyr is quite cautious about such assumptions. He comments that '[i]n a historical event like the Industrial Revolution, demand factors can only play a role under certain assumptions that have to be examined carefully' (p. 59). For example, an increase in demand for goods will only result in an increased supply 'if the economy has large underutilized resources that can be brought into production' (p. 60). The most Mokyr concedes at this point is that a strong demand for cotton goods stimulated inventors to increase output in that industry (p. 63). In this way, Mokyr judges the causal explanation by judging the adequacy of the theory upon which it rests. In the light of these qualifications, the solution Mokyr proposed seems a bit glib and in need of further consideration.

The various possible causes of the development of factories which Mokyr considered are those which historians have suggested on the basis of common general knowledge about the advantages of factory production. It proved difficult to find one which was clearly necessary and sufficient for the development of factories. Responsible historians will remain aware that sometimes the same kind of event can have different causes, and not feel obliged to find a single process to account for them all.

Chapter 8

Historical explanations

What causes should a responsible historian describe in order to explain an historical event? And what conditions should an historian mention to explain why one event occurred rather than another?

Some writers think there is no rational answer to these questions. Keith Jenkins, for example, assumes that there is an infinite number of causes for any event, and no rational way of deciding which should be included in an explanation. He says the causes apparently form

> an infinite chain spreading backwards and outwards [from the event being explained] which you somehow have to cut into despite the fact that no method (and no amount of experience) can provide you with any logical or definitive cut in (or 'cut out') points in order to give a sufficient and necessary explanation.
>
> (Jenkins, 1991, p. 52)

All historians can do, says Jenkins, is learn to play the game as others do, and produce explanations like those favoured by other historians.

In fact there has been no shortage of advice as to how historians should explain past events. Some have urged historians to look for explanations of historical change in certain features of society: in the furthering of class interests; in the pursuit of power; in the exploitation of women and underdeveloped countries. Robert Young, in a study of models of explanation, quotes Hélène Cixous's insight into historical processes as an Algerian French Jewish girl who witnessed the Algerian War of Independence:

> I saw how the white (French), superior, plutocratic, civilized world founded its power on the repression of populations who had suddenly become 'invisible', like proletarians, immigrant workers, minorities who are not the right 'colour'. Women. Invisible as humans. But, of course, perceived as tools – dirty, stupid, lazy, underhanded, etc. Thanks to some annihilating dialectical magic. I saw that the great, noble, 'advanced' countries established themselves by expelling what was 'strange'; excluding it but not dismissing it;

enslaving it. A commonplace gesture of History: there have to be *two* races – the masters and the slaves.

(Young, 1990, p. 1)

Others have prescribed certain formal models of explanation, which they think historians should follow. Some have proposed that historical explanations follow the example of the physical sciences, and explain events by using universal laws to relate them to causes sufficient to ensure their occurrence. Others have said that historical explanations should be quite different from scientific explanations, and explain historical events by describing the reasons people had for bringing them about, making them appear as rational as possible. Finally, others have urged historians to discover how people viewed events in the past, and to discover the cultural imperatives that moved people to act as they did. (For a fuller survey of some theories of historical explanation, see McCullagh, 2001.)

Both of these approaches, by those who promote a certain content for historical explanations and those who propose a certain form that they should take, are prescriptive. And without arguing the matter in detail, let me say that some widely accepted historical explanations do not fit any of the prescriptions offered. The causes of historical events are enormously varied, and not confined to the pursuit of class interests or power, nor do all involve the exploitation of the poor, the foreign or females. Causal explanations in history do not show that an effect had to happen. They simply point out causes that increased the probability of its occurrence. Nor do explanations which refer to people's reasons for acting always show that an action was rational. Sometimes the reasons are poor ones, and the action rather stupid. Finally, people do not always behave as their culture dictates. Some rebel against it, and find original ways of responding to situations.

My approach to the understanding of historical explanations is not prescriptive, but analytic and descriptive. I begin by analysing what the word 'explain' means, and note that it is a transitive verb, properly used with an object, a clause beginning with a pronoun, such as 'what', 'who', 'how' or 'why'. As the analysis proceeds, a fairly clear idea emerges as to what sort of information requests for explanation require. The kinds of explanation which are relevant to the subject of this chapter are explanations of why something happened, or why what happened was more probable than something else. I refer to these as 'genetic explanations' and 'contrastive explanations' respectively. The form of the question does not completely specify the kind of information required, however, so to discover precisely what is being asked for, I describe the kinds of answers which generally meet with approval. Genetic and contrastive explanations are sometimes augmented by further information, providing what I call 'profound explanations' of the events being explained.

One aspect of historical explanations that is difficult to analyse is the relation between explanations which refer to individual thoughts and actions, and those which refer to social structures and the relations between them. I shall discuss this relation in the section on structural genetic explanations. And it will also be examined in the final section, on a third type of historical explanation, namely reductive explanations, which explain changes in social structures by describing changes in the individual behaviour which constitutes those structures.

Genetic and contrastive explanations of individual actions

One can discover a lot about the ideal nature of historical explanations by considering the questions which they are designed to answer. The answer has to be appropriate to the question, if it is to be adequate.

The verb 'to explain' is a transitive verb, properly used in conjunction with a clause beginning with a pronoun such as 'what, 'who', 'how' and 'why'. The request to 'explain the French Revolution', for example, is incomplete. It could mean to explain what happened, who was involved, how the revolution succeeded in replacing the monarchy with a republic, and/or why it occurred. Without the question being amplified in some way, it is impossible to know precisely what information is being requested. One cannot judge the adequacy of an explanation without knowing precisely what question it was meant to answer.

When people speak about historical explanations, they commonly mean explanations of why historical events occurred. And what kind of information do such questions request? Rather than impose a preconceived view in answer to this question, I have found it very useful to study historical practice. The analysis of practice is quite legitimate, for the meaning of words and sentences in a community is best established by noticing the conditions under which they are used. By analysing the explanations that historians deem satisfactory, one can discover the ideal form of such explanations which 'why' questions apparently require. Often the explanations given in the course of an historical narrative are incomplete, because much of the information needed to complete the explanation has already been provided at earlier stages of the story. But the ideal form of historical explanations can be constructed from examples, nevertheless, especially when critics make plain the standards they expect to be met. In practice, then, what kind of information seems to supply a satisfactory answer to 'why' questions?

After studying a lot of historical explanations, I have noticed that there are two different senses in which the question can be asked and answered. The question can be a request for a genetic causal explanation, or it can be a request for a contrastive explanation, the contrast often being implied by the context in which the question was asked. The first version of the question asks: why did such-and-such an event occur? The second version asks: why did this event occur rather than that?

Before illustrating these two versions of the 'why' question, it is important to note a further feature they share. To ask why did such-and-such an event occur involves asking why did an event *of that kind* occur. It is often possible to describe the same event in a variety of ways, and an explanation is expected to be appropriate to the description given. Let me make the point clear with a homely example. Suppose I went shopping, and bought some steak. Someone might ask me: why did you go shopping? Reply: to get some food for dinner tonight. Why did you get meat? Because we normally eat meat for dinner, and I was following that custom. Why did you buy steak? Because I know everyone likes steak, and I think it is good for them. There are many more aspects of the event that could have been questioned: why I went to this butcher's shop, why I drove there, and so on. Historians do not attempt to explain every feature of an event, but only those which interest them. When they explain an event, therefore, they explain it as an event of a certain kind, having a certain characteristic. The kind of event is indicated by the words chosen when naming the event in asking for the explanation. Why go shopping? Why buy meat? Why buy steak? and so on. And they seek causes which increased the probability of the occurrence of an event of that kind in the circumstances.

Some philosophers, aware that people do not explain every feature of an event, have thought that the only way of specifying the feature to be explained is by asking for an explanation of a contrast (see, for example, van Fraassen, 1980, pp. 126–30). This is certainly one way of specifying precisely what is to be explained, but it is not the only way. For instance, one could ask 'Why did you go shopping rather than go to the movies?', in which case the correct answer might be: 'It never occurred to me to do so. I guess there was nothing I wanted to see at the movies at the time and I needed to get some food.' Notice that the states of affairs 'it never occurred to me' and 'there was nothing I wanted to see at the movies at the time' are not part of the causal story about what led me to go shopping. The other way to specify precisely what needs to be explained is that outlined in the last paragraph, of noting the words used to describe the event to be explained, and providing an account of the causes which increased the probability of such an event occurring.

Let me illustrate some of these points by considering explanations of Napoleon Bonaparte's seizure of power in France on 9–10 November 1799 (18–19 Brumaire), when the Directory was replaced by a triumvirate consisting of Bonaparte, Sieyès and Roger Ducos. Why did Napoleon seize power then? We know how he did so more clearly than why. But it seems likely that he was dismayed at the effects of a long period of economic depression upon France and the political instability produced by Jacobins on the left and Royalists on the right attempting to undermine the authority of the Directory (Tulard, 1985, pp. 78–9); and he doubtless believed that he was capable of providing strong, sensible government for France, with the enthusiastic support of the army; and he saw that a plan of Sieyès to get the government (the Directory, the Council of Ancients and the Council of Five Hundred) to change the constitution provided him with an opportunity to acquire power over the government for himself in the most legal fashion possible. Given these attitudes and beliefs, it appears reasonable for Napoleon to have intervened as he did.

Armand Lefebvre asked why Napoleon seized power for himself instead of siding with the Jacobins or the Royalists. This is a request for a contrastive explanation. Pieter Geyl sums up his explanation in these words, and concludes by confirming the explanation for Napoleon's seizure of power just given.

> He could have accepted the support of the royalists, and brought about a restoration [of the monarchy], but that would not appeal to a man who wished to be himself the master, and who was in any case aware that a restoration of the *ancien régime*, however strong the reactionary element, would arouse uncompromising resistance and bring to a head the latent civil war. He could have co-operated with the Jacobins, who wished for nothing better, but that would have meant a resumption of the war in its most revolutionary form, and European convulsion which would not have accorded with Bonaparte's ideas; moreover he would in that case have had to share control of France with Jacobin clubs and radical demagogues, hardly a prospect to please a general 'who only loved popular energy when clad in military uniform'. There remained the broad central mass of public opinion, tolerably satisfied with the social reforms of the Revolution and anxious to retain these, but longing for stability. Order, that was the slogan which Bonaparte understood, unity, an end to all that interminable bickering, a sweeping away of the parties, a chance to enjoy the fruits of the Revolution, work, reconstruction – and peace. But it must be a peace which would consolidate the powerful position that had been won.
>
> (Geyl, 1949, pp. 46–7)

Given this pattern of reasoning, it was probable that Napoleon would decide to take power for himself, rather than lend support to the Royalists or Jacobins.

Contrastive explanations provide information about a situation which made one outcome, an actual outcome, more probable than another, which might otherwise possibly have been expected.

At the conclusion of his book on Napoleon, Tulard offers this explanation of Napoleon's rise to power. The 'middle bourgeoisie' had profited from the revolution, acquiring a lot of property from the state and the church, and strongly desired their situation to be consolidated. They wanted no return to the *ancien régime*, nor an extension of the revolution, both of which would threaten their property. In Napoleon they found someone who would protect them from both these threats, and enable them to flourish in a well ordered state (Tulard, 1985, pp. 350–1).

Precisely what is being explained here? Tulard presents it as an explanation of Napoleon's rise to power. He begins the passage with these words: 'Faced with internal or external threats to its interests, the French bourgeoisie has always been able to invent a saviour . . . Napoleon is the archetype for these saviours' (p. 350). But in fact the bourgeoisie did not bring Napoleon to power: all they did was allow him to rule without opposition. So really what Tulard is doing here is explaining the support given to Napoleon's rule by the bourgeoisie. That was probably a condition of his success, but it does not explain his access to power.

Examples like these are familiar enough, but the challenge we face is to construct a theory about the nature of ideal causal and contrastive explanations. The examples in history books build upon an understanding of the subject which already is common knowledge or has already been provided in the book. Those examples, by themselves, do no necessarily provide all the information a reader needs to understand why an event occurred, or why one event occurred rather than another. I must admit that the suggestions which follow constitute a tentative theory about the ideal form of historical explanations, which will probably be improved with further investigation.

The key question is, which causes should be included in an ideal explanation? When Hugh Stretton examined historical practice, he drew the conclusion that historians take historical explanations back to causes which they hold to be important for personal reasons, 'according to their different interests, purposes and values' (Stretton, 1969, p. 19). He is able to illustrate this thesis with vivid examples. For instance, in explaining the causes of the First World War, he said, historians of the Left proposed 'an unbreakable causal chain' from capitalism, via imperialism, to war. Those on the Right preferred either a longer chain, attributing war to mankind's innate avarice and aggression, which would drive them to war in any economic system; or a shorter chain, seeing it as the result of failures of government or diplomacy (ibid., pp. 56–7). Stretton suggests that the causes identified by historians are often of a kind which they think should be changed to prevent a recurrence of harm. Such explanations, he says, are 'frankly manipulative: they single out controllable factors or balances to explain what these have done in the past and may therefore be made to do in the future' (pp. 60–1). Finally, Stretton thinks it a good thing that social scientists are guided by their values, because then the information they provide might be of value (p. 170).

The trouble with such an easy acquiescence to selection of causes based upon personal values is that the resulting explanation can be radically misleading, at least to readers who expect a fair, balanced account of the important causes of the event being explained. Stretton's reply to this objection would be that there are just too many causes and conditions of any event for a fair summary of the most important ones to be possible (pp. 54, 60). This is the same position as that of Jenkins, quoted at the beginning of this chapter. However, if one thinks of causes as events which produce a disposition or active tendency for an event of the kind being explained to occur in the circumstances, then the number of causes of any particular event of a certain kind is drastically limited. The causes of an event are then confined to those which significantly increased the probability of the effect's occurrence in the circumstances. The degree of significance will vary according to the degree of detail of the history. Brief histories will mention only those causes which considerably increased the probability of the outcome; lengthy histories will include causes of less significance.

Genetic explanations must not only describe causes of an event; they must describe all the causes which contributed to its occurrence, at the chosen level of importance. In other words, genetic explanations must be both true and fair. To omit important causes from an explanation is to give a misleading idea of why the effect occurred. A clear example of the need for fairness is found in discussion of the causes of the American Civil War. Why did the Northern and Southern states go to war in 1860? A.H. Stephens argued that the war was basically over the rights of states to govern themselves without interference from the national government. The issue which brought the conflict to a head was the right to keep slaves, which the Southern states argued should be determined by state, not national governments. C.A. Beard argued that the motives for the war were economic. When there was a Southern majority in Congress, laws were passed to foster free trade in the interest of Southern exports of tobacco and cotton. When Lincoln and the Northern Republican party came to power in 1860, Southerners feared that they would impose trade restrictions to protect growing industries and insist upon freeing labour for their farms in the north. J.G. Randall and Avery Craven, the 'revisionist' historians, denied that the differences between North and South were sufficient to cause a war, and blamed the leaders of each faction for arousing emotions to fever pitch, so that war became inevitable. Cultural and ideological explanations have been offered as well: Southerners feared the loss of their plantation life-style; Northerners worried that slavery was inconsistent with American values of freedom and equality, as well as with Christian values of the brotherhood of man. Historians have come to recognize the need to take all these causes into account in any explanation of the origins of sectional hostility and the outbreak of war. D.M. Potter does so, for example, in *The Impending Crisis 1848–1861*. He sums up his thesis in these words:

> [T]he slavery issue gave a false clarity and simplicity to sectional diversities which were otherwise qualified and diffuse. One might say that the issue structured and polarized many random, unoriented points of conflict on which sectional interest diverged. It transformed political action from a process of accommodation to a mode of combat. Once this divisive tendency set in, sectional rivalry increased the tensions of the slavery issue and the slavery issue embittered sectional rivalries, in a reciprocating process which the majority of Americans found themselves unable to check even though they deplored it.

(Potter, 1976, p. 43)

Potter's book describes this process in detail. His explanation is admirable because it includes and relates all the major causes of the war.

Profound explanations

Explanations which account for unusual features of a genetic explanation I call 'profound explanations'. They sometimes explain the elements of the first or major cause of an event, accounting for the disposition which was triggered then, or for the trigger itself. In the case of contrastive explanations they may explain the causes of the condition which was responsible for one outcome occurring rather than a designated other. The question which then arises again is: how far back down the causal tree should an historian go? My hypothesis is that they go back either until the occurrence of the disposition, belief or other trigger seems to be a normal response to the circumstances; or, if the disposition, belief or other trigger does not seem to be a normal response, until there is no other explanation available for it.

Let me illustrate at once. The explanation of why Napoleon seized power given above is like a condensed genetic explanation. It refers to Napoleon's growing dismay with the weakness of French government, and his growing desire to exercise the power he had acquired as the hero of the French army to remedy the situation in a forceful manner. Then it points out a situation which triggered his desire for power, namely Sieyès' plan to change the constitution and seize power, which gave Napoleon an opportunity he was determined to exploit. But an historian might say: 'I still do not understand. Successful generals do not normally want to seize control of the government of their country. Why did Napoleon want to do so?' It is probably with this question in mind that Tulard, in his account of the years before the 18th and 19th Brumaire, takes every opportunity to plot Napoleon's growing ambition. For example, after his spectacular success against Sardinian and Austrian troops in Lombardy in 1796–7, Napoleon became convinced that he could become a great leader. Tulard writes:

> Bonaparte himself was surprised by the rapidity of his military successes. It confirmed him in his opinion of his own merit and whetted his ambition. 'After [the battle of] Lodi,' Napoleon was to say later, 'I no longer saw myself as a mere general, but as a man called upon to influence the destiny of a people. The idea occurred to me that I could well become a decisive actor on our political scene.' . . .
>
> From the time of Lodi, Bonaparte's eyes were turned towards Paris, he was aware of the unpopularity of the Directory; he also knew that the power was there to be taken provided that all those who had profited in some way from the Revolution could be carefully handled.
>
> (Tulard, 1985, pp. 58, 62)

But if Napoleon wanted to take control in Paris after his victories in Italy, why did he obey the order of the Directory to take his army to conquer Egypt in 1798? Tulard suggests that he 'hoped by his victory [in Egypt] to increase his glory whilst the government in Paris continued to disintegrate' (p. 67). That he never lost sight of Paris is confirmed by his desertion of his troops in Egypt in August 1799, and his return to Paris. His expedition to Egypt had been unsuccessful: his fleet had been destroyed by Nelson, the people of Cairo had revolted and the Turks had marched on Egypt. Bonaparte, having heard of Sieyès' planned *coup d'état*, excused himself with these words: 'Extraordinary circumstances alone have persuaded me, in the interests of my country, its glory, and of obedience, to pass through enemy lines and to return to Europe' (quoted by Tulard, 1985, p. 70).

This additional information helps to explain Napoleon's ambition, and certainly plots its growing strength. It thus helps to allay doubts as to whether a successful general would have developed the degree of ambition required to act as Napoleon did in Paris in November 1799. Some might find the explanation of his ambition unsatisfactory still: what drives even a brilliantly successful general to seek the government of France? The answer seems to lie partly in Napoleon's passion for the ideals of the revolution, for social justice and strong government on behalf of the people; and partly in his personal ambition to be the saviour of France. Where did these passions come from? A psychologist might point to the frustrations of his youth and the humiliations of his life at a military academy, but not all who suffer hurts such as he did end up wanting to be dictators. One ends up simply affirming his uniqueness, as impossible to explain adequately.

Historians do not seek such a thorough explanation for the motives of everyone they study. Why not? Because most people's motives are commonplace, given their circumstances. Historians only augment genetic explanations when the causes or conditions which account for an outcome are themselves unexpected, such as the strength of Napoleon's ambition.

Profound explanations can augment genetic explanations in several different ways. We have seen how historians might account for Napoleon Bonaparte's ambition by describing events which quickened it. People's attitudes and desires are often responses to past events, and historians can explain them by describing the events which elicited them. But their actions are also a product of their beliefs, and if their beliefs are unusual, they too can be further explained, first by going further back within the agent's system of beliefs, and after that, to the ideas abroad in the agent's culture which he or she might have acquired. Napoleon, for example, was very moved as a young man by his reading of Rousseau to desire a government which would represent the will of the people, though this ambition was perhaps modified once he acquired power and the people were given fewer and fewer opportunities to express their will. Psychology, ideology and finally social structures can provide profound explanations. The bourgeoisie supported Napoleon as one who would ensure their rights to the property they had acquired during the revolution. Their social position gave them interests which drove them to support dictatorial government, so long as it served those interests. Commonly profound explanations refer to all three of these underlying causes or conditions, though some focus upon just one or two.

We have seen how an explanation of Napoleon's seizure of power can be augmented to make it more intelligible. Here are some examples of profound explanations augmenting accounts of the life of Winston Churchill. The first offers a psychological explanation for some of his behaviour. The others point to Churchill's underlying beliefs to explain his policies.

Anthony Storr (1969) has suggested that several characteristics of Churchill's behaviour can be understood as normal defences against depression. Storr produces a lot of evidence of Churchill's propensity towards depression, which he explains partly as a genetic inheritance, to be found in his father and other forebears, including the first Duke of Marlborough, and partly as a result of a social fact, his almost total neglect by his young social mother and busy political father, Lord and Lady Randolph Churchill (p. 247). Storr explains a long list of Churchill's characteristics as normal defences against depression: his great ambition, in the unconscious pursuit of self-esteem; his idealization of his parents and diversion of his hostility against them towards others in authority; his writing and painting and his romantic imagination to fill what he sometimes experienced as the emptiness of his life. In Hitler Churchill found the perfectly evil enemy against whom he could exercise all his hatred and energy (p. 259). His compassion, especially for prisoners, is attributed to his unhappy experiences at boarding school, and to his experience of futility as a prisoner of war during the Boer War (pp. 260–1). The only thing Storr says he cannot explain is Churchill's great courage in fighting depression so vigorously for most of his life (p. 273). In the end, unfortunately, it consumed him.

Notice that this psychological explanation not only goes deep into Churchill's psyche, showing that much of his behaviour can be understood as a defence against depression, but it relates that deep tendency to depression to antecedent events, in this case to his genetic inheritance and to his parents' neglect when he was a child.

As can be seen, psychological explanations account for people's attitudes rather than their ideas. Churchill acquired his beliefs about the glory of Britain from his study of history, in particular of his ancestors' contribution to it. In fact J.H. Plumb says that Churchill's interpretation of history reflected the beliefs of his father's generation.

> Both Empire and the people were problems which taxed English genius to its utmost, but it solved both. The British Empire was the most just the world had seen, and its people enjoyed the richest and freest democracy history had ever known. The English and their institutions were the result of time working on natural genius. And the centuries-old leaders of this miraculous historical development were those 'great Oaks,' as Edmund Burke called them – the great landed aristocratic families who were the guardians of England's destiny and its natural rulers.
>
> (Plumb, 1969, p. 135)

This version of English history, writes Plumb, 'helped him formulate his political ideas. It governed his attitude to India, to Ireland, to Europe. It invaded his strategy and his tactics. It inflamed his rhetoric with a measured and unforgettable passion. It regulated his political decisions. It imbued everything that he wrote' (ibid.).

Churchill's beliefs were also a product of his close study of his father's political speeches. 'As Churchill studied his father's career, he joined the ranks of those who believed that Lord Randolph had been the true successor to Disraeli: a prophet of "Tory Democracy"' (Charmley, 1993, p. 19). This was a party devoted to serving the nation, not to the conservation of traditional aristocratic privileges.

It is already apparent that some profound explanations refer to attitudes and beliefs which were expressed in many of the subject's (Churchill's) activities. In doing this, they perform a colligatory function, showing how many actions were related to the same set of underlying attitudes and beliefs. One could say, therefore, that as well as explaining certain features of many of Churchill's actions, these profound explanations also provide a colligatory interpretation of aspects of his life.

What then is the difference between a general interpretation of someone's life, and a profound explanation of his or her behaviour? It is hard to say, but I suggest that a general interpretation supplies a framework in which an historian casts the narrative of the subject's life, whereas a profound explanation is added to a genetic narrative and does not necessarily structure it. Clearly general beliefs and dispositions can serve both functions, interpretative and explanatory. People behave as they do because they hold the beliefs they do, and have the temperament and attitudes they do.

A.J.P. Taylor has provided some useful insights into Churchill's beliefs and attitudes which could be used both to explain and to interpret his actions. Here are some of his observations: 'He was always ambitious to serve the greatness of the British Empire and to promote the principles of democracy and ordered freedom' (Taylor, 1969, p. 26). 'He wished to remove poverty and injustice, not to achieve any fundamental change, and claimed rightly to be at heart a conservative even in his most radical days.' He 'did not regard the Dominions as equals, and he saw the Commonwealth . . . as a family of children, loyally sustaining the venerable mother to whom they owed so much' (p. 16). Then Taylor remarks: 'Despite the seeming rationality with which his state papers were composed, Churchill was strongly swayed by emotions – usually generous, sometimes the reverse' (ibid.).

> He believed in concessions from strength, not from weakness. When he was powerful, his benevolence brimmed over. When challenged – either at home or by foreign enemies – he sought total victory first and advocated conciliation only when victory had been won. This was the attitude he adopted in two World Wars, in the Boer War, and in the Irish troubles also.

He had the same attitude toward the British workers: social reforms if they were well-behaved and stern action against them if they dared to strike . . .

His deeper weakness was impatience, particularly in his earlier years. When he was set on a course, he wanted results at once and was angered by the dead weight of habit.

(p. 17)

In the pages which follow, Taylor illustrates these beliefs and attitudes again and again. He also notes apparent inconsistencies in his policies which remain to be explained (p. 26). Some irrational decisions are attributed to 'a romantic devotion to British greatness' (p. 27), others to boyish impulse (p. 50).

Profound explanations of group behaviour

The next example is of a profound explanation supporting a contrastive explanation. People have often wondered why the Light Brigade was ordered to ride to its certain death during the Crimean War between Britain (and France) and Russia (1854–5). The Light Brigade of about 700 British horsemen was ordered to attack the enemy at the end of a valley, which had guns trained upon these troops from three sides. The order was absurd, suicidal. They were all killed. The charge of the Light Brigade occurred because the horsemen had been trained to obey their officers, and they had been ordered to make the charge. What cries out for explanation is why such a dreadful order was given in the first place, and why more reasonable battle plans were not formulated and followed instead.

Cecil Woodham-Smith has investigated the background of the officers involved, to provide a profound explanation of their stupidity. Those who led the charge of the Light and Heavy Brigades, Lords Cardigan and Lucan, were inept and arrogant, and totally lacking in experience. The commanding officer, Lord Raglan, had been a diplomat, and at 65 years of age, he had never led troops into battle in his life (Woodham-Smith, 1957, p. 168). His staff were no better, five of them being his nephews (p. 177). The Crimean War was, from beginning to end, a British fiasco. Why was the British army led by such incompetent officers? According to Woodham-Smith, the British thought of war as 'an aristocratic trade' (p. 11), which required courage and little else. It was not thought important that officers receive training in war, or be at all experienced (pp. 146–7). The rank of officer had to be bought, and the cost of commissions excluded all but the wealthy. In particular, it excluded experienced soldiers who simply could not afford them (pp. 31–3). So those who were officers were neither trained nor experienced in war, and those who were trained and experienced could not become officers. But this explanation is still not enough. Why on earth did the British government tolerate such a dreadful state of affairs? Apparently the government remembered the outstanding successes of Marlborough and Wellington under this system, and simply overlooked the fact that there was nothing to prevent fools from acquiring a commission. The system was generally approved as a way of ensuring that revolutionaries, from the lower classes, never gained control of the army.

Notice how this explanation works. The stupidity of the commanding officers is explained as the result of both an ideology which saw war as an adventure for aristocrats, and a number of practices which allowed men to become officers who were temperamentally unsuited for the job, and who had inadequate training and experience. It even explains these practices as the result of a determination, following the English Civil War, to prevent the army from falling into the hands of revolutionaries. Without this information, the stupidity of the officers during the Crimean War is difficult to understand. The profound explanation makes the foolishness of the order given to the Light Brigade intelligible.

Sometimes it is difficult to tell whether an explanation is causal or contrastive because it can be regarded as both. Consider this explanation of a massacre in Nanjing. It both explains what caused the soldiers to behave so badly, and in doing so, explains why they did not behave more humanely. It refers to ideology, attitude, common practices and structural facts to account for what happened.

According to some historians, over 200,000 Chinese civilians and prisoners of war were murdered over a period of six weeks after Nanjing fell to Japanese forces on 13 December 1937, and about 20,000 cases of rape occurred in the city. The basic narrative is plain enough, even though the numbers involved are uncertain. The question historians have asked is what explains such dreadful behaviour by the Japanese troops? Daqing Yang, in a review of recent writing about the massacre, records the ever more complex explanation of the event being developed by historians (Yang, 1999). At first some ascribed it to a breakdown of discipline in the Japanese army, which would explain why they were not kept in check. More recently historians have looked to 'modern Japanese militarism' for an explanation. Japanese soldiers were trained to be brutal, so their training established a disposition to treat their enemy badly. There were also ideologically implanted beliefs at work. One was the importance of conquering Nanjing, the capital of China, which may have driven them to kill the Chinese so ferociously. Another was a contempt they had acquired for the Chinese people, and, according to some witnesses, a willingness to condone the sexual abuse of women. Others have noted social facts about the soldiers involved, 'the high proportion of poorly disciplined reserve soldiers in the China theatre and . . . the narrow military education of commanders and staff officers, which contributed to the lack of respect for civilian lives and international law' (p. 856). Daqing Yang concludes that 'the atrocity in Nanjing is increasingly seen as an outcome of both the brutalization of war in China and deep-rooted tendencies in pre-war Japan' (p. 859). Once again, an extraordinary event is made more intelligible once a profound explanation of it is provided. The culture and training of the Japanese troops go some way towards explaining their horrific treatment of the Chinese.

Profound explanations and colligatory interpretations

Sometimes historians look for a 'profound explanation' for a range of events which serves to colligate them, to display them as all outworkings of the one basic cause or condition. The point to be made about these explanations is that while they might have considerable colligatory success, their explanatory power is usually very limited. Indeed, in the search for a simple unifying explanation, historians are in danger of overlooking other quite important causes of the events they are trying to explain.

Sometimes historical changes which seem to have no common explanation can eventually be seen to have one. For example, the most salient fact about German politics in the 1930s was the consolidation of Nazi power. There were several different elements in that consolidation. Voter support for the National Socialist Party increased. As Chancellor from 1933, Hitler replaced the existing government administration with his own, and set up additional police forces, the S.A. and the S.S. His party attacked the Communists, the Trade Unions, and other political parties, effectively eliminating their opposition to his rule. The army supported Hitler's regime, even his elevation in August 1934, after the death of President von Hindenburg, to the new position of Head of State. The theme 'consolidation of Nazi power' neatly sums up much of the politics of Germany in that period. However, it seems that there is no single explanation of every element of that consolidation. Voters supported the Nazi Party for a variety of reasons: many, especially the youth, were captured by Hitler's promise to build a great nation after the humiliation of the Treaty of Versailles. The bourgeoisie and industrialists looked for stability and prosperity after a period of economic depression. The army's reasons for tolerating Hitler's government are unclear, but winning its tacit support was vital to his success. Hitler's ideology and charismatic leadership explain a lot of his behaviour and his success, but the interests of others also explain their support of his rule. There seems to be no single explanation for the consolidation of Nazi power in the 1930s.

John Hiden and John Farquharson, however, have offered a single profound explanation of Hitler's rise to power. Using a theory derived from the work of Barrington Moore, they suggest that when the people of Germany realized how poorly their new democracy coped with the challenges of reconstruction after Germany's defeat in the First World War, and how it entirely failed to protect the country from the ravages of the massive economic depression at the end of the 1920s, they were willing to accept an authoritarian regime instead (Hiden and Farquharson, 1983, pp. 161–2). This explanation accounts in very general terms for many different groups in Germany supporting the National Socialists, and for the National Socialists themselves believing that a dictatorship under a strong visionary such as Hitler was the best form of government to adopt. Obviously this explanation needs to be supplemented to explain what each group hoped for from the new regime, which they had not enjoyed under the postwar democracy. The very generality of this profound explanation is in danger of obscuring important differences.

In the search for a unifying profound explanation, historians often prefer single factor explanations, even at the risk of misrepresenting the complexity of the causal process. That this is a matter of professional concern is evident in a review by D. Cannadine of a long book on British imperialism. In it Cannadine deplores the tendency of historians to look for single explanations of the establishment of Britain's empire. He lists several different theses, which attribute the empire to accident, to capitalism, to the pursuit of glory, to strategic interests, and to the need to ensure good government in colonized countries. He shows that each is quite inadequate, and concludes that 'to suppose that an Empire so vast, so varied and so multiracial could have come into being for one single or simple reason is clearly absurd' (Cannadine, 1995, pp. 181–3). His review is of a two-volume history of the British Empire by P.J. Cain and A.G. Hopkins (*British Imperialism*, Longman, London, 1993), which attributes the growth and control of empire to 'gentleman capitalists' in London, who invested very large sums of money overseas, and then acted to ensure that their investments were protected and profitable. After 1945, British investments in the Empire were not very significant, and instead money was invested in Europe and America. Cannadine denies that the development of the empire had such a simple origin. The connections between the City of London and the government of Britain were not always very close; and many counties outside London invested in the empire, as indeed did Wales, Scotland and Ireland. He concludes that 'the analysis is excessively monocausal, and gives inadequate weight to the many other explanations for Empire – not just political-diplomatic-strategic, but also religious, humanitarian, ideological and cultural' (p. 194).

The issue we confront is the tension between a desire to produce a nicely unified history, illustrating an interesting theme which has, perhaps, been unappreciated before; and the desire to offer a comprehensive, fair explanation of the major events being described. When unifying explanations ignore causes of considerable importance, they are misleading.

Structural explanations

The term 'structural explanations' refers to two different things: one is the way in which social structures influence individual behaviour; the other is the way in which changes to social structures are explained. (In Chapter 3, I distinguished three kinds of social structure: social organizations, social systems and general social structures.)

Social structures and individual behaviour

Profound explanations are often provided by referring to unconscious psychological facts, as can be seen from the examples described above. Another source of human behaviour often overlooked by commonsense are social pressures. People commonly respond to social expectations, for instance in the language they speak and in what they say by means of it. There is a lot of interest these days in the influence of common discourse upon individuals' thinking and acting, a subject which used to be studied under the heading of ideology. People often structure their understanding of historical situations according to the discourse they think relevant, and the discourse often also prescribes appropriate and inappropriate responses.

Social organizations impose special pressures on their members. Authorized rules and practices stipulate patterns of behaviour members should follow, in the interests of the organization. At the extreme, laws and regulations govern the decisions of judges, civil servants and military personnel to a quite extraordinary degree. Nevertheless, individuals retain the freedom to act contrary to those laws if they wish to. They normally conform to them, partly because they approve of the functions of the organization, and partly no doubt from self-interest, for disobedience could result in punishment or dismissal.

While organizations constrain individual behaviour on the one hand, they facilitate it on the other. The resources of an organization enable people to achieve things they could not otherwise manage to do. Universities, for example, provide the opportunities and facilities for research which it would be difficult to find otherwise. An army enables its general to win a battle; a court enables a judge to reach a just sentence; a hospital enables a doctor to perform a complex operation; and so on.

It is difficult to assess the degree of pressure an organization places upon its members. But this pressure has been blamed for the decision by the German Nazi government to kill the Jews in countries it controlled, and for the way in which so many Germans helped to carry out that policy. In his book *Modernity and the Holocaust* (1989), Z. Bauman explains the appallingly immoral treatment of the Jews as largely the product of bureaucratic tradition. Bauman says that once the German government had decided that the Jews could have no part in the new Nazi Aryan state, then genocide, the policy of exterminating the Jews, was a bureaucratic decision made when other ways of excluding the Jews from the new German state seemed impracticable. The cost and logistics of expelling the Jews from Germany and from the lands Germany conquered, and colonizing them elsewhere, became impossible, so another administrative decision had to be made. Extermination was 'the rational solution'. Bauman comments: the 'spirit of instrumental rationality, and its modern, bureaucratic form of institutionalization, . . . made the Holocaust-style solutions not only possible, but eminently "reasonable" – and increased the probability of their choice' (p. 18). Once Hitler had expressed his wish for a German state free of Jews and other misfits, the bureaucracy simply sought practical ways of implementing his policy, without any concern for the morality of what was being sought.

Bauman points out that genocide on the scale envisaged and achieved by the Nazi government required an immense, efficient and unimpeded bureaucracy, which was provided by the state. He writes: 'When the modernist dream [of a perfect state] is embraced by an absolute power able to monopolize modern vehicles of rational action, and when that power attains freedom from effective social control, genocide happens' (pp. 93–4). Not only did the German bureaucracy implement the government's policy efficiently, it also succeeded in impeding moral outrage at what it was doing. Bauman points out that the SS men and women who obeyed the government's orders were not all pathological killers, but most were quite normal citizens (p. 19), obeying their superiors as they had always done.

Modern bureaucracy reduces any moral inhibitions people might have in carrying out immoral acts. Citing the work of H.C. Kelman, Bauman states three conditions reducing moral inhibitions: 'the violence is *authorized* (by official orders coming from the legally entitled quarters), actions are *routinized* (by rule-governed practices and exact specification of roles), and the victims of the violence are *dehumanized* (by ideological definitions and indoctrinations)' (p. 21). Later he added that bureaucracies distance people from the effects of their actions, thereby reducing any sense of personal responsibility for the suffering they cause, and they reward technical competence as the most desirable quality in a bureaucrat, not moral responsibility. Furthermore, they tend to refer to the people affected by their decisions in an inhuman way, as cargo or statistics, not humans for whom one is morally responsible (pp. 98–104).

Historians refer to social systems, or rather to elements of social systems, to explain individual behaviour which conforms to them. For example, suppose an historian discovers that a firm has just lost a major market for its products, and that the management then dismisses a number of employees. The historian would assume the dismissals were in response to the loss of income incurred by the loss of markets, because this is the normal, rational response in such circumstances, according to economic theory

Jon Elster, in *Nuts and Bolts for the Social Sciences* (1989), has drawn attention to the fallibility of rational generalizations as descriptions of human behaviour. There is not always a rationally optimal response to a situation, and even when there is, people do not always act rationally, he said. Even when people do act in accordance with rational economic theory, Elster said we do not understand why they do so unless we study the small 'mechanisms' which made them act individually as they did (p. 10). I suggest that when people act according to a rational theory, historians simply assume that they acted rationally. It is only when they fail to act as the theory predicts that historians need to examine the 'mechanisms' that caused them to behave so irrationally.

Changes in general social structures can cause individual, and more commonly group, action when those changes are recognized as contrary to the interests of the group. E.P. Thompson has documented the ways in which English labourers in the mid-nineteenth century, suffering from the enclosure of common lands and the mechanization of industry, longed for their own plots of land, and the prosperity and independence they imagined went with them

(Thompson, 1968, pp. 253–5, 326). Thompson focussed on the writings of the groups he studied, attributing their actions to their perceptions of social change. Charles Tilly, in his analysis of the counter-revolutionary wars in the Vendée in France in 1793, tried to get away from rational explanations, and look for socio-economic interests to explain group behaviour. He noted that the counter-revolutionaries included a lot of peasants involved in 'localized, subsistence agriculture', in areas where 'market-oriented, rationalized agriculture' threatened to absorb them; and they included a lot of weavers, who resented the poor treatment they received from their masters during a crisis in the industry (Tilly, 1963, p. 55). He assumes that people will do what they can to defend their interests, and since the counter-revolutionaries can be seen to be doing that, there is no need to investigate their individual perceptions of the predicaments facing them (ibid., p. 34).

Those sceptical of the reality of social structures might point out, quite correctly, that people who rebel against what they think are changes in general social structures are really responding to their ideas about society, or to prevailing discourse about society, but not to any real social structures at all. I defended the reality of social structures in the last section of Chapter 3. Here it is enough to say that when historians investigate the origins of discourse and beliefs about social structures, they usually discover precisely that kind of evidence which warrants belief in their reality. In some cases, no doubt, people believe on insufficient evidence; and in some cases, discourse about social structures is fabricated for political purposes. But often change in the general wealth or power of distinct social groups is plain for all to see.

Explaining changes in social structures

The importance of distinguishing social organizations, social systems and general social structures is particularly evident when it comes to explaining changes in social structures. For change in each of these kinds of social structure is explained in a different way.

Explaining changes in social organizations

Changes in social organizations can either be authorized from above or just implemented from below. Most organizations have rules outlining procedures for considering and deciding changes to the organization, and if these are properly followed, the changes are regarded as duly authorized. Some procedures allow for input from those affected by the changes; others give a lot of discretion to those in charge. To explain changes from above, historians study how these rules were implemented, who came up with a plan for a change, who lobbied whom to support the proposal, and who finally voted for it, for what reasons. Changes from below are those departures from regulations which become so regular as to constitute a new practice governing a section of the organization.

Explaining changes in social systems

Changes in social systems have been more difficult to explain. Certainly there are ways of explaining changes in the quantities of variables within a system, for example changes in investment, prices, wages and employment within an economic system can often be explained as fairly rational. Similarly, it is often fairly easy to explain changes in the fortune of parties within a political system, in terms of their ideology, organization, wealth, and charisma, though voting patterns are not entirely rational. What are more difficult to explain are changes to the systems themselves.

For a while some social theorists looked for a general theory of social change. Some thought social systems to be in a state of equilibrium, and that if some event disturbed the system, it would adjust to restore the equilibrium. For example, if the market for one product disappeared, farmers or industrialists would turn to produce another for which there was a demand. Presumably, if royal government proved to be entirely incapable, as were the governments of the King of France and the Czar of Russia just before the revolutions in those countries, then a new form of government would be formed to take its place. The trouble was that social systems do not always adjust to change efficiently, as this theory supposes. Chalmers Johnson had developed a theory of revolutionary change based upon this theory, but he acknowledged that it was not universally applicable (see McCullagh, 1998, pp. 282–3). Ralf Dahrendorf preferred to think of society as a field in which groups with opposing interests contest for authority and power. He explained social changes as a result of such conflict. But he had to admit that sometimes social changes were the result of agreement between various groups in society, not conflict at all (ibid., p. 284).

The failure to find a general theory of systems change suggests that historians should stop looking for a general, theoretical explanation of such changes, and account for each particular instance of social change by providing a common-sense narrative of how it took place. The important advantage of this procedure is that such narratives clearly indicate the influence of contingencies, unexpected events or particular states of affairs, upon the process of change. The main reason why no general theory of systems change is adequate is that none can allow for contingencies interrupting the general process it describes.

However, general explanations of change in particular social systems are very useful for identifying the general causes which, taken in sequence, produced change in those social structures. These summaries do not describe a process which was necessary as a whole. But they do reveal general causal processes which were essential for its occurrence. Here is an example of a summary by R.M. Hartwell of the changes in the British economy during the second half of the eighteenth century which produced the Industrial Revolution.

> Growth was prompted by the increasing supply of factors [raw materials and labour], by the changing technology and by the increasing demand [result-

ing from a growth in population]. Investment plus invention increased productivity in industry, created further employment and tended to push up
wages. However, since interest rates remained low, and wages rose only
slowly, there was neither a capital nor labour shortage to inhibit enterprise.
Although demand remained buoyant, the costs of enterprise remained relatively low, and investment was encouraged. The turning-point came in the
eighties, when the mounting pressure of demand, both real and potential,
created pressures on industry to further increase productivity. This resulted
in a series of notable technical breakthroughs which so reduced the price of
industrial goods that not only was domestic demand greatly increased, but
English goods were cheap enough also to invade, even over tariff and trans-
port barriers, the mass market of Europe. The industrial revolution had
begun.

(Hartwell, 1967, p. 28. This quotation is discussed
in McCullagh, 1998, pp. 285–6)

Commonsense descriptions of particular changes within the British economy
would not reveal the causal connections described in this passage. So they are no
substitute for such general causal analysis. Clearly descriptions like this draw
upon economic theory, a theory which describes ways in which different economic variables can influence certain kinds of outcome. To produce such
descriptions of social systems, historians must be very familiar with the theory
involved, and especially sensitive to the range of possible causes and effects of
the kinds of event they study.

In order to test the adequacy of a theory, or its relevance to an historical
episode, historians see whether particular events in fact had the causes or effects
that the theory predicted. Political historians sometimes use theories to explain
events. In a recent essay on political history, Susan Pedersen points out that
Marxist theories which described political parties as serving class interests were
found unable to account for the popularity of Gladstonian liberalism among the
working class in nineteenth-century Britain (Pedersen, 2002, pp. 42–3). Glad-
stone's liberalism did not offer the working class greater power. Rather, it
lightened the demands made upon the people by government, which appealed to
an 'older dissenting, radical and working-class hostility to an oppressive and pat-
rimonial state' (ibid., p. 43). Pedersen is here pointing to an alternative theory of
politics, which relates support for political parties to the ideas they promote in
their rhetoric and to existing cultural traditions. But attention to rhetoric should
not displace the analysis of political structure, says Pedersen. In eighteenth-
century Britain there was much concern about 'old corruption', the old influence
of great families of Britain over parliament and government. But historians have
discovered that in fact British government of that time was remarkably efficient.

Not only was it able to extract a strikingly large proportion of GNP to
sustain the functions of the state (and pre-eminently to sustain its wars), but

the collection and dispersal of these funds was never (as it was in France) actually delegated to parasitic private interests.

(ibid., p. 48)

This is the language of political theory, of particular use in comparing the political system of one country (Britain), with that of another (France). The survival of the British government during revolutionary times was doubtless a result of its efficiency, compared with the inefficiency and collapse of the French. Pedersen concludes: 'Popular understandings of the institutions of . . . state, however critically important to the social history and party politics of the period, do not give us a very good analytical understanding of these states . . .' (ibid., p. 49). (For a fascinating discussion of the interaction between political history and theory, see *Debating Revolutions*, ed. N.R. Keddie (1995).)

While political theory can often account for the popularity and strength of some governments, and the unpopularity and weakness of others, changes to social systems are often brought about by government decree, particularly after episodes of great social disturbance, such as revolutions, wars and natural catastrophes, which require a new political organization to cope. The best political histories of systems change, therefore, combine an analysis of social predicaments with an explanation of the decisions made to cope with them. An impressive example of such a history is Barrington Moore's book *Soviet Politics* (1950), in which he identifies the structural dilemmas faced by the Bolsheviks from time to time, and explains their response by noting background 'ideological constraints [the desire for social equality], functional imperatives [of promoting economic production and the distribution of goods], and international relations', and then explaining the 'costs and benefits' of the policies adopted (D. Smith, 1984, pp. 322–5). For example, in 1921 the government introduced a New Economic Policy which permitted some private enterprises to continue, but leaders of these enterprises were opposed to bolshevism. 'The tensions that resulted meant that an authoritarian response was bound to follow' (ibid., p. 323).

Explaining changes in general social structures

Finally we come to explanations of changes to general social structures. The most popular subject for Western historians of general social structures has been the transition from feudal agrarian societies to democratic, industrial capitalist societies. The attempt to find one general theory to explain this very rich and complex pattern of change has proved fruitless. The Marxist theory that capitalists would overthrow feudal structures to promote their better means of producing wealth foundered on the fact that the English Civil War, which resulted in the formation of a republican government under Oliver Cromwell, was motivated as much by religious concerns as by economic ones. R.J. Holton, in his book *The Transition from Feudalism to Capitalism* (1985), examined several theories of change, but concluded that 'there is no single pattern of capitalist development within the nation-states of early modern Europe' (p. 146). He concluded:

> Instead of the search for a unitary causal force behind the emergence of capitalism, what seems called for is a greater tolerance of causal pluralism, multilinear patterns of social change, analyses of particular unrepeatable historical conjunctures and explanation in terms of contingent rather than historically necessary patterns of social development.
>
> (p. 145)

To determine the causes of change in a general social structure, historians have to refer to the properties which define that structure. For example, if one is describing the structure of power in a society, then the changes which are most likely to affect that structure are political. W.G. Runciman has identified three common kinds of social power, economic, ideological, and coercive, and from this he infers that there are 'three dimensions of social structure' (Runciman, 1989, p. 15). It comes as no surprise then that when Peter McPhee wants to explain changes to French society between 1780 and 1880, 'focusing on social relations of power', he should pick out 'the two great social crises of this century – the French Revolution of 1789–95 and the Second Republic, 1848–51' as the events responsible for the most striking changes in the social structure (McPhee, 1993, pp. 2–3). These involved changes in all three kinds of power named by Runciman. The first saw the replacement of a feudal system of government with a bourgeois bureaucratic one.

> In 1789–91, revolutionaries reshaped every aspect of institutional and public life according to bourgeois assumptions of rationality, uniformity and efficiency. Underpinning this sweeping, energetic recasting was an administrative system of departments, districts, cantons and communes. These departments were henceforth to be administered in precisely the same way within an identical structure of responsibilities, personnel and powers. Diocesan boundaries now coincided with departmental limits, and cathedrals were usually located in departmental capitals.
>
> (pp. 98–9)

McPhee notes that the 'institutional, legal and social changes' brought about by the revolution created 'the environment within which capitalist industry and agriculture would thrive' (p. 101). The social transformation of France as a consequence of the revolution was massive (see ibid., ch. 5). As for the Second Republic, McPhee says that it 'marked the end of royalist régimes in France and the definitive victory of universal manhood suffrage' (p. 195), promised by Louis-Napoleon when he seized power in 1851 (p. 190). 'In the long run . . . the consolidation of universal suffrage was to undermine the predominance of great landowners as typical of the ruling élite' (p. 268).

Towards the end of his book, McPhee criticizes the assumptions of 'modern-ization theory'. It provides a good, closing example of the danger of top-down history, driven by general assumptions of the nature of historical change which have not been tested against the evidence. McPhee explains

> The premises of modernization theory have had a powerful but negative impact on the writing of social history: they presuppose that in society and politics, as in the marketplace economy, the bourgeoisie of the nineteenth century was the repository of 'modern' values and behaviour taught or dif-fused to the urban and rural masses through a 'trickling-down' process.
>
> (p. 275)

One elaboration of this modernization theory is the suggestion that popular support for liberal parliamentary government was a consequence of bourgeois values being accepted by the lower classes. McPhee points out that it was the élites who did not want parliamentary democracy to be extended, and the working classes who did:

> the victory of parliamentary democracy by 1880 was due more than any-thing else to deeply held beliefs among working people that popular sovereignty implied manhood suffrage and electoral choice. In the end, this was a victory won by revolution 'from below'. . . . Resistance to the practice of parliamentary democracy came from entrenched élites, not from insuffi-ciently 'enlightened' working people with a predilection for violent protest.
>
> (p. 276)

Then again, the theory of modernization presented the processes of urbanization and mass eduction 'as inevitably secularizing beliefs' about the place of people in the world, and as 'sapping the habit of religious worship'. In fact, however, between 1830 and 1860 there was a great religious revival in France, particularly among women (p. 277).

These examples show the fundamental importance of historians knowing the detailed history of their subject before they attempt an interpretation or explana-tion of it. Those who confine their histories to the illustration of politically correct or academically popular theories leave themselves open to refutation.

Conclusion

Those who teach history in schools and universities often value the subject for providing training in critical thinking. They teach students critical interpretation of evidence, and critical assessment of interpretations and explanations. They hope that the skills students acquire by studying history will be useful in other contexts. Such teachers will, I hope, welcome this book as it introduces readers to the forms of argument found in the discipline of history.

A question that needs to be asked, however, is why does history have to be rational? To add to its entertainment value, why not embellish it with colourful details for which we lack evidence, but which could have been true? As propaganda, why not simplify the story and perhaps exaggerate aspects of it to make its message clearer? Why should historians insist that professional history be rationally defensible?

These questions force us to consider the social value of professional history. There are three social functions of history which require that history be as rational as possible. The first is that history establishes the identity of social groups, institutions and nations. It describes the character of instances of these by studying how they have behaved in the past. In so doing, it draws attention to characteristics which people identify with those particular groups, institutions or nations, to which they respond with approval or hostility. In war, politicians generally denigrate the enemy, to encourage hatred and justify killing. Historians have a vital responsibility to ensure that the accounts they give of groups, institutions and nations are as accurate and fair as they can make them, so that responses to them can be just.

A second valuable contribution history makes to present society is that it identifies trends at work that can enhance or diminish its quality of life. The globalization of liberal capitalism has had good and bad effects which are likely to continue, and the bad ones, which range from the exploitation of cheap labour to the loss of many community values and services, need to be addressed. Another trend of recent concern has been the exploitation and degradation of the environment, with dramatic effects upon the world's climate and the loss of natural species. More recent trends involve difficult relations between Muslim and Christian communities; and a worrying disregard for international law.

Historians must report these trends accurately, if we are to respond to them appropriately.

Finally, history has many lessons to teach us about the value or disvalue of the beliefs and practices, traditions and institutions which we have inherited, enabling us to see the value of those worth preserving and the need to change those which are not. History is also a rich field for the discovery of causes of historical change, of wars and revolutions, of economic prosperity and depression, which inform many of our political and economic judgements. Once again, we will act foolishly if the historical basis of our decisions is not as accurate as possible.

Historians as a profession have a social responsibility to protect the community from false and biased propaganda. Individual historians will have their own personal biases no doubt, but the profession has standards of rational justification, set out above, which can be applied to correct most personal biases. Culture-wide biases are harder to rectify: we must rely upon people from other cultures to help us detect those. (For a discussion of bias in history, see McCullagh, 2000.)

There are other benefits which history can provide, but these are personal rather than social. In describing the fortunes of great and ordinary people in the past, and of their projects and communities, historians help us understand the variety of ways in which peoples' lives can unfold, which is a source of personal wisdom. By describing the struggles of a person's own family, group or community, how they have reached the point they are currently at, history can foster a sense of corporate identity, an ability to see one's own life as part of that of a greater social whole. And finally, history can be very entertaining, as it describes how people overcame difficulties in achieving their goals, or were finally defeated by them. Fiction can provide entertainment as well as history, but it cannot yield wisdom and a sense of corporate identity nearly as convincingly.

To fulfil these social and personal functions responsibly, history should be credible, intelligible and fair. Historians should ensure that their descriptions of the past are well supported by evidence, so that they are entirely credible. One cannot prove descriptions of the past that are absolutely true, but one can have so much evidence in support of them that it is quite reasonable to believe them true. When historians explain significant events, they should do so accurately and comprehensively. The causes they identify must actually have influenced the outcome, and no important causes should be ignored. Otherwise readers will not properly understand how such outcomes are produced. Finally, descriptions, explanations and interpretations must be fair, not omitting features of a subject or process so as to give a misleading impression of its nature. In judging the value of people, policies and institutions, people need to know their good points and their bad points alike. A partial, one-sided account will produce a mistaken idea of their value.

Given the importance of providing credible, intelligible and fair history, it is incumbent upon serious students of history to know how they should justify their conclusions.

References

Philosophical and reflective works

Adams, W.P., 1999. 'The historian as translator: an introduction', *The Journal of American History*, 85: 1283–8.

Ankersmit, F.R., 1983. *Narrative Logic. A Semantic Analysis of the Historian's Language*. The Hague, Martinus Nijhoff.

Barrett, Michele, 1988. *Women's Oppression Today. The Marxist/Feminist Encounter*, rev. edn. London, Verso.

Bauman, Z., 1989. *Modernity and the Holocaust*. Cambridge, Polity Press.

Berghahn, V.R. and Schissler, H. (eds), 1987. *Perceptions of History: International Textbook Research on Britain, Germany and the United States*, Leamington Spa, Berg.

Berkhofer, Robert F. Jr., 1995. *Beyond the Great Story. History as Text and Discourse*. Cambridge, MA, The Belknap Press of Harvard University Press.

Blackmore, Susan, 1999. *The Meme Machine*. Oxford, Oxford University Press.

Bloch, Marc, 1954. *The Historian's Craft*, trans. Peter Putnam. Manchester, Manchester University Press.

Boggs, Carl, 1976. *Gramsci's Marxism*. London, Pluto Press.

Bonnell, V.E. and Hunt, L. (eds), 1999. *Beyond the Cultural Turn. New Directions in the Study of Society and Culture*. Berkeley, University of California Press.

Bourdieu, Pierre, 1977. *Outline of a Theory of Practice*, trans. R. Nice. Cambridge, Cambridge University Press.

Brown, Robert, 1973. *Rules and Laws in Sociology*. London, Routledge and Kegan Paul.

Butterfield, Herbert, 1951. *History and Human Relations*. London, Collins.

Cabrera, M.A., 2001. 'On language, culture, and social action', *History and Theory*, 40: 82–100.

Carr, David, 1986. 'Narrative and the real world: an argument for continuity', *History and Theory*, 25: 117–31.

—— 1991. 'Discussion: Ricoeur on narrative' in *On Paul Ricoeur. Narrative and Interpretation*, ed. David Wood. London, Routledge, pp. 160–74.

Certeau, Michel de, 1984. *The Practice of Everyday Life*, trans. S. Rendall. Berkeley, University of California Press.

—— 1988. *The Writing of History*, trans. Tom Conley. New York, Columbia University Press.

Chartier, R., 1991. *The Cultural Origins of the French Revolution*, trans. L.G. Cochrane. Durham, NC, Duke University Press.

—— 1997. *On the Edge of the Cliff. History, Language, and Practices*, trans. L.G. Cochrane. Baltimore, MD, The Johns Hopkins University Press.

Cohen, G.A., 1988. *History, Labour and Freedom: Themes from Marx*. Oxford, Clarendon Press.

Collingwood, R.G., 1946. *The Idea of History*. London, Oxford University Press.

—— 1970. *An Autobiography*. Oxford, Oxford University Press.

Crapanzano, Vincent, 1986. 'Hermes' dilemma: The masking of subversion in ethnographic description', in *Writing Culture. The Poetics and Politics of Ethnography*, ed. J. Clifford and G.E. Marcus. Berkeley, University of California Press.

Dallin, A., 1988. 'Commentary on "A Stalin Biographer's' Memoir"', in *Psychology and Historical Interpretation*, ed. W.McK. Runyan. New York, Oxford University Press, pp. 82–5.

Danto, Arthur, 1965. *Analytical Philosophy of History*. Cambridge, Cambridge University Press.

Derrida, Jacques, 1982. *Margins of Philosophy*, trans. A. Bass. Brighton, The Harvester Press.

Dilthey, W., 1959. 'The understanding of other persons and their life-expressions', in *Theories of History*, ed. P. Gardiner. Glencoe, NY, The Free Press, pp. 213–25.

Dray, W.H., 1957. *Laws and Explanation in History*. Oxford, Oxford University Press.

Durkheim, Emile, 1952. *Suicide. A Study in Sociology*. London, Routledge and Kegan Paul.

—— 1964. *The Division of Labour in Society*, trans. George Simpson. New York, The Free Press.

Elster, Jon, 1983. *Explaining Technical Change. A Case Study in the Philosophy of Science*. Cambridge, Cambridge University Press, and Oslo, Universitetsforlaget.

—— 1989. *Nuts and Bolts for the Social Sciences*. Cambridge, Cambridge University Press.

Ermarth, E.D., 2000. 'Beyond "the subject": individuality in the discursive condition', *New Literary History*, 31: 405–19.

—— 2001. 'Beyond history', *Rethinking History*, 5: 195–215.

Escobar, Arturo, 1993. *Encountering Development. The Making and Unmaking of the Third World*. Princeton, NJ, Princeton University Press.

Fay, Brian, 1975. *Social Theory and Political Practice*. London, Allen and Unwin.

Fein, H., 1994. 'Genocide, terror, life integrity, and war crimes: the case for discrimination', in *Genocide. Conceptual and Historical Dimensions*, ed. G.J. Andreopoulos. Philadelphia, University of Pennsylvania Press, pp. 95–107.

Firestone, Shulamith, 1970. *The Dialectic of Sex: The Case for Feminist Revolution*. New York, Morrow.

Floud, Roderick, 1988. 'What is economic history?', in *What is History Today?*, ed. Juliet Gardiner. Basingstoke, Hampshire, Macmillan.

Foucault, Michel, 1973. *The Order of Things. An Archaeology of the Human Sciences*. New York, Vintage Books.

—— 1976. *The Archaeology of Knowledge and the Discourse on Language*, trans. A.M. Sheridan Smith. New York, Harper and Row.

Freud, S., 1986. *The Essentials of Psycho-analysis*, ed. A. Freud, trans. J. Strachey. Harmondsworth, Penguin.

Friedlander, S., 1978. *History and Psychoanalysis. An Inquiry into the Possibilities and Limits of Psychohistory*. trans. S. Suleiman. New York, Holmes and Meier.

Fukuyama, F., 1992. *The End of History and the Last Man*. London, Hamish Hamilton.

Giddens, Anthony, 1984. *The Constitution of Society*. Cambridge, Polity Press.

Goble, F.G., 1971. *The Third Force. The Psychology of Abraham Maslow*. New York, Washington Square Press.

Greenblatt, S.J., 1980. *Renaissance Self-Fashioning: From More to Shakespeare*. Chicago, University of Chicago Press.

Harlan, David, 1989. 'Intellectual history and the return of literature', *The American Historical Review*, 943: 581–609.

Harris, Marvin, 1978. *Cows, Pigs, Wars and Witches. The Riddles of Culture*. New York, Vintage Books.

—— 1979. *Cultural Materialism. The Struggle for a Science of Culture*. New York, Random House.

Held, David, 1980. *Introduction to Critical Theory: Horkheimer to Habermas*. London, Hutchinson.

Helmer, O. and Rescher, N., 1959. 'Exact or inexact sciences: a more instructive dichotomy?', reprinted in *The Nature and Scope of Social Science*, ed. L.I. Krimerman. New York, Appelton-Century Crofts, 1969, pp. 181–203.

Holton, R.J., 1985. *The Transition from Feudalism to Capitalism*. Basingstoke, Macmillan.

Horney, K., 1988. 'A Stalin biographer's memoir', in *Psychology and Historical Interpretation*, ed. W.McK. Runyan. New York, Oxford University Press, pp. 63–81.

Hughes, J.M., 1989. *Reshaping the Psychoanalytic Domain. The Work of Melanie Klein, W.R.D. Fairbairn, and D.W. Winnicott*. Berkeley, University of California Press.

Humphreys, P., 1989. *The Chances of Explanation. Causal Explanation in the Social, Medical, and Physical Sciences*. Princeton, NJ, Princeton University Press.

Jenkins, Keith, 1991. *Re-Thinking History*. London, Routledge.

—— 1995. *On 'What is History?'* London, Routledge.

—— (ed.), 1997. *The Postmodern History Reader*. London, Routledge.

—— 1999. *Why History? Ethics and Postmodernity*. London, Routledge.

Johnson, Chalmers, 1983. *Revolutionary Change*, 2nd edn. London, Longman.

Kaufmann, W., 1956. *Nietzsche. Philosopher, Psychologist, Antichrist*. Cleveland, OH, The World Publishing Company.

Kaye, H.F. and McClelland, K. (eds), 1990. *E.P. Thompson, Critical Perspectives*. Cambridge, Polity Press.

Keddie, N.R., 1995. *Debating Revolutions*. New York, New York University Press.

Lake, Peter, 1993. 'Defining Puritanism – again?' in *Puritanism. Transatlantic Perspectives on a Seventeenth-Century Anglo-American Faith*, ed. F.J. Bremer. Boston, Massachusetts Historical Society, pp. 3–29.

Lloyd, Christopher, 1986. *Explanation in Social History*. Oxford, Blackwell.

—— 1993. *The Structures of History*. Oxford, Blackwell.

Loptson, P., 1995. *Theories of Human Nature*. Peterborough, Ontario, Broadview Press.

Lyotard, J-F., 1984. *The Postmodern Condition: A Report on Knowledge*, trans. G. Bennington and B. Massumi. Manchester, Manchester University Press.

McCullagh, C. Behan, 1978. 'Colligation and classification in history', *History and Theory*, 17: 267–84.

—— 1984. *Justifying Historical Descriptions*. Cambridge, Cambridge University Press.

—— 1991. 'How objective interests explain actions', *Social Science Information*, 30: 29–54.

—— 1998. *The Truth of History*. London, Routledge.

—— 2000. 'Bias in historical description, interpretation, and explanation', *History and Theory*, 39: 39–66.

—— 2001. 'Theories of historical explanation (philosophical aspects)', in *The International Encyclopedia of the Social and Behavioral Sciences*. Kidlington, Elsevier Science.

—— 2004, forthcoming. 'What do historians argue about?', *History and Theory*, 43.

Margolis, J., 1999. 'Pierre Bourdieu: *habitus* and the logic of practice', in *Bourdieu. A Critical Reader*, ed. R. Shusterman. Oxford, Blackwell, pp. 64–83.

Mellor, D.H., 1995. *The Facts of Causation*. London, Routledge.

Mitchell, J., 1974. *Psychoanalysis and Feminism*. London, Allen Lane.

Munslow, Alun, 1999. *Deconstructing History*. London, Routledge.

Neale, R.S., 1985. *Writing Marxist History. British Society, Economy and Culture since 1700*. Oxford, Blackwell.

Newton, J.L., Ryan, M.P. and Walkowitz, J.R. (eds), 1983. *Sex and Class in Women's History*. London, Routledge and Kegan Paul.

Norris, C., 1996. *Reclaiming the Truth. Contribution to a Critique of Cultural Relativism*. London, Lawrence and Wishart.

Novick, Peter, 1988. *That Noble Dream. The 'Objectivity Question' and the American Historical Profession*. Cambridge. Cambridge University Press.

Olafson, F.A., 1979. *The Dialectic of Action. A Philosophical Interpretation of History and the Humanities*. Chicago, The University of Chicago Press.

Pedersen, Susan, 2002. 'What is political history now?' in *What is History Now?*, ed. David Cannadine. Basingstoke, Palgrave Macmillan, pp. 36–56.

Rosenberg, Alexander, 1995. *Philosophy of Social Science*, 2nd edn. Boulder, CO, Westview Press.

Runciman, W.G., 1989. *A Treatise on Social Theory*, vol. 2: *Substantive Social Theory*. Cambridge, Cambridge University Press.

Runyan, W.M., 1988. 'Alternatives to psychoanalytic psychobiography', in *Psychology and Historical Interpretation*, ed. W.M. Runyan. New York, Oxford University Press, ch. 12.

Said, E.W., 1993. *Culture and Imperialism*. London, Chatto and Windus.

Scott, Joan, 1996. *Only Paradoxes to Offer. French Feminism and the Rights of Man*. Cambridge, MA, Harvard University Press.

—— (ed.), 1996a, *Feminism and History*. Oxford, Oxford University Press.

Scriven, M., 1966. 'Causes, connections and conditions in history', in *Philosophical Analysis and History*, ed. W.H. Dray. New York, Harper and Row, pp. 238–64.

Seidman, S. (ed.), 1994. *The Postmodern Turn. New Perspectives on Social Theory*. Cambridge, Cambridge University Press.

Seliger, M., 1977. *The Marxist Conception of Ideology. A Critical Essay*. Cambridge, Cambridge University Press.

Shapiro, Ann-Louise (ed.), 1994. *Feminists Revision History*. New Brunswick, NJ, Rutgers University Press.

Silverman, Max, 1999. *Facing Postmodernity. Contemporary French Thought on Culture and Society*. London, Routledge.

Skinner, Quentin, 1974. 'Some problems in the analysis of political thought and action', *Political Theory*, 2: 277–303.

—— 1998. *Liberty before Liberalism*. Cambridge, Cambridge University Press.

Smith, J.M., 2001. 'Between *discourse* and *experience*: agency and ideas in the French Revolution', *History and Theory*, 40: 116–42.

Spiegel, G.M., 1990. 'History, historicism, and the social logic of the text in the Middle Ages', *Speculum*, 65: 59–86.

Stannard, D.E., 1980. *Shrinking History. On Freud and the Failure of Psychohistory*. New York, Oxford University Press.

Stretton, Hugh, 1969. *The Political Sciences*. London, Routledge and Kegan Paul.

Szaluta, J., 1999. *Psychohistory. Theory and Practice*. New York, Peter Lang.

Thelan, David, 1999. 'Individual creativity and the filters of language and culture: Interpreting the Declaration of Independence by translation', *The Journal of American History*, 85: 1289–98.

Tilly, Charles, 1963. 'The analysis of a counter-revolution', *History and Theory*, 3: 30–58.

—— 1978. *From Mobilization to Revolution*. Reading, MA, Addison-Wesley.

—— 1981. *As Sociology Meets History*. New York, Academic Press.

Turner, Victor, 1981. 'Social dramas and stories about them', in *On Narrative*, ed. W.J.T. Mitchell. Chicago, University of Chicago Press, pp. 137–64.

van der Dussen, W.J., 1981. *History as Science. The Philosophy of R.G. Collingwood*. The Hague, Martinus Nijhoff.

van Fraassen, Bas C., 1980. *The Scientific Image*, Oxford, Clarendon Press.

Waite, R.G.L., 1977. *The Psychopathic God: Adolf Hitler*. New York, Basic Books.

Walsh, W.H., 1958. *An Introduction to Philosophy of History*, London, Hutchinson.

Weber, Max, 1947. *The Theory of Social and Economic Organization*, trans. A.M. Henderson and Talcott Parsons, ed. Talcott Parsons. Glencoe, NY, The Free Press.

White, Hayden, 1975. *Metahistory. The Historical Imagination in Nineteenth-Century Europe*. Baltimore, MD, The Johns Hopkins University Press.

Wiseman, T.P., 1988. 'What is political history?' in *What is History Today...?* ed. J. Gardiner. Basingstoke, Macmillan, pp. 18–30.

Wittgenstein, L., 1958. *Philosophical Investigations*, 2nd. edn., trans. G.E.M. Anscombe. Oxford, Blackwell.

Wolfe, Patrick, 1997. 'History and imperialism: a century of theory, from Marx to postcolonialism', *American Historical Review*, 102: 388–420.

Young, Robert, 1990. *White Mythologies. Writing History and the West*. London, Routledge.

Historical works

Adamson, J.S.A., 1989. 'Parliamentary management, men-of-business and the House of Lords, 1640–49', in *A Pillar of the Constitution: The House of Lords in British Politics, 1640–1784*, ed. C. Jones. London, Hambledon.

Alford, B.W.E., 1996. *Britain in the World Economy since 1880*. London, Longman.

Baldwin, G., 2001. 'Individual and self in the late Renaissance', *The Historical Journal*, 44: 341–64.

Baron, Ava, 1994. 'On looking at men: masculinity and the making of a gendered working-class history', in *Feminists Revision History*, ed. Ann-Louise Shapiro. New Brunswick, NJ, Rutgers University Press, pp. 146–71.

Beard, C.A., 1972. 'The approach of the irresistible conflict', in *The Causes of the American Civil War*, ed. E.C. Rozwenc, 2nd edn. Lexington, MA, D.C. Heath, pp. 68–99.

Bennett, J.M., 1994. 'Medieval women, modern women: across the great divide', in *Feminists Revision History*, ed. Ann-Louise Shapiro. New Brunswick, NJ, Rutgers University Press, pp. 47–72.

Berger, R., 1996. Review of *Men at Work: Labourers and Building Craftsmen in the Towns of*

North England, 1450–1750, by Donald Woodward, *The American Historical Review*, 101: 1539–40.

Bernard, G.W., 2000. 'New perspectives or old complexities?' *English Historical Review*, 115: 113–20.

Biernacki, R., 1995. *The Fabrication of Labor: Germany and Britain, 1640–1914*. Berkeley, University of California Press.

Blainey, G., 1973. *The Causes of War*. London, Macmillan.

Blassingame, J.W., 1979. *The Slave Community*, 2nd edn. New York, Oxford University Press.

Bloch, Marc, 1965. *Feudal Society*, 2 vols., trans. L.A. Manyon. London, Routledge and Kegan Paul.

Boles, J.B. (ed.), 1988. *Masters and Slaves in the House of the Lord. Race and Religion in the American South 1740–1870*. Lexington, University of Kentucky Press.

Breen, T.H., 1997. 'Ideology and nationalism on the eve of the American Revolution: revisions once more in need of revising', *The Journal of American History*, 84: 13–39.

Briggs, Asa, 1959. *Chartist Studies*. London, Macmillan.

Bush, M.L., 2000. 'Protector Somerset and the 1549 rebellions: a post-revision questioned', *English Historical Review*, 115: 103–12.

Butterfield, H., 1957. *George III and the Historians*. London, Collins.

Cannadine, David, 1984. 'The present and the past in the English Industrial Revolution 1880–1980', *Past and Present*, 103: 131–72.

—— 1995. 'The empire strikes back', *Past and Present*, 147: 180–94.

Charmley, John, 1993. *Churchill: The End of Glory. A Political Biography*. New York, Harcourt Brace.

Clark, G.K., 1962. *The Making of Victorian England*. London, Methuen.

Clarke, M.V., 1937. 'The Wilton Diptych', in M.V. Clarke, *Fourteenth Century Studies*, eds L.S. Sutherland and M. McKisack. Oxford, Clarendon, pp. 272–92.

Conrad, S.A., 1993. 'Putting rights talk in its place. *The Summary View* revisited', in *Jeffersonian Legacies*, ed. P.S. Onuf. Charlottesville, University Press of Virginia, pp. 254–80.

Crafts, N.F.R., 1995. 'Exogenous or endogenous growth? The Industrial Revolution reconsidered', *The Journal of Economic History*, 55: 745–72.

Crafts, N.F.R. and Mills, T.C., 1997. 'Endogenous innovation, trend growth, and the British Industrial Revolution: reply to Greasley and Oxley', *The Journal of Economic History*, 57: 950–6.

Cronon, William, 1992. 'A place for stories: nature, history, and narrative', *The Journal of American History*, 78: 1347–76.

Cust, R., and Hughes, A. (eds), 1989. *Conflict in Early Stuart England. Studies in Religion and Politics 1603–1642*. London, Longman.

—— (eds), 1997. *The English Civil War*. London, Arnold.

Davidson, James, 2001. 'Dover, Foucault and Greek homosexuality: penetration and the truth of sex', *Past and Present*, 170: 3–51.

Davis, J.A., 1989. 'Industrialization in Britain and Europe before 1850: new perspectives and old problems', in *The First Industrial Revolutions*, ed. Peter Mathias and J.A. Davis. Oxford, Blackwell.

Derry, T.K., 1957. *A Short History of Norway*. London, Allen and Unwin.

Doyle, W., 1999. *The Origins of the French Revolution*, 3rd edn. Oxford, Oxford University Press.

Dunn, John, 1980. *Political Obligation in its Historical Context. Essays in Political Theory*. Cambridge, Cambridge University Press.

Elkins, S.M., 1968. *Slavery. A Problem in American Institutional and Intellectual Life*, 2nd edn. Chicago, University of Chicago Press.

—— 1971. 'Slavery and ideology', in *The Debate over Slavery. Stanley Elkins and His Critics*, ed. A.J. Lane. Urbana, University of Illinois Press.

Elton, G.R., 1955. *England under the Tudors*. London, Methuen.

—— 1962. *The Tudor Revolution in Government*. Cambridge, Cambridge University Press.

Ely, R., 2000. 'Ordinary Germans, Nazism, and Judeocide' in *The 'Goldhagen Effect'. History, Memory, Nazism – Facing the German Past.*, ed. G. Eley. Ann Arbor, University of Michigan Press, pp. 33–87.

Ferguson, Niall, 1998. *The Pity of War*. London, Allen Lane.

Fischer, F. 1967. *Germany's Aims in the First World War*, London, Chatto and Windus.

Fliegelman, Jay, 1982. *Prodigals and Pilgrims. The American Revolution against Patriarchal Authority, 1750–1800*. Cambridge, Cambridge University Press.

Floud, R. and McCloskey, D., 1994. *The Economic History of Britain since 1700. Volume 3: 1939–1992*, 2nd edn. Cambridge, Cambridge University Press.

Foucault, M., 1979. *Discipline and Punish. The Birth of the Prison*, trans. A. Sheridan. Harmondsworth, Penguin.

—— 1981. *The History of Sexuality, vol. 1: An Introduction*, trans. R. Hurley. Harmondsworth, Penguin.

Friedan, Betty, 1963. *The Feminine Mystique*. Harmondsworth, Penguin.

Geyl, Pieter, 1949. *Napoleon. For and Against*, trans. O. Renier. London, Jonathan Cape.

Gilson, Étienne, 1960. *Heloise and Abelard*, trans. L.K. Shook. Ann Arbor, University of Michigan Press.

Goldhagen, D.J., 1996. *Hitler's Willing Executioners. Ordinary Germans and the Holocaust*. London, Little, Brown and Company.

—— 1998. 'The failure of the critics', in *Unwilling Germans? The Goldhagen Debate*, ed. R.R. Shandley, trans. J. Riemer. Minneapolis, University of Minnesota Press, pp. 129–50.

—— 1998a. 'What were the murderers thinking?', in *Unwilling Germans? The Goldhagen Debate*, ed. R.R. Shandley, trans. J. Riemer. Minneapolis, University of Minnesota Press, pp. 151–61.

Gordon-Reed, A., 1997. *Thomas Jefferson and Sally Hemings*. Charlottesville, University Press of Virginia.

Greasley, D. and Oxley, L., 1997. 'Endogenous growth or "Big Bang": two views of the first Industrial Revolution', *The Journal of Economic History*, 57: 935–49.

Greene, J.P., 2000. 'The American Revolution', *American Historical Review*, 105: 93–102.

Haines, R. and Shlomowitz, R. 2000. 'Explaining the mortality decline in the eighteenth-century British slave trade', *Economic History Review*, 53: 262–83.

Hampson, N., 1991. 'The heavenly city of the French revolutionaries', in *Rewriting the French Revolution, The Andrew Browning Lectures 1989*, ed. C. Lucas. Oxford, Clarendon, pp. 46–68.

Hanham, Alison, 1972. 'Richard III, Lord Hastings and the historians', *The English Historical Review*, 87: 233–48.

—— 1975. 'Hastings Redivivus', *The English Historical Review*, 90: 821–7.

Harriss, G.L., 1963. 'A revolution in Tudor history? Medieval government and statecraft', *Past and Present*, 25: 8–38.

Hartwell, R.M. (ed.), 1967. *The Causes of the Industrial Revolution in England*. London, Methuen.

Haskins, C.H., 1957. *The Renaissance of the Twelfth Century*. New York, Meridian Books.

Hays, J.N., 1998. *The Burdens of Disease. Epidemics and Human Response in Western History*. New Brunswick, NJ, Rutgers University Press.

Hiden, J. and Farquharson, J., 1983. *Explaining Hitler's Germany. Historians and the Third Reich*. London, Batsford Academic and Educational.

Hill, Christopher, 1955. *The English Revolution, 1640*, 3rd edn. London, Lawrence and Wishart.

Higman, B.W., 2000. 'The sugar revolution', *Economic History Review*, 53: 213–36.

Holmes, G., 1969. *The Florentine Enlightenment 1400–1450*. New York, Pegasus.

Holton, R.J., 1985. *The Transition from Feudalism to Capitalism*. Basingstoke, Macmillan.

Hughes, Ann, 1998. *The Causes of the English Civil War*, 2nd edn. Basingstoke, Macmillan.

Hunt, Lynn, 1992. *The Family Romance of the French Revolution*. Berkeley, University of California Press.

Hunter, Allen (ed.), 1998. *Rethinking the Cold War*. Philadelphia, PA, Temple University Press.

Isaac, Rhys, 1982. *The Transformation of Virginia 1740–1790*. Chapel Hill, University of North Carolina Press.

Jones, Archer, 1992. 'Military means, political ends: strategy', in *Why the Confederacy Lost*, ed. G.S. Boritt. Oxford, Oxford University Press, pp. 43–78.

Jones, Colin, 1995. 'A fine "romance" with no sisters', *French Historical Studies*, 19: 277–87.

Jones, E.T., 2001. 'Illicit business: accounting for smuggling in sixteenth-century Bristol', *The Economic History Review*, 54: 17–38.

Jones, J.R., 1993. *Marlborough*, Cambridge, Cambridge University Press.

Karras, R.M., 2000. 'Active/passive, acts/passions: Greek and Roman sexualities', *The American Historical Review*, 105: 1250–65.

Kershaw, Ian, 1989. *The Nazi Dictatorship. Problems and Perspectives of Interpretation*, 2nd edn. London, Edward Arnold.

Leffler, M.P., 1994. 'National security and US foreign policy', in *Origins of the Cold War. An International History*, eds M.P. Leffler and D.S. Painter. London, Routledge, pp. 15–52.

—— 1999. 'The Cold War: what do "we now know"?' *American Historical Review*, 104: 501–24.

Leffler, M.P. and Painter, D.S. (eds), 1994. *Origins of the Cold War. An International History*. London, Routledge.

Levine, L.W., 1977. *Black Culture and Black Consciousness*. New York, Oxford University Press.

McGwire, M., 1994. 'National security and Soviet foreign policy', in *Origins of the Cold War. An International History*, eds M.P. Leffler and D.S. Painter. London, Routledge, pp. 53–76.

McKitterick, Rosamond, 2000. 'The illusion of royal power in the Carolingian Annals', *The English Historical Review*, 110: 1–20.

McPhee, Peter, 1993. *A Social History of France, 1780–1880*. London, Routledge.

McPherson, J.M., 1988. *Battle Cry of Freedom. The Civil War Era*. New York, Ballantine Books.

—— 1992. 'American victory, American defeat', in *Why the Confederacy Lost*, ed. G.S. Boritt. Oxford, Oxford University Press, pp. 15–42.

Manning, Brian, 1992. *1649. The Crisis of the English Revolution*. London, Bookmarks.

—— 1996. *Aristocrats, Plebians, and Revolution in England 1640–1660*, London, Pluto Press.

Martin, John, 1997. 'Inventing sincerity, refashioning prudence: the discovery of the individual in Renaissance Europe', *American Historical Review*, 102: 1309–42.

Mathias, Peter, 1989. 'The industrial revolution: concept and reality', in *The First Industrial Revolutions*, ed. Peter Mathias and J.A. Davis. Oxford, Blackwell, pp. 1–24.

Mayer, A.J., 2000. *The Furies. Violence and Terror in the French and Russian Revolutions*. Princeteon, NJ, Princeton University Press.

Mews, C.J., 1999. *The Lost Love Letters of Heloise and Abelard. Perceptions of Dialogue in Twelfth-Century France*. Basingstoke, Macmillan.

Meyerowitz, Joanne, 1993. 'Beyond *The Feminine Mystique*: a reassessment of postwar mass culture, 1946–1958', *The Journal of American History*, 79: 1454–81.

Mokyr, Joel (ed.), 1999. *The British Industrial Revolution: an Economic Perspective*, 2nd edn. Boulder, CO, Westview Press.

Mommsen, H., 1998. 'The thin patina of civilization: anti-Semitism was a necessary, but by no means sufficient, condition for the Holocaust', in *Unwilling Germans? The Goldhagen Debate*, ed. R.R. Shandley, trans. J. Riemer. Minneapolis, University of Minnesota Press, pp. 183–96.

Moore, Barrington, 1950. *Soviet Politics – the Dilemma of Power: The Role of Ideas in Social Change*. New York, Harper and Row.

Morrill, John, 1997. 'The religious context of the English Civil War', in *The English Civil War*, eds R. Cust and A. Hughes. London, Arnold.

Morrison, M.A., 1997. *Slavery and the American West. The Eclipse of Manifest Destiny and the Coming of the Civil War*. Chapel Hill, University of North Carolina Press.

Muslin, H.L. and Jobe, T.H., 1991. *Lyndon Johnson: The Tragic Self: A Psychohistorical Portrait*. New York, Insight Books.

Namier, L., 1963. *The Structure of Politics at the Accession of George III*. London, Macmillan.

Nevins, A. and Commager, H.S., 1966. *America. The Story of a Free People*, 3rd edn. Oxford, Clarendon Press.

O'Neill, R.J., 1968. *The German Army and the Nazi Party, 1933–1939*, 2nd edn. London, Cassell.

Pirenne, Henri, 1936. *Economic and Social History of Medieval Europe*, London, Routledge and Kegan Paul.

Plumb, J.H., 1969. 'The historian', in *Churchill Revised. A Critical Assessment*. New York, The Dial Press, pp. 133–69.

Ponting, Clive, 1994. *Churchill*. London, Sinclair-Stevenson.

Potter, David, 1960. 'Jefferson Davis and the political factors in Confederate defeat', in *Why the North Won the Civil War*, ed. David Donald. Binghamton, NY, Louisiana State University Press, pp. 91–114.

—— 1976. *The Impending Crisis 1848–1861*. New York, Harper and Row.

Richardson, R.C., 1998. *The Debate on the English Revolution*, 3rd edn. Manchester, Manchester University Press.

Roesdahl, Else, 1991. *The Vikings*, trans. S.M. Margeson and K. Williams. London, Allen Lane.

Russell, Conrad, 1990. *The Causes of the English Civil War*. London, Clarendon.

Ryan, Alan, 1965. 'Locke and the dictatorship of the bourgeoisie', *Political Studies*, 13: 219–30.

Shagan, E.H., 1999. 'Protector Somerset and the 1549 rebellions: new sources and new perspectives', *English Historical Review*, 114: 34–53.

—— 2000. '"Popularity" and the 1549 rebellions revisited', *English Historical Review*, 115: 121–33.

Sharpe, Kevin, 1999.' Representations and negotiations: texts, images, and authority in early modern England', *The Historical Journal*, 42: 853–81.

Smith, Dennis, 1984. 'Discovering facts and values: the historical sociology of Barrington Moore', in *Vision and Method in Historical Sociology*, ed. Theda Skocpol. Cambridge, Cambridge University Press, pp. 313–55.

Sommerville, J.P., 1989. 'Ideology, property and the constitution', in *Conflict in Early Stuart England. Studies in Religion and Politics, 1603–1642*, eds R. Cust and A. Hughes. London, Longman.

Stampp, K.M., 1965. *The Peculiar Institution. Slavery in the Ante-Bellum South*. New York, Alfred A. Knopf.

Stone, L., 1972. *The Causes of the English Revolution*. London, Routledge and Kegan Paul.

—— 1981 *The Past and the Present*. Boston, Routledge and Kegan Paul.

Stone, N., 1999. *Europe Transformed, 1878–1919*, 2nd edn. Oxford, Blackwell.

Storr, A., 1969. 'The man', in *Churchill Revised. A Critical Assessment*. New York, The Dial Press, pp. 229–74.

Tackett, T., 2000. 'Conspiracy obsession in a time of revolution: French élites and the origins of the terror, 1789–1792', *American Historical Review*, 105: 690–713.

Taylor, A.J.P., 1969. 'The statesman', in *Churchill Revised. A Critical Assessment*. New York, The Dial Press, pp. 15–62.

Thompson, E.P., 1968. *The Making of the English Working Class*. Harmondsworth, Penguin.

Thompson, M.P., 1987. 'Significant silences in Locke's *Two Treatises of Government*: constitutional history, contract and law', *The Historical Journal*, 31: 275–94.

Tulard, Jean, 1985. *Napoleon, The Myth of the Saviour*, trans. T. Waugh. London, Methuen.

Underdown, David, 1996. *A Freeborn People. Politics and Nation in Seventeenth-Century England*. Oxford, Clarendon.

Walter, James, 1981. 'Studying political leaders from a distance: the lessons of biography', in *Reading Life Histories. Griffith Papers on Biography*, ed. J. Walter. Nathan, Queensland, Griffith University, pp. 29–38.

Watts, Sheldon, 1997. *Epidemics and History. Disease, Power and Imperialism*. New Haven, CT, Yale University Press.

Weinrich, J., 1990. 'Reality or social construction?', in *Forms of Desire, Sexual Orientation and the Social Constructionist Controversy*, ed. E. Stein. New York, Garland Publishing, pp. 175–208.

Wolffe, B.P., 1974. 'When and why did Hastings lose his head?', *The English Historical Review*, 89: 835–44.

Woodham-Smith, Cecil, 1957. *The Reason Why*. London, Constable.

Woods, R.B., 1995. *Fulbright. A Biography*. Cambridge, Cambridge University Press.

Yang, Daqing, 1999. 'Convergence or divergence? Recent historical writings on the Rape of Nanjing', *American Historical Review*, 104: 842–65.

Zagorin, Perez, 1998. *The English Revolution: Politics, Events, Ideas*. Brookfield, VT, Ashgate.

Name index

The names in this index include the names of authors quoted; the names of those whose ideas have been discussed; and the names of people who were the subject of historical inquiry, mentioned in the text.

Subject index

American Civil War: battle of Antietam 74; battle of Fredericksburg 74–5; causes of 176; reasons for Southern secession 73; why the North won 157, 163–5
American Revolution 39, 40–1, 141–2
anthropological interpretation 37
arguments to the best explanation 44, 49–52
authority 66–7

Balinese cockfights 37
bias: in reading texts 20, 26, 31–4
British economy: twentieth century 160–1, 162
British imperialism: explanations of 184

causes 63, 152–62, 165–9; mental 71–99; social 99–113
Chartists 80–1
Cold War 130–2
colligation 125–32
conditions 63, 157–8

direct inferences 44–5, 46–8

English Civil War: causes of 144–50
English Revolution 128–9, 133–7
explanations: analysis of 171–3; causal 158–62, 166–9, 175; comprehensive 113–15; contrastive 63, 162–5, 173–84; of evidence 44, 49–52, 113; fairness of 146–8; genetic 176; profound 160, 177–84; psychological 85–91, 115, 179

feminist theory 160; see also women: subordination of

French Revolution 38, 93–5; terror 114–15
French society: nineteenth century 191–2
Freudian theory 85–6, 90

generalizations: accidental 59–63; causal 62–3; credibility of 140–2; lawlike 54–9

habits 100
hermeneutical circles 35–6, 138–9
Holocaust 7; and bureaucracy 185–6
homosexuality 96–7
hybrid inferences 52–4

ideology 79–83, 93
imitation 100
Industrial Revolution in Britain: causes of 57–8, 168–9, 188–9; characteristics of 59–60, 129–30
interests: class 81–2; human 83–5
interpretation of events: colligatory 125–32; credibility of 138–44; fairness of 144–50; intelligibility of 150–1; summary 132–7

knowledge: historical 12–14, 43; reasons for scepticism 7–8, 14–16

Light Brigade: charge of 181–2

Marxist theory 78–83, 189, 190
meaning of actions, events and practices 37–42
meanings of texts: coherence of 34–6; contexts (textual, social and intellectual) 24–6; conventional (= basic) 18–19, 23, 24; hermeneutical